The Amazing Transforming Superhero!

The Amazing Transforming Superhero!

Essays on the Revision of Characters in Comic Books, Film and Television

Edited by TERRENCE R. WANDTKE

McFarland & Company, Inc., Publishers
Jefferson, North Carolina, and London

LIBRARY OF CONGRESS CATALOGUING-IN-PUBLICATION DATA

The amazing transforming superhero! : essays on the
revision of characters in comic books, film and television /
edited by Terrence R. Wandtke.
    p.   cm.
Includes bibliographical references and index.

ISBN-13: 978-0-7864-3189-2
softcover : 50# alkaline paper ∞

1. Comic books, strips, etc.—History and criticism.
2. Heroes in literature.   3. Heroes in motion pictures.
4. Heroes on television.   I. Wandtke, Terrence R.
PN6714.A43   2007
741.5'352—dc22   2007015953

British Library cataloguing data are available

Cover art ©2007 Digital Vision

Manufactured in the United States of America

McFarland & Company, Inc., Publishers
Box 611, Jefferson, North Carolina 28640
www.mcfarlandpub.com

For Mom and Dad:
I was saddened when I didn't grow up to be a superhero but am grateful not to have grown up as an orphan.

For Anna:
I find you to be everything Wonder Woman should be minus the invisible jet, superpowers, and skimpy outfit.

For Bella and Ripley:
I don't know what the future holds for you except that you'll someday take center stage and no longer be my faithful sidekicks.

Acknowledgments

I would like to give special thanks to the following: Jules Feiffer, Umberto Eco, and Richard Reynolds for inspiration; Georgia Johnston, Rob McManus, and Gary Burns for opportunities; Anna Wandtke, Doug Miller, and Half Price Used Books for support; and, of course, God for truth, justice, and all that stuff.

Contents

Preface

I remember many things about my first superhero comic book. Some of those memories are clear and some are vague; some describe the comic book itself and some describe the circumstances surrounding its purchase and the reading experience that followed. I remember standing in front of a tall magazine rack in a local supermarket, gazing with fierce longing at the pamphlet-like "books" filled with words but more importantly with the vibrant colors of men in tights. I remember reading it at home, overwhelmed by the smoky smell of the low-quality paper on which the superhero story was splashed; I read and re-read the story countless times on that day, seemingly unable to fill the Superman-shaped hole in my heart that I never knew existed before then. I remember begging my parents to buy another for me; I wasn't so worried about my father's response (I had already caught him poring over my comic book) but was greatly relieved to hear my mother say, "We don't care what you read as long as you read." Needless to say, I was immeasurably grateful at the time but to my surprise, I remain so today. While my mother's comment introduced me to the dubious esteem in which superhero comic books were held by society at large, her desire to have a reader in the family allowed me to participate in a popular culture experience that captured the dreams of millions and continues to grow in surprising and strange new ways.

I don't remember how much my first comic book cost; this was perhaps the result of someone else making the purchase. But in years to come, as I became a comic book collector, I have no clear recollection of the cost of any one particular comic book (except to say more generally that comic books were much less expensive than they are now). I know that I always found the money to buy my regular titles and that I reached a point in the late eighties when I stopped collecting because the comic books cost too much (although I don't remember how much was too much). I don't remember the details of the story in my first comic book, only that Superman was the sole hero and that he *flew* and demonstrated feats of *immense* strength; this is likely the result of the marvel that such feats held in an era before they could be depicted convincingly in any other medium.

But in years to come, even as I became more discriminating as an appreciator of the arts and even after *Superman: The Movie* "made me believe a man can fly," I still sometimes felt that the complexities of a comic book story written for an adult audience remained secondary to the comic book image of a man lifting a skyscraper above his head. I know that in the late eighties Frank Miller convinced me that Superman was a stooge of an ineffectual and simple-minded American government, but I was even more affected by the majesty of Miller's rendering of a silhouetted Superman in flight—likely his intention. Often, I think the things that I can't remember clearly about my experience of superheroes are just as important as the things I can. Often, I think I want to experience superhero stories to remind me of the things I only vaguely remember about superheroes.

In some ways, these statements could establish me as a reader nearly aware of the way a commodity culture manufactures not just products but my desire for those products (certainly a popular way for scholars to describe superheroes). In other ways, these statements could establish me as a reader on the verge of recognizing the archetypes in my unconscious mind on which superheroes are based (certainly another popular way for scholars to describe superherocs). While interpretations of superheroes are not limited to these two perspectives, I would assert that the superhero doesn't need to be solely understood one way or the other; the superhero could be understood as both (although most who engage in the above-mentioned Marxist reading and above-mentioned psychoanalytic reading would probably beg to differ). Moreover, sometimes I feel it's important to recognize the simple things about the subject that we study before we begin to apply sophisticated criteria that supposedly reveal its complexities.

Superheroes are unquestionably an integral part of the world's heroic mythologies. Without ever having been an asthmatic who served an easy target for the local bully, I fell in love with superheroes. And as best as I can tell by the large section of superhero "graphic novels" at Borders, the summer offerings at the local AMC multiplex, and the content of most of my brother-in-law's video games, the rest of the world has fallen in this way too. The stories of superheroes in all those mediums always revisit the traumatic point of the superhero's origin and we go along for the visit in a way that would be masochistic unless we had faith that something other than the experience of trauma could be gained from their stories. I'm not always sure what that something is or whether that something is in fact very valuable at all. But sometimes, when I close my eyes, I find myself in a strange place. I am an academic full of the ideas that invigorate my critical studies and yet I still believe a man can fly.

I hope this preface doesn't seem coy or sloppily sentimental because I really don't have those things in mind. I agree with the sentiment of the fantasy writer Madeleine L'Engle when she suggests the transcendent nature of reading lies in the fact that you do not read as the someone you are now but as all the someones that you once were. I don't mention this to reconstruct a stereotypical dichotomy that falsely associates imaginative wonder only with childhood and critical analysis only with adulthood. Children view their world very critically even though their critical faculties are different than those of an adult and adults view their world very imaginatively even though their imaginative abilities are different than those of a child. In some ways, this is a reassuring and important fact to keep in mind, as some haven't read superhero comic books since childhood and others have only read them as adults. In my own case as a young boy reading about superheroes, I remember wanting to see through my hand the way the comic book advertisements promised me I could if I owned their X-ray glasses (but I had a sneaking suspicion that no such glasses really existed). Even though I'm embarrassed to admit it, I remember reading the first issue of Marvel's *What If?* in which Spiderman joined the Fantastic Four and crying over the conclusion when Sue Richards left not only the Fantastic Four but also Reed Richards, her husband; I was able to talk myself back from the edge of emotional ruin by reminding myself that it was only an imaginary *What If?* story and not a real Fantastic Four (but then I wondered what it meant to have a "real" story with fictitious characters).

Now, I soar to great heights with the complex imaginings of stories such as Alan Moore's "Whatever Happened to the Man of Tomorrow?" wherein I'm allowed to see a possible ending to the story of Superman. The last lines of the poem which introduces the story states, "This is an imaginary story ... / Aren't they all?" And now, I wonder how Lacan's definition of the imaginary might be employed to clarify the psychology of sequential art in the modern age's superhero graphic novels....

Introduction: Once Upon a Time Once Again

It seems that in the beginning, there was Superman. And then came a revolution in the medium of "comic" books that embraced the superhero. And with that revolution came ... revision. Over the course of about seventy years, since *Action Comics* #1 was published in 1937, the superhero clearly has been a vibrant presence in the United States and the world through not just comic books but a variety of other media forms as well. Superheroes now exist on an international stage in Hollywood blockbusters, internet fanfiction, Wal-Mart t-shirts, and even copyright law (all in unique ways and distributed worldwide).

Some would argue that the superhero has existed or at least been "in the making" both inside and outside the United States for much more than the seventy years since the creation of Superman (now one of the world's most recognizable figures). Whether the superhero finds its roots in ancient mythologies or takes shape as the quintessential commodity of the 21st century's world marketplace, it must be acknowledged that as long as the superhero has been in existence, the superhero has been "in the making," working through a series of revisions. While this is certainly not a profound observation, the revisionism inherent within the narratives of superhero comic books, films, and television deserves greater scrutiny.

Obsessed with superhero continuity, the superhero aficionado known as the fanboy may try to identify various strands of superhero revisions as canonical and non-canonical.[1] However, the fanboy fights a losing battle in superhero worlds filled with imaginary cities (with an ever-changing landscape), informed by conceits of the medium (in which heroes almost never age), and redeveloped by regularly changing writers and illustrators (in ways that are sometimes slight and sometimes dramatic). In addition, when suggestions from letter pages, innovations of television incarnations, and wild tangents of fanfiction at least partially reshape the current story arc of the comic book source material, the idea of origin and canon becomes nebulous at best. And especially in an era in which superhero comic books are no longer subject to the burden of popularity associated with their pulpy heyday and have changed radically for the sake of an older audience,[2] the time has come to carefully examine one of the most unique aspects of superhero characters: their survival. This survival is due largely

5

to the willingness of the public at large to see them grow and change and be constantly updated, and be expanded into other media forms. As unavoidable components of the cultural milieu of the world, superheroes must be acknowledged as important means by which we come to understand ourselves. Therefore, the revisionism which is widely accepted as part of and integrally related to our experience of superheroes must also be recognized as critical to our identity. While this volume doesn't promise to provide certain answers so much as open the debate on the issue of superhero revisionism, the introduction does seek to provide a general framework for the ways that superhero revisionism has manifested itself.

REVISION AND NOT EVOLUTION (PER SE)

A brief explanation is in order of why the terms *revision* and *revisionism* are so well suited to describe the development of the superhero. Even though the rapid turnover of writers and artists (and readers) in charge of the direction of any one superhero is common knowledge, many still assert that superheroes evolve over time. After all, the truly popular superheroes have continuity editors who protect the "property," proceed from a fairly well-known origin story, and work with basic mythic archetypes.[3] While I don't seek to dispute any of those three items exactly, I believe other factors are at work which prevent a simple linear evolution of characters (not the least of which are their long lives in many different mediums).

Trends in superhero revisionism do not in any significant way conform to an evolutionary model that would only benefit from a strict historical analysis. Those who argue that superheroes evolve would argue, for instance, that Frank Miller's Batman is a linear descendent of Bob Kane's original vision of Batman created in 1938: a portrayal of dark justice that emblematically confronts the brokenness of the American dream. With this evolutionary model in mind, the camp of the 1960s' television series (and the comics that were published at the same time) would have to be understood as an aberration, an exception to the otherwise orderly rule of development. However, the grim and gritty Dark Knight has not (via some aesthetic version of natural selection) qualitatively conquered the fabulous Batman open to gay readings.

Tim Burton's Batman films (cribbed largely from Miller's Batman ideas) were followed by Joel Schumacher's Batman films (based more on the comical elements drawn largely from the television series). Even more notable in demonstrating that these threads coexist and inform one another would be Alan Moore's *The Killing Joke*. Perhaps the most grim and gritty depiction of the Joker's psychosis ever put to paper with the permission of DC Comics, the graphic novel is also well known for its inclusion of all components of Batman's mythology, including the Batcave's giant T-

Rex and Bruce Wayne's photograph of the Bat-family which features the ever ridiculous Batmite.

Therefore, although it may seem counter-intuitive to begin at the end, it would be most fruitful to exemplify the nature of superhero revision by drawing some examples from recent incarnations of superheroes. This approach works best because the current state of the most popular superheroes demonstrates the most interesting consequences of superhero revisionism. Initially, it seems the newest version of a superhero is always privileged over that which preceded it, with current fans asserting that Grant Morrison's Superman (written in the 2000s)[4] is not only more relevant but also more "authentic" than Jerry Siegel's Superman (written in the 1930s and '40s). Consider that the twenty-something youthfulness of the 1960s' Superman was explained by the assertion that this current version of Superman represented another earth's Superman (thus allowing that the 1940s' Superman might, like mere mortals, be getting a bit long in the tooth); however, the 1960s' Superman, the primary focus of the ongoing Superman comic books, was said to hail from Earth *One* and the 1940s' Superman from Earth *Two* (an interesting paradox considering that in basic literary terms, Earth One's Superman would not exist without the mythological framework provided by what would thereafter be known as Earth Two's Superman).

The simple explanation for this is that new audiences are introduced to the superhero and the current audience does not want to read about "their father's" Superman. However, at the same time, the psychic trace of the original is never completely lost, despite the best efforts of comic book writers to obliterate the partially hidden past; this is best represented by Marv Wolfman's *Crisis on the Infinite Earths* in which a villain destroyed all earths except for Earth One. In the decades since this series was written, writers seemed incapable of making references only to the new post–*Crisis* history of superheroes. Thus, Geoff Johns' *Infinite Crisis* brings back Earth Two's Superman as well as all the other earths destroyed in *Crisis on the Infinite Earths*. Past versions of superheroes are never completely lost and those past versions continue to shape the most recent versions.

HOW DO YOU LIKE YOUR REVISIONISM?

At the same time, it is necessary to keep in mind that there are different degrees to which revisions find popular acceptance. In order to effectively profile these degrees, it's important to note that superhero narratives, like all serial narratives, are based on a series of tropes and conceits. Fundamental tropes of the "classic" superhero story include aspects of the character such as the costume as both a disguise and a marker of the self; fundamental conceits include aspects of the character such as the superhero's refusal to age as the world continues to change around the superhero. Dealing with the way these two things interact, a greater appreciation can be gained for the way revisions to any one superhero might be accepted.

For instance, Superman went through a variety of revisionary changes in the 1990s, a reaction to the general darkening of the superhero narratives in the wake of Frank Miller's *The Dark Knight Returns* and Alan Moore's *Watchmen*. With these texts serving as the new models for superhero relevance, the boy scout of the DC universe would have to make some changes to maintain his popularity. Two of those changes are fairly well known; the "death" of Superman (a shakeup that seems to participate in the grim and gritty tenor of other contemporaneous superhero narratives) and the marriage of Superman to Lois Lane (a shakeup that domesticated Superman and seems quite the opposite of "grim and gritty"). The third notable change in this era is not as well known but is similar to the death of Superman storyline in that it found its basis in one of the popular 1960s "imaginary" stories: "The Amazing Story of Superman-Red and Superman-Blue."

The original story begins with Superman's experiment with kryptonite that causes him to be split into two beings, one wearing a mostly red Superman costume and the other wearing a mostly blue Superman costume. After Superman frees the people of Kandor from their bottle and marries Lois Lane and Lana Lang (Superman-Red and Superman-Blue, respectively), the story was ended with the narrator's firm promise that this was merely an imaginary story of Superman. In seeming contrast, the 1990s story of Superman-Red and Superman-Blue was written as a central part of the mainstream titles and was meant to be regarded as part of Superman's "real" continuity. After problems developed that Superman believed to be an evolution of his classic powers, Superman would gain energy-based abilities that required him to be held together by a blue "containment" suit. Shortly thereafter, Superman would split into two beings representing different aspects of his personality (the second Superman, of course, wore a red costume). Remarkably unpopular with the readers, this publicity stunt to again raise Superman's profile in the 1990s had quite the opposite of the intended effect. Therefore, the two Supermen were quickly merged back together and Superman returned to his classic costume, discovering he again had his classic powers (with a trite explanation to excuse it all).[5] Unlike the death of Superman story, which became an official part of the Superman mythology, the 1990s' story of Superman-Red and Superman-Blue was willfully pushed from the memory of most, making it at least as imaginary as the original version.

Another costume change that startled faithful readers of classic superhero comic books occurred for Spiderman roughly a decade before the blue energy Superman. Conventionally thought to be an attempt to quickly copy DC's superhero universe-spanning cross-over mini-series *Crisis on the Infinite Earths*, Marvel's poorly written *Secret Wars* was released before *Cri-*

sis on the Infinite Earths. Promising profound changes to the Marvel universe, the gimmick was that one month superheroes were magically swept away and the next they were returned with incredible differences; readers then had to read a monthly twelve-issue mini-series to discover where they went and how those changes took place. (A god-like being who referred to himself as the Beyonder transported superheroes and supervillains to another planet, thus setting the stage for lots of superhero and supervillain "team-ups" and lots of superhero victories through lots of bombastic superhero violence.)

Ironically, these "radical" revisions, such as replacing the Fantastic Four's Thing with She-Hulk, had little staying power. One of the most controversial was the one which might seem most superficial; Spiderman gave up his red and blue webbed costume for a more sleek black and white costume. However, as previously noted, a superhero's costume is a signifier of the character's self and for that reason fans of a beloved superhero will not easily part with the original costume. In a way that may seem as gimmicky as the simplistic plot of *Secret Wars* itself, the likely return of Spiderman's classic costume was written into the new costume storyline; Spiderman's new costume was not clothing at all but a sentient alien symbiote he discovered on the *Secret Wars* planet (without really understanding what would become its nefarious nature). As fan opinion weighed in generally against the new costume, Spiderman slowly became aware of the way his new costume was influencing him for the worse. Eventually Spiderman rejects and defeats the symbiote, but unlike Superman-Red and Superman-Blue, this incident would be far from willfully forgotten within the canon of Spiderman.

While Spiderman would return to his classic costume and never again wear the black costume, the alien symbiote would continue to live on in the Marvel universe (in a near classic example of the return of the repressed). The symbiote would find another host in Eddie Brock, a reporter rival of Spiderman's alter ego, Peter Parker. Thereafter, he would be known as Venom, initially one of Spiderman's vilest enemies, but in the dark age of 1990s comic books, Venom becomes a popular anti-hero in the vein of Todd McFarlane's Spawn (appropriately representing the mixed opinions of fans at the debut of Spiderman's new costume). Moreover, the character of Venom cannot be seen as simply an aberration because he exists beyond the confines of classic Spiderman continuities in alternate Spiderman narratives that cannot easily support Venom's origin story. For instance, the "Ultimate" line of Marvel superhero titles ostensibly seeks to retell superhero stories from the beginning for a new generation of readers. Within the Ultimate universe, stories are updated and streamlined and cross-over events like *Secret Wars* almost never take place. Nevertheless, while Spiderman *again* never completely loses his classic look, the symbiote story resulting in the creation of Venom is deemed central to Spiderman mythology and an alternate origin story is created (the symbiote becoming a genetically engineered suit created by the fathers of Peter Parker and Eddie Brock). And as an even further testament to the symbiote's curious sideline centrality, the symbiote story becomes the essential thread in Sam Raimi's *Spiderman 3* (Venom is one of only four Spiderman villains featured in the three Spiderman films).[6]

Another possible outcome of a superhero's costume change is neither outright rejection nor anxious assimilation but enthusiastic acceptance. This is most frequently seen with superheroes that do not have a clearly established identity or fan base; this certainly is the case with Blade, premiering first in 1973 as an adversary to the title character in Marv Wolfman's *Tomb of Dracula*. While some might argue that Blade doesn't in the strictest sense have a secret identity, he definitely had a costume at his debut. Ordinary except in the fact that he was immune to vampire bites, Blade identifies himself as a vampire killer. Part of the black superhero phenomenon of the 1970s, Blade takes shape as a character alternately interesting and flat, too often mired in the stereotyped image of blackness in comic books at the time. Speaking in a way that weakly approximated street slang of the 1970s, Blade sports an afro and a costume with enormous goggles that smack of disco fashion. While never completely falling out of circulation in the Marvel universe (even after the cancellation of *Tomb of Dracula*), Blade would never capture enough popular interest to support a series on his own; he would occasionally surface in superhero comic books geared to appeal to the horror subculture subsumed by superhero comics in the comics code era of the 1960s. However, with the reinvention of Blade in his self-titled 1998 film, the character would find new "life" on the silver screen, in comic books, and eventually on the small screen.

Since Blade could hardly be considered an important property by Marvel, he would be licensed with few restrictions placed on his reimagining (unlike Spiderman, whose image is highly guarded). Therefore, the film's Blade looks quite different than his comic book incarnation; he is played by Wesley Snipes as a leather-clad half-vampire with sinister weapons he uses to hunt full-blooded, evil vampires. In a paradoxical way, by constructing vampirism as a metaphor for racial otherness, the film version rejects the tokenism of his original creation by making race a central issue in the narrative. In addition to being a black vampire in a sea of white vampire enemies, Blade is constantly taunted by vampires for trying to "pass" as human. Moreover, the only way he resists the vampire thirst at the film's end is through a new serum concocted by a researcher in sickle cell anemia, a blood disease the primarily affects African Americans. This version of Blade became extremely popular, spawning two film sequels and a television series which followed the same basic story arc. In fact, it would be most accurate to say that this version became more important than the

Spiderman doesn't wear the black and white costume anymore (or at least not for long in retellings of his story); however, the costume refuses to go away, regularly resurfacing as the monstrous Venom. From *Ultimate Spiderman, Vol. 6: Venom* (New York: Marvel Comics, 2005).

original, largely replacing the memory of the "first" Blade (as much as it existed) and creating fan desire that the comic book version of Blade might be more like the film version. As a consequence, Blade is bitten by the vampire Morbius and gains all the vampire strengths that the film version of Blade possesses. Eventually, an Ultimate version of the character would be created that would not only lack 25 years of baggage but also be fashioned almost exclusively on ideas created within the narrative of the film.

Certainly part of the explanation for this greater degree of revision would lie in the fact that Blade was meant to be a supporting character, written in a marginalized context (that of the black superhero), and never recognized as a classic hero who transcended the historical situation of his creation. (Whether superheroes can ever truly transcend their historical situation is less important than whether their fan base believes they can.) However, the current version of Blade would not exist without the original version of Blade and in that regard, both versions still do exist.

EXAMPLES (AND STILL MORE EXAMPLES) OF SUPERHEROES

While it's important to take into account the relative popularity of the entrenched notions of the superhero to see how revisions may or may not become part of the superhero's canon, it's also important to recognize that sometimes the popular superhero's life can be changed with the handy disclaimer of a story as noncanonical. The many ongoing Superman comic books may have an editor who assures that their stories logically relate to each other but they exist alongside *All Star Superman*, a stand-alone Superman comic book that follows its own story arc independent of the other Superman titles. This doesn't even take into consideration the popularity of trade paperback collections of past Superman comic books that have stories of the Superman of Earth Two, the Superman of Earth One, and the post–*Crisis* Superman sitting alongside one another. Despite the fact that the century of their creation was still in part informed by the Enlightenment which privileged objective truth and authoritative sources, classic superheroes exist simultaneously in multiple forms in different contexts that do not logically cohere with one another. Moreover, they do not exist in multiple forms just for a stereotypical audience for superheroes: the juvenile comic book reading audience that one might speculate is intellectually incapable of identifying these inconsistencies. In addition to the fact that the typical comic book reader is more anxious and aware than the public at large about such inconsistencies, it has been quite some time since the majority of the comic book audience has been young enough to be classified as juvenile. Also, current superhero fans no longer move away from the superheroes of their youth in the same way as that previous generations of fans have. The artistic accomplishment of recent superhero stories has increased and readers approach past material with a somewhat fashionable ironic detachment; therefore, current fans no longer feel the same sort of pressure to graduate to socially acceptable literature (felt so very acutely in the era shaped by Frederic Wertham's tirades against the medium of comic books). Superheroes live out multiple, sometimes contradictory, lives for their fans within culture at large and for our best examples, one need look no further than the same superhero standard mentioned often thus far: Superman.

From his start, Superman was a multi-media phenomenon rendered almost immediately in radio, cartoon, and film versions. These versions have often related to one another organically and developed in a way that enacts the above mentioned ideas. While the radio program based its ideas primarily on the mythos detailed in Jerry Siegel's comic book adventures of Superman, the radio program added kryptonite and Clark Kent's editor, Perry White, to the mix; these subsequent additions made outside the medium that gave birth to the superhero were seen as essential to original conception of Superman in years to come, now represented as essential part of the Superman canon (inside and outside his comic book renderings). While many claim there is an essential urtext from which all things Superman flow, the truth remains that Superman mythology is very organic. In the recent history of Superman, he exists in comic books not only in the multiple versions mentioned above, but also in various alternate histories (the evil Superman of John Francis' *The Dark Side* and the Russian Superman of Mark Millar's *Red Son*) and in various future histories (the emasculated Superman of Frank Miller's *Dark Knight* and the disillusioned Superman of Mark Waid's *The Kingdom*). DC's Elseworld series, whose volumes explore various alternative histories, was instituted in the 1990s but is really the linear descendent of the imaginary Superman stories of the 1960s (stories that most famously include "The Death of Superman" and the already discussed "The Amazing Story of Superman-Red and Superman-Blue").

While some incarnations of Superman in other media have tried to maintain the conventional comic book story arc (such as the animated *Adventures of Superman* series by traditionalist Paul Dini), most often we see the "biblical" truth of Superman's story eventually incorporating the most admired flights of imagination. This includes the "Death of Superman" arc in the canonical Superman titles, which may introduce a new Kryptonian villain but owes a debt to the imaginary story of the 1960s; this also includes Superman marrying Lois Lane in the canonical titles, which made into a stately affair the farcical marriage in the television series *Lois and Clark* (but nevertheless was undoubtedly inspired by the television plot). Both events would be considered inconceivable by writers of Superman in the 1940s and yet are now part of our collective knowledge of Superman.

Three versions of Superman existing outside the medium of comic books that provide some of the most interesting contemporary revisions to the character can be found on both small and big screens. The television series *Smallville* takes a look at Clark Kent's youth and imagines that Clark may have grown up with Lex Luthor (his future arch-enemy) as his best friend. (Again, this would be incorporated into a comic book retelling of Superman's origin in Mark Waid's *Birthright*.) In addition to requiring a remarkable amount of knowledge about Superman's mythos from its viewers, the series also asks its viewers to willingly suspend what they know in order to reimagine the story, surprisingly finding viewers willing to deconstruct and reconstruct the narrative.

Although it may seem a trite example, the American Express commercials (with live action footage of Jerry Seinfeld interacting with an animated Superman) enact a very similar dynamic. The commercials represent Superman in a recognizable form (animated, barrel-chested, and full of superpowers) but also in an unrecognizable form (self-conscious, self-deprecating, and full of Seinfeld-esque observational humor), thus evoking sentimentalism and ironic detachment at the same time. And in Brian Singer's *Superman Returns*, Brendan Routh picks up where Christopher Reeve left off but not exactly; the film presents a continuation of 1980s *Superman II* that quite intentionally ignores the existence of *Superman III* and *IV* (and invites the viewer to participate in this willful ignorance). Moreover, the film offers us a continuation of a familiar Superman story which then takes Superman into radically new territory (after his five year absence, he comes to realize that he is the father of Lois Lane's son).

Perhaps the most important thing to note when comparing the three above mentioned Superman stories is that none of them work together in terms of characterization or continuity. Nevertheless, the three existed simultaneously with *Smallville* airing on television, the American Express commercials available for download on the internet, and *Superman Returns* gracing the screens of multiplexes across the country. As the simultaneous existence of these Supermen does not create collective outrage among consumers, it may be speculated that revisionism is not only part of the phenomenon of the superhero, but also that this revisionism is indicative of contemporary consciousness.

Superman and his briefly mentioned counterpart, Batman, are easy choices to exemplify superhero revisionism simply because their history is so long; nevertheless, the revisionism seen in their incarnations is not unique. While the above examples were drawn from the lives of superheroes created in the golden age of superhero comic books (also including Wonder Woman and Captain America), they could just as easily have been drawn from the silver age (Spiderman and the X-Men), the bronze age (Power Man and the Punisher), or the modern age (the New Teen Titans and Spawn).

Superheroes exist in their previous forms in graphic novel collections of comic books, DVD collections of television series, and internet recreations of superhero stories that reinterpret "canonical" superhero mythology outside the boundaries of copyright law. Consequently, superheroes exist within a fascinating cultural dialectic. The superhero seems to be a transhistorical presence that serves as a consistent moral reference point for people around the world; and yet the superhero seems to be a mutable persona subject to the passing needs of a time recorded in specific cultural histories. The superhero is an emblematic representation of conservative values of nationalism with story arcs built around the basic components of the hero monomyth; yet the superhero is reinscribed by different authors in different mediums so that the superhero becomes endlessly multiple with an identity that is quintessentially post-modern. While this dialectic results in part from media conglomerates striving to keep their properties consistent and yet relevant, the superheroes exist only partially within the control of companies that own them. These characteristics of the superhero revisionism persist despite the increasing emphasis and presence of creator-owned superhero properties. Comic book authors such as Grant Morrison and Neil Gaiman enact revisionism within their own creator-owned material, such as Morrison's retooling of superhero ideas in *The Invisibles* and *The Filth* and Gaiman's playful revisions of his own stories in *Sandman*; this is a testimony to the idea that forces other than the hegemony of corporate culture cause the superhero to be what it is. In addition, despite being advocates for creator rights, they are consistently enticed to write company owned properties such as the X-Men and Superman in Morrison's *The New X-Men* and *All-Star Superman* and the entire Marvel universe in Gaiman's *1602*. With superheroes "living" as complex and contradictory concepts endlessly revised inside and outside the controlling force of history, transformed by and operating beyond the mediums they inhabit, and alternately moved by the earnestness of classicism and the self-awareness of post-modernism, there is a need to more clearly define the types of revisions that we see in superhero narratives in order to fully encourage the debate on superheroes as pervasive global tropes.

While establishing some basic categories for superhero revisionism becomes something of a necessity for this discussion to proceed, a disclaimer must be made about establishing such categories. The walls separating these categories are porous at best. Although the separations are valid, one type of revisionism easily relates and often leads to another. However, taken with the proverbial grain of salt, these categories can lead to a fuller discussion of superheroes and their significant role in the new media forms that are redefining contemporary thought. Four basic categories present themselves, with the porous walls separating them being most indistinct between the first two types of revisionism. These basic types of revisionism include additive, fundamental, conceptual and critical.

ADDITIVE REVISIONS

Additive revisions are the type seen most often: seemingly minor additions that can be read as the logical outgrowth of the basic premise established within a superhero narrative. Such revisions are incremental and expand the world of the superhero by adding abilities, characters, and elements of society in such a way that they reinforce motifs central to the story from the "start." Of course, the exact starting point of superhero narratives generally remains difficult to determine for reasons already mentioned (most significantly, the way recent incarnations often take precedence and the most current versions appear most authentic). Nevertheless, most superheroes that come to be regarded as "classic" (such as Wonder Woman and the Hulk) have an essential starting point at the beginning of their run in comic books. With Wonder Woman, most of the additive revisions revolve around idealistic Diana Prince's Amazonian heritage left behind in part to serve the larger needs of the world from which the Amazons separated themselves. In the case of the Hulk, they are connected to brilliant Bruce Banner's over-reaching which pushes the scientific envelope too far and creates a traumatic event that awakens the angry monster within him.

Perhaps due to the fact that his origin seems less well developed than the above mentioned superheroes at his first appearance in *Detective Comics* #27, Batman demonstrates how even a delayed origin story can be seen as an outgrowth of the initial framework. Within the first Batman story, the rich and lazy Bruce Wayne rides along with his friend Commissioner Gordon to a murder scene; in short order, he becomes bored and leaves Gordon to his work. Soon thereafter, the Batman appears on the trail of the serial murderer who threatens the business elite of the city. While it could be argued the first story is set up to showcase the dark knight in violent confrontation with criminals (resulting in the climactic revelation that Bruce Wayne is the Batman), the initial story does establish basic elements that lead to the classic origin story: Batman's inscrutable dual identity, his dark form of justice, and his outsider status in regard to most officers of the law. Thereafter, the soon added explanation for Bruce Wayne's costumed fight for justice flows directly from these precepts; his parents, the millionaire Waynes, were killed by a common mugger. Training his body and mind, young Bruce Wayne would eventually don a disguise to strike fear into criminals, a "cowardly" lot nevertheless beyond the reach of law enforcement. Since Batman is a non-powered superhero, the expansion of his arsenal—his utility belt with many gadgets and his vehicles which ranged from the Batgyro to the Batmobile—seems logical.

Although most of his early foes were street criminals, Batman did face some supernatural villains as well (such as the Monk, later revealed as a vampire). On one hand this could be seen as a precedent which sets up the introduction of Batman's regular array of garish villains, including the Joker, the Penguin, and Two-Face. On the other hand, the rogues' gallery needs no certain precedent, portrayed by many as the natural outgrowth of the presence of a costumed superhero; consider Frank Miller's *Batman: Year One* or Christopher Nolan's *Batman Begins* which portray Batman donning a terrifying costume as the equivalent of a policeman using an automatic rifle and causing an escalation among those who commit crimes on the street. Batman initially works alone but would be joined by confidantes such as his loyal butler Alfred and his boy wonder sidekick Robin. Authors have explained this widening of the Batman family as a natural outgrowth of Batman's vigilante justice, an inspiration to others in the midst of a crime-ridden city; consider Edmond Hamilton's introduction of Batwoman in the 1950s *Batman* or Jeph Loeb's retelling of Robin's origin in *Dark Victory*, in which Batman inspires individuals to be more than they were.

Of course, identifying these changes to be simply additive must be acknowledged as a debatable claim. Despite those who argue that these revisions grew from the initial vision of Batman, others would argue that Batman's rogues' gallery separated Batman from grimmer reality of common crime that was largely the focus of the comic book up to that point; in addition, the introduction of Robin is read by some as a fundamental revision that steered stories toward a juvenile audience and changed Batman's world from that of film noir drama to Technicolor comedy. And this brings up the next category of revisionism.

FUNDAMENTAL REVISIONS

Fundamental revisions are major changes which signal a departure from what has been presented before in a specific superhero narrative. Since the difference between the first and second type of revisionism is a matter of degree, an example is necessary (while humbly noting that level of departure is debatable). In the case of Captain America, who faded away with World War II patriotism, Jack Kirby would resurrect his creation in the 1960s within the pages of *The Avengers*. As a patriot frozen in a block of ice during a wartime skirmish, Captain America would awake in a 1960s era not only no longer awash with American idealism but also informed by paranoia and eventually a deep cynicism toward American institutions. Therefore, in contrast to his initial run, which at times tonally bordered on jingoism, the second run of Captain America would be a contemplation of the validity of American ideals and inability of society to live up to those ideals. This radical rewriting of Captain America has had a permanent impact on the character (and it could be argued that this rewriting made him a round, viable character able to exist beyond the simplistic war-time sentiment of his original series).

Therefore, fundamental revisions are those which do not necessarily proceed in a logical way from the basic premise established within a superhero narrative. And with this definition in mind, fundamental revisions are those changes which take the superhero to a new audience and reshape the basic understanding of that superhero's significance within the pantheon of superheroes. Therefore, this does not include the "major" revisions promised but seldom delivered by so many DC and Marvel cross-over events. However, this does include alternative timelines and imaginary stories, especially when those alternative timelines and imaginary stories impinge upon the original storyline.

One of the best examples in this category would be the X-Men stories as written by Chris Claremont, for a number of reasons. Originally created during Stan Lee's creative boom in 1960s, the X-Men would be superheroes born with abilities arising from genetic abnormalities (known as mutants). Gathered together by Professor Xavier at his School for Gifted Youngsters, the X-Men stories would often be read as parables describing anti–Semitism or racial intolerance, but it's unclear that such a reading is inherent within the initial run. The five students at the school are notably white and middle to upper class while their enemies are Jewish (Magneto) and gypsy (Quicksilver and the Scarlet Witch), part of the ridiculously titled supervillain team, the Brotherhood of *Evil* Mutants.

The development of mutanthood as a flexible metaphor for otherness only truly took place once Chris Claremont began writing the series in 1975 (after it floundered and became a reprint-only series). While not disavowing the initial series, Claremont decided to work with a mostly new, international team, replacing all but one of the original team (Cyclops).[7] Rather than tepidly deal with the social implications of mutanthood, Claremont made the outcast status of mutants central to the storyline, with the team divided amongst itself (lacking the idealistic teamwork of the original X-Men) and the "villains" like Magneto much more sympathetic with viable other perspectives on mutanthood. The traditional lines between the good superheroes and the evil supervillains were blurred as pressure of social prejudices became the chief culprit in the series. The initial story arc would culminate in Claremont's "Days of Future Past" in which he depicts a future where not only mutants but all superheroes are killed (or put in concentration camps by government engineered robot technology).

Similar to the disagreement about how to classify the introduction of supervillains and a teenage sidekick to Batman's universe, some could argue that Claremont simply pushed forward Lee's ironic treatment of superheroism. While it is a potentially valid argument that could be dealt with at some length, many others agree that Claremont adds a degree of self-consciousness rarely seen in superhero narratives before his run with the X-Men. For instance, the loss of the traditional good-evil dichotomy within the X-Men could be emblematically represented within the break-out character of Claremont's new X-Men: Wolverine. With a loner mentality that worked at odds with the team, Wolverine comes to represent an antithesis to the traditional superhero; he is violent without a clear moral center, unconcerned with hiding his identity from the world, and unaware of his origin. While at times a flat character (simply a Dirty Harry with claws), Wolverine works primarily as a foil by which the traditional super-heroism of a character like Cyclops might be reevaluated.

As the series developed through Claremont's run, it became clear that both of these characters would be incomplete without the other (the two symbolically linked to one another through their love of Jean Grey). Just as Magneto's violent assertion of superiority and Professor Xavier's wish for peaceful coexistence deals with the "other" in society, Wolverine and Cyclops represented two fundamental attitudes toward superheroism, a sort of metanarrative formed by the X-Men. And this reevaluation of super-heroism in general is magnified in one of Claremont's most well-known storylines, "The Dark Phoenix Saga," dealing with the third person in their love triangle. When Jean Grey becomes the incredibly powerful Phoenix only to be driven insane by the magnitude of her power, her story could be understood as a rewriting of the impossibly powerful Superman (capable of doing anything but doing little besides fighting the villain of the month). However, this type of revisionism takes the next step forward in this framework.

CONCEPTUAL REVISIONS

Conceptual revisions rewrite the basic ideas not of a superhero but of the superhero as a general idea with wide-ranging social impact. In other words, this type of revisionism doesn't take place simply when a new writer or artist takes over an old series. Instead, this type of revisionism only takes place in a new series which may intentionally resemble a series that pre-ceded it, but does so only to drastically rework the archetypal superhero narrative. While self-consciousness may be a component of Claremont's X-Men and Claremont may venture into conceptual revisions, the texts which more purely represent conceptual revisionism view the superhero seriously and playfully as the same time, earnestly embracing the conventions of superhero narratives while foregrounding those conventions in a way that indicates skeptical detachment. While it's apparent that revisions can only take place over the course of time, conceptual revisions would be the revisions that seem to require the most distance between the source material and the revision.

Although Stan Lee has often been overcome by his enthusiasm for his own work and therefore has not been the perfect model of self-con-sciousness, his work on Spiderman would be a good introduction to this type of revisionism. While some see the adolescent sidekick trend of the 1940s as an attempt to appeal to comic books' largest audience at the time, Lee would be the first to clearly centralize a character who represented

the stereotypical comic book reader. Peter Parker is the teenage intellectual (teenagers being the largest audience for comic books in the 1960s)
who is cast out of the social cliques of his high school. After being bitten
by a radioactive spider and receiving spider-like powers, Parker did not
put on a costume and fight crime (seemingly the only option in conventional superhero narratives); he fought with a mask in exhibition wrestling
matches in order to make money that he never had. Adding this realistic
character motivation causes the reader to move outside the conventions
of past comic book narratives toward a more critical viewpoint. An orphan
like most superheroes, Parker lived with his uncle and aunt, who served
as surrogate parents. As the greedy world encourages him to look out for
himself, he allows a burglar to escape (only to find out that burglar later
killed his uncle). Again, exposing the trappings of superhero origins (such
as the need to be an orphan), Parker only becomes Spiderman once his
"father" is lost and he is motivated by the guilt he feels; ironically, his
superpowers physically enable him to stop the murder but also psychologically disable him. Spiderman will regularly be regarded as a menace to
society and more importantly to Peter Parker's "real" life (again a narrative move that causes the reader to question the nature of superheroism
as conventionally portrayed).

Although Spiderman serves well as a prototypical example of conceptual revisionism, the best and typical example of such revisionism is Alan
Moore's *Watchmen*. With a cast of characters loosely based on Charlton
characters such as the Blue Beetle, Captain Atom, and the Question
(owned by DC comics, the publisher of Moore's series), *Watchmen* had
goals that are more ambitious than even fundamental revision, bringing
a sense of realism to superhero narratives. Moore accomplishes this in a
paradoxical way by constructing an alternate timeline leading to 1985 (the
year before the publication of the series) in which costumed crime fighters
had existed but are outlawed and in which the United States is poised on
the brink of nuclear war with the Soviet Union.

Rather than vigilantes welcomed into the larger fold of society (as
with Golden Age superheroes), the costumed crime fighters of *Watchmen*
are objects of fear, seen as representatives of misappropriated power. When
the Comedian, one of the former "costumes" (who continued to operate
through government assignment) is killed, Rorschach, one of the only
remaining costumes still working independently, investigates the crime.
With an uncompromising moral code, Rorschach is as paranoid as the culture around him, believing this to be the beginning of a plot to eliminate
all costumes. Ultimately, he discovers that his paranoid fantasy is true, that
Ozymandias, a former costume made rich by selling his image, planned
the killing and subsequent events to eliminate costumes. Hardly a quintessential supervillain, Ozymandias engineers a faux alien invasion scenario that kills half the people of New York but prevents the impending

nuclear war between the United States and the Soviet Union; the two super-powers pledge to work together to face this "extraterrestrial" threat.

By making Rorschach's paranoid fantasy the truth and the supervil-lain's plan that of world peace, the narrative of *Watchmen* questions the conventional superhero story with its convenient dividing lines between good and evil. Moreover, the narrative prevents Rorschach and his once again partner, Nite Owl, from engaging in a necessary component of the superhero power fantasy: violent confrontation that results in the defeat of a great evil. In this case, they are stymied by the questions of greater good with only Rorschach resolving to tell the world of Ozymandias' "crime." He is ultimately prevented from doing so by Dr. Manhattan, the superpowered human who finds himself curiously detached from the human experience by virtue of his superpowers. Unlike Siegel's Superman but like Nietzsche's superman, he finds himself above tragedy and the human devotion to morality. (In fact, his last words indicating that noth-ing ever ends directly refer to Nietzsche's idea of eternal recurrence.) Dr. Manhattan maintains his connections to such human concerns only through his tenuous connections to human beings such as his wife, Lau-rie Juspeczyk (also known as the costumed crime fighter, the Silk Spec-tre).

By showing the general ugliness, sadness, and doubt in the lives of superheroes, Moore reverses the veneration that regularly accompanies the reading of superhero stories. In addition to forcing the reader into a crit-ical position by resisting conventions and forcing the reader to analyze superhero narratives in general, *Watchmen* more directly addresses aspects of the superhero through the newly developing relationship between Nite Owl and the Silk Spectre. Unable to sexually consummate their relation-ship in their lives as ordinary people, they only do so after donning their costumes with the assertion that the costumes made it better (thus expos-ing the widespread fetish of the second skin superhero costume).

Perhaps most significant is the metafictive elements within the story which range from epigraphs to excerpts from books written by the char-acters. Among these, a comic book read within the comic book narrative by an inconsequential character forms a parallel with the story that pro-foundly illuminates the central narrative. *Tales of the Black Freighter* portrays a castaway's attempts to return home in order to warn his family of the impending arrival of a phantom pirate ship, attempts which become more and more gruesome. With parallels to the culture of *Watchmen* and the warped psyches of Rorschach and Ozymandias, this comic book story also exists within an alternate history in which horror comics, not superhero comics, became dominant. With the horror piece speaking so clearly of and descriptively to the world around it, this metafictive element suggests that superhero comics do the same for our world. Although intended to be a salvo to superhero comic books (rather than inspire the grim and gritty period that followed), *Watchmen* also serves as a desperate plea to read conventional superhero narratives carefully, critically, and self-consciously. And this brings up the final category of revisionism.

Rather than using the trickery of a villain to pit superheroes against one another, Alan Moore uses moral conundrums; in the final chapter of *Watchmen*, Rorschach realizes that Dr. Manhattan (with his super-powered hand aimed at Rorschach) will not allow him to inform the world of Ozymandias' "crime." From page 24 of the 12th chapter of *Watchmen* (New York: DC Comics, 1987).

CRITICAL REVISIONS

Critical revisions operate outside the mediums typically associated with superhero narratives such as comic books, animation, and film. Instead, these are interpretative positions taken by critics of popular culture who study superheroes, interpretive positions that ultimately have an impact on the way that superhero stories are told (or retold as the case may be). In this category, the term "critics" is being used in the broadest sense, not only referring to someone editing a collection on superhero revisionism but also to people who write letters to comic book letter pages,[8] provide commentary to DVD editions of superhero television series, or produce superhero fanfiction on the internet. In fact, since superheroes had been recognized as an important cultural product in terms of their ability to generate revenue long before they had been recognized as an important cultural product deserving of scrutiny by the higher echelons of academia, the non-academic criticism may be more important overall; companies have recognized that they are dependent upon fan appreciation and have often directly responded to fan input.

One of the most universally decried stories (which some say demonstrates that superhero stories are in the hands of people who don't take their artistic potential seriously) is the death of Jason Todd storyline ending in *Batman* #428. After setting up Jason Todd as the second Robin (Dick

Grayson had then become Nightwing), writers develop Todd, perhaps already in reaction to negative fan response, as a fairly annoying character. Within a story involving the Joker, Robin is caught in an explosion and fans are allowed to call DC (for a small fee) and indicate their preference for him to live or die. While perhaps indicative of a sort of blind devotion to the consumer and making money from Batman as a product, this stunt certainly demonstrates the influence of forces outside those directly responsible for producing superhero narratives, such as editors, writers, artists, etc.

In order to see how such outside forces influence superhero revisionism, one need look no further than the intended and unintended influences of the notorious Fredric Wertham, author of the poorly written *Seduction of the Innocent.* His 1954 tome argues that comic books ultimately have a negative social impact on youth and at the time resulted in Congressional hearings on the subject. As a consequence of those hearings, the comic book industry agreed to regulate itself through a list of prohibitions detailed in "the comics code" (prohibitions against overt expressions of sex, violence, drug use, etc.). Two intended effects would be the sanitization of comic books and the death of the horror comics industry (the central target of Wertham's attack), which could not survive within the restrictions of the comics code. In addition, this event would keep comics in the ghetto as kids' stuff until the underground comix movement of the 1960s again brought comic books to an adult audience (limited though that audience for art comics may have been).

There would also be two unintended effects, one of which would be the resurrection of superhero comic books (which could be more easily rewritten to adhere to the code than the horror comic books which had been stealing their audience). Perhaps more significant would be a specific case seen in the rewriting of Batman, also a target of the attack. Wertham would be the first to make the homophobic charge that something unsavory was taking place between Bruce Wayne and his ward, Dick Grayson. In order to redress this charge, the characters of Batwoman and Batgirl were introduced to the Batman titles, supposedly as love interests for Batman and Robin. However, due to prohibitions against violence and sexual expression, Batman and Robin became even less stereotypically masculine in their renderings. In fact, when Batwoman regularly sought a kiss from Batman, he would respond with a quick excuse about crime to fight (as such a display of physical affection was in spirit prohibited by the comic code). Nevertheless, this sort of side-step (immortalized in the TV series with Adam West) made Batman look more gay than he had before.

Due to its more direct and intentional nature, a more potent example can be found in one of the new lives of Superman: the film *Superman Returns.* Over the years, many interpretations of Superman's mythology have been set forth, ranging from Superman as a Christ-figure to Superman as a Jew, Superman as an immigrant to Superman as a gay man. Within the scholarship of Superman, the idea of Superman as Christ has been most persistent.[9] The claim is regarded as ironic by some when considering the Jewish identities of his creators,[10] but those who argue for Superman as Christ have suggested that not only did Jerry Siegel and Joel Schuster choose to hide their own Jewishness but that subsequent writers pulled Superman more in line with the Christianity of mainstream American culture.[11] Nevertheless, recent critics have been very interested in unearthing the intended or unintended Jewish characteristics of the Superman story. In line with the idea of Superman as an outsider are the readings of him as an immigrant and as gay; however, while the reading of him as immigrant takes a look at him as the bearer of the American flag in the colors of his costume and stresses his assimilation to the ideals of American culture,[12] the reading of him as gay takes a metaphorical reading of his secret identity and stresses his need to hide from culture at large.[13]

Quite curiously, Brian Singer's film rendition of Superman chooses to stress the interpretation of Superman as Christ. Picking up where the film *Superman II* ended (with Superman replacing the flag on the White House), *Superman Returns* clearly deals with Superman as a Christ-like savior. Superman directly discusses with Lois why the world needs a savior and later in the film sacrifices himself to save the world. Falling to earth with his arms outstretched in the pose of the crucified Christ, Superman seems to die but is later resurrected to promise his son that he will never be without him.[14] The reason that this is curious (and shows the power of the most popular critical position on Superman to influence the shape of this reincarnation of Superman) is that Brian Singer is both Jewish and gay. Even more ironically, he is widely understood to have been chosen as the director of *Superman Returns* on the strength of his work with the X-Men films which used mutanthood as a metaphor to describe both Jewish and homosexual identity.[15]

Some Possible Explanations of Revisionism Up for Revision

The fact that superheroes have been revised is not a profound observation, but it is a phenomenon that deserves to be dealt with more centrally in critical discussions of superheroes. In some ways, revisionism has been dealt with both directly and indirectly in some of the major scholarship on superheroes that precedes this collection. This scholarship will be profiled in order to provide: (1) a yet broader basis for the discussion on superhero revisionism and (2) a sense of how critical attitudes toward superheroes have changed over the years in which they've been studied.

This overview is not meant to be an historically exhaustive study, but works with several texts that I consider by the author to be the most representative of distinctive attitudes toward superhero revisionism. The starting point for superheroes scholarship is diffuse, but Jules Feiffer's *The Great Comic Book Heroes* would be the best single work to mark the beginning. Written in 1965 by an illustrator who produced several notable comic books, Feiffer's book would be part of an era (against which Will Eisner would fight) that insisted comic books would never be regarded as an art form. Curiously, Feiffer would be part of the group of people who both produced and consumed comic books and yet who insisted that comic books could never be art. Referring to them as "junk," he found in them a relief from the oppressive junk of culture which pressured the individual to conform. His treatment of superheroes is often affectionate but that doesn't prevent him from making some great analysis about the meaning of Superman's secret identity, the significance of Batman as a counterpoint to Superman's idealism, and the impact of World War II on the integrity of superheroes. Most clearly related to the issue of revisionism would be his claims about how the culture and industry worked together to create something "new" that satisfied every expectation. "When *Superman* at last appeared, he brought with him the deep satisfaction of all underground truths: Our reaction was less 'How original!' than 'But, of course!'" (Feiffer 9). Although in love with the medium, Feiffer's discussion deals in a sort of cynicism that is often nearly Marxist. In reference to World War II superheroes, he acknowledges that superheroes in general may speak to our more basic selves but are also changed as need be to better satisfy the most recent cultural phenomenon (therefore updated not to be new, but more familiar).

The Great Comic Heroes was initially marketed to a wide audience; in its fully illustrated form, it was intended to be sold less as a cultural commentary and more as a nostalgic reference to the Golden Age of superheroes. The gentrification of superhero studies would only be fully accomplished with the work of Umberto Eco, whose cachet as a semiologist allowed him to deal in popular culture in the same way as cultural critics like Roland Barthes or media critics like Marshall McLuhan. With "The Myth of Superman" (a chapter in *The Role of the Reader*), Eco inaugurated an era in which scholars saw comic books as fair game.[16] Eco's study would be the first of many that looked at the essential narrative of Superman as it intersected with the reader in history. While he didn't call superhero comics junk, he certainly understood them as market-driven. As he puzzles through Superman's ability to seem timeless and timely at the same time, he states, "Superman, then, must remain 'inconsumable' and at the same time be 'consumed' according to the ways of everyday life. He possesses the characteristics of timeless myth, but is accepted only because his activities take place in our human and everyday life" (Eco 111). Therefore, Eco contends that the writers of Superman develop a clever way of portraying the timeline of Superman's life in which what has happened previously is always unclear. "The stories develop in a kind of oneiric climate—of which the reader is not aware—where what has happened before and what happened after appear extremely hazy. The narrator picks up the strand of the event again and again, as if he had forgotten to say something and wanted to add details to what had already been said" (Eco 114). In this way, Eco identifies the device he sees used to excuse the consistent return to the origin story or to retell variations on the same story.[17] Whether this description of superhero storytelling is limited to the earliest eras of comic books or still holds true is debatable, but Eco is regularly referenced by critics seeking to perform an historical analysis of comic books by examining how the same superhero story is told differently in different time periods.[18]

Probably the most well known scholarly work on superheroes is Richard Reynolds' *Superheroes: A Modern Mythology*, due at least in part to the fact that its central position justifies superhero studies. In his 1992 work, Reynolds contends that the superhero retains a series of conventions in almost all permutations (including a traumatic origin, superpowers, and a secret identity). Implicitly working the notion of archetypes and Joseph Campbell's heroic monomyth, Reynolds ties superheroes to a much older tradition of heroic mythologies. Thus, superhero comic books are not junk, may be art, but certainly are myth in an academic sense of the term. In this way, he not only makes the superhero narrative a cross-cultural and transhistorical construct, he also connects the superhero narrative to much older forms of literature, like *The Odyssey*, which already have a place within the academy. In his discussion of various types of comic book continuities, Reynolds states:

> Because there is such a focused determination among writers and fans that continuity shall be kept up at all costs, there always remains plenty of room for the reinterpretation of consistent facts within the style of a particular creative team. One element of the character's myth (for example, the character's origin) can be used to generate a potentially unlimited number of texts, even texts which seem to 'tell the same story.' Continuity implies an agreed body of material which exists independently of any specific text—analogous perhaps to the way in which medieval poets could retell the 'Matter of Britain' before Malory attempted a systematizing of the Arthurian 'continuity' in the *Mort D'Arthur* [Reynolds 47–48].

Again, in relation to the issue of revisionism, Reynolds' explanation of revisions is much less tied to the superhero as commodity and much more to the superhero as an element of a cultural unconsciousness. The near-infinite variation of the superheroes merely belies the consistency offered by the core of the story.

The soundest rejection of Reynolds came in 2002 within Geoff Klock's *How to Read Superhero Comics and Why*; Klock states, "These kinds of observations in regard to popular culture have become tedious ... they are designed to make us recognize something previously latent in our mind rather than tell us something we did not know before" (Klock 10). With an intensely theoretical text which contends contemporary comic books can be regarded as art alongside high literature, Klock sets out quite a bit of work for himself. This is due largely to the fact that his theory of choice is Harold Bloom's "anxiety of influence" and as an advocate of the traditional literary canon, Bloom would be unlikely to consider comic books suitable for inclusion in the category of high literature. However, Klock's choice of material for his study is limited to a small sample of Modern Age comic book works such as Grant Morrison's *JLA* and Warren Ellis' *The Authority*; the authors take comic books seriously as an art-form and willfully flaunt their self-conscious approach to the medium. Although most interested in fundamental and conceptual revisions in the Modern Age, Klock offers a clear motivation for repetition with a difference in superhero narratives: "[S]uperhero comic books are an especially good place to witness the structure of misprision, because as a serial narrative that has been running for more than sixty years, reinterpretation becomes a part of its survival code. Bloom would suggest that novels, poems, and plays, often viewed as closed structures, are best seen in a continuous line with the history of their literature, a paradigm Batman fans have known for years" (Klock 13–14).

With the proficient reader's intentional interaction with superhero narratives and their culture as a necessary part of the experience of superheroes, the Freudian-based anxiety of influence determines that a reader will engage in misprision, an intentional and poetic misreading that reorients the text; this self-conscious move on the part of individuals who produce superhero narratives not only makes the texts they produce more personally relevant but also reveals to the culture the implications of the meaning inherent within the source material. Now that these major texts in superhero scholarship have been profiled, it should again be made clear that my intention is to offer a sense of how the phenomenon of revisionism has been described within the major trends they represent. Since the goal is to further the discussion on this phenomenon, my intention is not to show preference to one approach over another; in fact, vestiges of all these approaches make their appearance within the essays presented in this collection.

Revisionism Throughout Superheroic History and in this Mild Mannered Collection

The basis for this collection resides in part with my fascination with the widespread embrace of superhero revisionism that coincides with a greater willingness by the public at large to take the superhero "seriously." However, it resides in larger part and more particularly with panels I've organized for conferences and festivals, conversations that I've had with colleagues and associates, and inspirations from primary resources and scholarship. While I find the framework presented in this introduction quite useful (and hope you do as well), I quite intentionally refrained from making it a springboard for all essays in this collection. Instead, I preferred to choose essays that seemed to form unintentional connections, a strange sort of synergy that developed on its own.

By responding to a Zeitgeist that was at work within the world of superhero scholarship, I believe that this collection has a greater integrity than anything that I could forcefully manufacture. That's not to say that some papers didn't come from calls-for-papers for a panel on the subject (and actually a few even came from a call-for-papers for this collection). Nevertheless, I believe I merely am helping to push forward something that I recognized had already begun rolling. Even though revisionism extends beyond the imposition of a strict historical schema, I've created a loose way to group the following essays based on the eras or mediums with which each primarily deal. The first section is "Superheroes in the Golden and Silver Ages," the second, "Superheroes in the Modern Age," and the third, "Superheroes in the Multi-Media Age." Obviously, this is not an attempt to definitively establish historical periods, as superheroes from their inception have always been part of a multi-media age. (With that stated, the third section does deal quite intentionally with the more recent developments in superhero revisionism outside the medium that made them famous.)

"Superheroes in the Golden and Silver Ages" employs terms popularly used to describe the first age of superheroes, beginning with the comics of the late 1930s, and the second age of superheroes, beginning with the comics of the early 1960s. Some call the "age" of superhero comics in the 1970s the "Bronze Age," but that takes too far the Golden/Silver spilt suggested by a fan in a letters page. While the split between Golden and Silver Ages does have some significant value, the further split of the Bronze Age doesn't have nearly as much value.[19]

The Golden Age represents Superman, Batman, Wonder Woman, and a wide array of others created or purchased by the company that would come to be known as DC Comics. The basic framework for the superhero—heroes with lost parents who donned costumes and fought for justice outside the law—would be formed simultaneously from American idealism and doubt and often from the collective experience of World War II.

The Silver Age represents Spiderman, the Hulk, and The Fantastic Four, and a wide array of others owned by Marvel Comics, which breathed new life into the genre of superhero comics. Fundamentally questioning many of the central tenets of superhero enshrined within the Golden Age, these superheroes would be written with some of the same idealism of the Golden Age but would be also informed by cynical detachment that seemed a necessary part of the Cold War's atomic anxieties. (Curiously, they are both now often regarded with nostalgia, together forming the fundamental foundation of the superheroes known worldwide.) As the superhero industry grew (and grew notorious for its treatment of superhero creators), several key issues that formed the foundation of these comics are represented here, ranging from America's national identity and gender politics in the wake of World War II to the evolution of American ideals as seen through Jewish eyes.

"Superheroes in the Modern Age" uses a regularly mentioned, if not universally agreed upon, term used to describe the third age of superheroes beginning with the comics of the 1980s. (Some have called it the "Dark Age" to keep up with the above ages schema and also to describe the tone of superhero comics of this era, but this seems as uselessly poetic as the Bronze Age; others have called it the revisionist era to describe the treatment of the superhero motif, but this seems to ignore the possibility that fundamental revisions could take place in other eras and might take place beyond it as well.)

While some new superheroes were developed during this period (such as Todd McFarlane's Spawn), the Modern Age represents a general darkening and maturing of the superhero narrative. As the comic book audience became more thoroughly older, adult themes were regularly introduced to the fantasy world of superhero narratives. While still maintaining the trappings of superhero stories like the secret identities and superpowers, there seemed to be more psychological realism in the stories of Alan Moore's *Swamp Thing* and Frank Miller's *Daredevil* (incidentally, this was also the era of knowing your comic book writer and artist); superheroes were imagined as if they might exist in the real world and *Watchmen* and *The Dark Knight Returns* ushered into superhero narratives self-conscious political commentary about the dangers of hero worship. In the wake of these watershed titles came excessive violence and sexual content, the proliferation of comic book antiheroes (such as the Cable, Lobo, and Spawn), and some highly literate narrative (and meta-narrative) work that threatened to develop a mainstream audience for comics. As the superhero comic book buyers market grew (and then went bust with the industry managing to soldier onward), several key issues that formed the foundation of these comics are represented here, including the supposed post-modernity of new comic book narratives, the increasing globalization of American superheroes, and the nagging question of where the superhero might go from here.

"Superheroes in the Multi-Media Age" is simply a descriptive label and shouldn't raise the hackles of anyone with a political investment in what the ages of superheroes might be called. As previously noted, superheroes have always been part of a multi-media age and the other mediums that have represented them have been far from inconsequential in shaping the superhero as a whole. Nearly from his inception, Superman was recognized as a property to be sold, and selling a character to be used in other visual or narrative mediums increases the exposure and awareness of that character. However, selling a character also gives the buyer the artistic license to redesign the character. Although trying to maintain the character's integrity, comic book companies have also been trying to make money from the start. Therefore, strategic compromises are made with artists who have other visions of the superhero and how that superhero might look in a new medium. Superman reached a vast new audience through the Superman radio show, Batman through the Batman television show, and the Spiderman through the Spiderman cartoon. In each case, none of these other versions would be easily forgotten as these other versions revised the superhero and then worked organically to revise their representations in other mediums, including comic books.

As the seemingly insatiable appetite for all things superhero continues to grow in recent years, several key issues mentioned above and several others dealing with their translation are represented here, ranging from the tension to the interdependence of various superhero mediums and including the way traditional philosophies of gender and society are seen in new ways. (With one essay introducing this section and serving as a bridge between the three sections, this section focuses primarily on late 20th and early 21st century developments in the superhero: things that have taken place as culture at large can no longer ignore the multi-media omnipresence of the superhero.)

Ultimately, the collection develops a sense of coherency by taking a very serious critical and theoretical look at superheroes as myth, commodity, and much more. However, it hopefully also does this while still encouraging an enthusiastic debate enabled by the playful consciousness of a superhero world that is endlessly revised.

NOTES

1. For a fuller description of the fanboy (the adult superhero comic book fan who grows up with the supposedly juvenile stories of superheroes), see the excellent overview of comic book fandom in Matthew J. Pustz's *Comic Book Culture*.

2. As listed in endnote 1, Pustz gives an excellent sense of the development of comic book fandom, what it once was and what it is now.

3. This often repeated characterization of superhero stories is most often credited to the work of Richard Reynolds in *Superheroes: A Modern Mythology*, profiled later in this introduction.

4. Grant Morrison was entrusted with the new millennium version of Superman in a title supposedly starting with a clean slate and unburdened by over a half century of continuity issues: *All Star Superman*.

5. Unlike so many other stories from this era, this 1997 story has yet to be collected in a single volume (and considering its lack of popularity with fans, it is not likely to be collected anytime soon).

6. In this case, I'm counting the two incarnations of the Green Goblin as one villain.

7. In order to give credit where it is due, it must be noted that the new team first appeared in *X-Men* Giant Size #1, which was written by Len Wein. Despite introducing the

contentious and international feel of the new version of the old super-team, this issue was primarily an adventure story that didn't establish much of what became central to Claremont's X-Men.

8. An excellent discussion of the power of the intellectual nitpickers who wrote to letters pages in the heyday of the letters pages can be found in Pustz's *Comic Book Culture*, particularly in the chapter titled "From Comicons to Web Pages."

9. This interpretation of Superman is probably best represented in the article by Thomas Andrae that describes Superman's historical transition, "From Menace to Messiah."

10. For a treatment of the Jewish roots and general Jewishness of Superman and other superheroes, see Weinstein Simcha's *Up, Up, and Oy Vey!*

11. This pull is made most painfully obvious when Superman marries Lois Lane in the ongoing comic book storyline and Jerry Siegel serves as the *priest* who marries them.

12. This interpretation of Superman is represented in an impressive essay by Gary Engle titled "What Makes Superman So Darned American?"

13. Due to the controversy surrounding it, this position is most notably represented in Alonso Duralde's "What I Learned from Superman" featured in *The Advocate*; the release of the article immediately preceded the release of *Superman Returns* and the issue's cover sported the title "How Gay is Superman?"

14 Superman's son could complicate a straightforward reading of Superman as Christ but need not, as the Christ comparison is metaphorical.

15. In terms of the focus on mutants as representative of racial and sexual others, Magneto is quite clearly a Jewish concentration camp survivor, seen in a flashback in concentration camps in the first film and making reference to the tattooed number on his arm in the third; less clearly but more humorously as the metaphorical gay man, Iceman "comes out" as a mutant to his parents in the second film, to which they reply: "Have you ever tried not being a mutant?"

16. With the release of the *Superman: The Movie* written by Mario Puzo and starring Marlon Brando, culture at large began to take superheroes a bit more seriously as well.

17. Marvel's Ultimate line and DC's All Star line was ostensibly designed to attract new readers but by colloquial evidence actually seems to attract old readers.

18. One of the best examples of this trend is "From Menace to Messiah," which uses Eco to further its aim as a historical analysis and cultural studies work.

19. Some might suggest that race was the issue that distinguished superhero comic books in the 1970s from their predecessors; however, as previously noted in the analysis of Blade, that issue is portrayed too often at a superficial level to deserve a separate designation.

WORKS CITED*

Andrae, Thomas. "From Menace to Messiah: The History and Historicity of Superman." *Discourse* 2 (1980): 84–111.

Batman. Dir. Tim Burton. Warner Bros., 1989.

Batman and Robin. Dir. Joel Schumacher. Warner Bros., 1997.

Batman Begins. Dir. Christopher Nolan. Warner Bros., 2005.

Batman Forever. Dir. Joel Schumacher. Warner Bros., 1995.

Batman Returns. Dir. Tim Burton. Warner Bros., 1992.

Blade. Dir. Stephen Norrington. New Line, 1998.

Duralde, Alonso. "What I Learned from Superman." *The Advocate* 23 May 2006: 38–40.

Eco, Umberto. "The Myth of Superman." *The Role of the Reader: Explorations in the Semiotics of Texts*. Bloomington: Indiana University Press, 1979. 107–124.

On the works cited pages, I have chosen to use the writer's name as a reference point. This is done for the sake of convenience and should not be read as a suggestion that writers are more important than the artists in the ultimate effect created by a comic book experience.

Engle, Gary. "What Makes Superman So Darned American?" *Superman at Fifty!: The Persistence of a Legend.* Eds. Dennis Dooley and Gary Engle. New York: Macmillan, 1987. 79–87.
Feiffer, Jules. *The Great Comic Book Heroes.* Seattle: Fantagraphics, 2003.
Francis, John. *Superman: The Dark Side.* New York: DC Comics, 1999.
Gaiman, Neil. *1602.* New York: Marvel Comics, 2005.
_____. *Sandman: Preludes and Nocturnes.* New York: Vertigo, 1995.*
Johns, Geoff. *Infinite Crisis.* New York: DC Comics, 2006.
Klock, Geoff. *How to Read Superhero Comics and Why.* New York: Continuum, 2002.
Loeb, Jeph. *Batman: Dark Victory.* New York: DC Comics, 2001.
Millar, Mark. *Superman: Red Son.* New York: DC Comics, 2004.
Miller, Frank. *Batman: Year One.* New York: DC Comics, 1997.
_____. *The Dark Knight Returns.* New York: DC Comics, 1996.
Moore, Alan. *The Killing Joke.* New York: DC Comics, 1988.
_____. *Watchmen.* New York: DC Comics, 1987.
Morrison, Grant. *The Filth.* New York: Vertigo, 2004.
_____. *The Invisibles: Say You Want a Revolution.* New York: Vertigo, 1996.*
_____. *The New X-Men: E is for Extinction.* New York: Marvel Comics, 2001.*
Pustz, Matthew J. *Comic Book Culture: Fanboys and True Believers.* Jackson: University Press of Mississippi, 1999.
Reynolds, Richard. *Superheroes: A Modern Mythology.* Jackson: University Press of Mississippi, 1992.
Simcha, Weinstein. *Up, Up, and Oy Vey!: How Jewish History, Culture, and Values Shaped the Comic Book Superhero.* Baltimore: Leviathan, 2006.
Spiderman 3. Dir. Sam Raimi. Columbia Pictures, 2007.
Superman II. Dir. Richard Lester. Warner Bros., 1980.
Superman III. Dir. Richard Lester. Warner Bros., 1983.
Superman IV: The Quest for Peace. Dir. Sidney J. Furie. Warner Bros., 1987.
Superman Returns. Dir. Brian Singer. Warner Bros., 2006.
Superman: The Movie. Dir. Richard Donner. Warner Bros., 1978.
Waid, Mark. *Kingdom Come.* New York: DC Comics, 1997.
_____. *Superman: Birthright.* New York: DC Comics, 2005.
Wertham, Fredric. *Seduction of the Innocent.* New York: Rinehart, 1954.
Wolfman, Marv. *Crisis on the Infinite Earths.* New York: DC Comics, 2001.
X-Men. Dir. Brian Singer. 20th Century–Fox, 2000.
X-Men 2: X-Men United. Dir. Brian Singer. 20th Century–Fox, 2003.
X-Men: The Last Stand. Dir. Brett Ratner. 20th Century–Fox, 2006.

In each of these cases, I'm only listing the first collected edition in a series of collected editions.

PART I

SUPERHEROES IN THE GOLDEN AND SILVER AGES

Retconning America: Captain America in the Wake of World War II and the McCarthy Hearings

Jason Dittmer

Since 1940, Captain America has served as a bellwether for changing attitudes about the values and policies of the United States. At some points in time, the hero's activities have been the subject of national debate and at other times, he has been ignored to the point of cancellation. Whether fighting against government conspiracies following the Watergate debacle, waging the "War on Drugs" in the 1980s, or using guerrilla tactics to oppose government surveillance during the current "War on Terror," the Star-Spangled Avenger has been there for many (but not all) of the American Century's most definitive ideological conflicts. For instance, one controversial narrative located Captain America squarely in the debate over representations of the 9/11 attacks both in the popular and academic press (see Medved and Lackner 1–8; Dittmer 642–643). Therefore, more than simply reflecting America, the hero actively helps shape the national myth. This essay documents one of the ways in which the creative staff in charge of Captain America has altered the history of Captain America in order to keep the character within the bounds of an ever-changing conception of what America is and what America stands for. It begins, however, with an outline of the theoretical basis for this study, focusing on the relationship between the power to shape popular culture and notions of identity and belonging.

THE NATION AS SERIALIZED NARRATIVE

The world in which we live is fundamentally a creation of our imaginations. While philosophers may argue about the ontological existence of "reality," it should be readily clear that nobody fully understands this alleged reality, even at the cosmically local scale of our planet. Rather, as a species, we function on this planet through the use of our geographical imaginations (Said 54–55; Gregory 205), which are cognitive maps of the world that associate certain values, ideas, and objects with various places in the world. This simultaneously reduces the complexity of these places to manageable levels and provides a mental framework that allows individuals to operate, even if with imperfect knowledge. One of the fundamental features of modern geographical imaginations is the division of the earth's surface into discrete units that are believed to have special ontological status: nation-states. While this particular type of cognitive map dominates popular discourse (one need only read a newspaper to see the centrality afforded to the nation-state), among academics it has long been criticized as a reified discursive construction that benefits certain elites at the expense of alternative forms of social and political organization (Anderson 6–7).

The nation-state's primacy in popular discourse stems, in part, from popular culture, which immerses consumers in "national culture" such that nationality becomes a taken-for-granted part of each individual's identity. Antonio Gramsci has argued that coercing loyalty from population over a large territory is well nigh impossible and it is more efficient for elites to exercise hegemony over mind and motivation (Adamson 170): "Gramsci's concept of hegemony posits a significant place for popular culture in any attempt to understand the workings of society because of the very everydayness and apparently nonconflictual nature of such productions. Any political analysis of the operation of dominance must take full account of the role of institutions of popular culture in the complex milieu that ensures the reproduction of cultural (and thus political) norms" (Sharp 31).

Once the nation-state has become a reified and hegemonic basis for society, popular culture is still needed to continually buttress the nation-state's existence. Further, popular culture is necessary to sculpt the national identity in ways that reinforce the goals and status of cultural and political elites. Thus, national identity can be thought of as an ultimately contested concept, with various ideological, economic, or political groups competing to have their form of discourse emerge as hegemonic.

Ultimately, national identity is not a static and timeless concept, as national mythmaking would have it, but instead a continually changing discourse that structures the nation's sense of collective self and its relationship with others. Because of this, serial narratives such as monthly comic books, the nightly news, and weekly television dramas can be seen not only as a venue in which national identity is constructed in regular chronological intervals, but also as an archive of discourses that can be studied longitudinally. If a serial narrative lasts long enough, it will certainly have to change in order to maintain a link to the society that is consuming it. However, serial narratives have a general inability to produce systemic social change and are therefore innately conservative. This is because they continually require conflict that is similar to that of the contemporary "reality" in order to draw readers. For instance, the character

Superman never became significantly involved in World War II because his power is such that no human army could stand up to him.[1] Were he to fight the Nazis, he would win in short order. While the reader might thrill to such a sight, it would leave no storyline to tell the next month, as Superman's world would no longer resemble the one in which the reader resides. Thus, the intersection of a serial narrative's need for storytelling continuity and its commercial need to resemble the reader's reality means that these narratives can never lead the way in systemic change; instead they can only reflect it. I will subsequently refer to this as the "tyranny of the serial" (see also Wolf-Meyer 499–502).

However, it would be a mistake to think of national identity and popular culture as entirely separate, with one reflecting the other. The link is instead more intimate, as the seriality of popular culture parallels and constitutes the seriality of the national narrative. National identity is, in many ways, a serialized narrative in which characters evolve and events occur, but with certain themes emerging discursively as threads that hold the narrative together. For example, an American history course not only teaches events in the national history, but also reifies the nation through the very scope of the course. American history is unveiled as a changing pastiche of "others" such as Communists, the British, Nazis, etc. with a timeless and essentialized America as the protagonist. Similarly, the nightly news is a daily reminder of national identity that enables citizens to participate in national life, engaging in political behavior that assumes the primacy of the nation-state and distracts from alternative forms of political organization. Homi Bhabha reminds us of the ways in which national experience is drawn out temporally (quoted selectively, 1–8):

> Nations, like narrative, lose their origins in the myths of time and only fully realize their horizons in the mind's eye. Such an image of the nation—or narration—might seem impossibly romantic and excessively metaphorical, but it is from those traditions of political thought and literary language that the nation emerges as a powerful historical idea in the west.... To encounter the nation as it is written displays a temporality of culture and social consciousness more in tune with the partial, overdetermined process by which textual meaning is produced.... These approaches are valuable in drawing our attention to those easily obscured, but highly significant, recesses of the national culture from which alternative constituencies of peoples and oppositional analytic capacities may emerge....

Hence, there is very little difference between the nationalist effects of a history class or the nightly news and that of a comic book like *Captain America*, which features a hero that embodies a particular set of values and asserts them as the American ideal. Comic books in particular hold value for the inculcation of nationalist values because unlike a high school American history textbook, they are easily dismissed as children's entertainment, yet similar to the textbook, they are generally consumed at an age when young adults' geographic imaginations are being initially formulated (Dijkink 3).

The remainder of this essay focuses on Captain America as an icon of the American ideal and on his comic book as a medium for disseminating that ideal to the nation. The next section will outline the politics of the hero's creation and summarize the values he embodied in the 1940s and 1950s. Following that, this essay will turn to Captain America's revival as a major comic book superhero in the 1960s, and how the continuity of the character was modified via a process called "retconning" to incorporate revisionist history of the nation that effectively "othered" prior national discourses (particularly the McCarthyite red baiting of the 1950s). Finally, the essay will illustrate how those prior national discourses were deployed subsequently to help sculpt a hegemonic affirmation of national anti-racist virtue as well as a narrative that offered redemption as a possibility for all Americans.

CREATION OF A HERO, EMBODIMENT OF A NATION

In 1938, Superman debuted in the pages of *Action Comics*, demonstrating the sales potential of comic books; an average issue sold 1.3 million copies, about three to six times more issues than an average comic book (Wright 13). A frenzy of superhero creation ensued, including many who looked and acted like Superman. However, DC Comics publishers Harry Donenfeld and Jack Liebowitz threatened to sue everyone who published a Superman clone, prompting a search for different superheroes that might connect with the audience equally well. Captain America emerged from this creative ferment, and although he was not the first patriotic superhero (that honor belonging to the Shield, from whom Captain America clearly borrowed), he was the first to ignite the newsstands.

Even though the war in Europe and in the Pacific had been underway for quite a while, the comics industry had not written about it. This was in part because of the tyranny of the serial, described above, but also because America itself was divided, with Hitler attracting significant support from significant elements of American society (such as the German American Bund organization) and with isolationists refusing to take overt positions in the world's conflicts. However, the largely Jewish comic book industry began to take sides as news of *Kristallnacht* and the "final solution" became common knowledge in the community: "Maybe this was the strangest thing of all: that the Jews were eager for battle, the Jews who had never trusted governments or militaries and had always tried to keep their sons away from the front were rooting for Roosevelt to get us over there and spit in Hitler's eye" (Jones 162).

Thus, the idea of a patriotic superhero to battle against Hitler was intuitive to Captain America's creators, Joe Simon and Jack Kirby. Simon saw the narrative potential: "There never had been a truly believable villain in comics. But Adolf was alive, hated by more than half of the world" (quoted on Ro 13). Their creation was both a commercial and a political project: "The United States hadn't yet entered the war when Jack and I created Captain America, so maybe he was our way of lashing out against the Nazi menace" (Simon, quoted in Ro 16). The second-generation immigrant Kirby had always seen comic books as a way of promoting his own view of America:

> He [Kirby] ... cited his experiences growing up in a tough neighborhood where good boys learned to survive by acting tough and standing up to bullies as a primary inspiration for his comic book work and his politics.... Kirby later recalled that he had been drawn to comic art because of its simplicity and directness, which he equated with the American way. "I thought comics were a common form of art and strictly American," he said. "America was the home of the common man, and show me the common man that can't do a comic" [Wright 35–36].

Captain America debuted in 1940, selling over a million issues and presenting Hitler as an enemy of America. Although controversial at the time (10 months before Pearl Harbor), the attack on Pearl Harbor and subsequent American entry into the war against the Axis inspired the geopolitical position represented by Captain America to become the mainstream acceptable position.

Captain America's appearance is clearly intended to invoke the symbolism of the flag of the United States. Its main color is blue, with white forearms culminating in red gloves. Red and white vertical stripes adorn his stomach, with red pirate boots on his feet. Finally, the uniform is completed by a white "A" on his forehead, a white star on his chest, and two tiny wings on the temples that hearken back to the winged ankles of the Roman god Mercury.[2] His uniform clearly situates Captain America within what Renan has referred to as the "cult of the flag" (17). Thus, when Captain America was featured on the cover of *Captain America Comics* #1 punching Hitler in the face, there was little doubt that he represented the United States. What was less clear, however, was what type of United States he represented. As the first issues were released, Simon and Kirby's vision of America became more apparent. First, Captain America's main weapon was indeed not a weapon at all, rather an indestructible shield. This made a very particular claim about America—that even its most powerful super-soldier was purely a defensive instrument of national policy. Captain America's main goal, as outlined in the origin story, was to protect the territorial integrity of the United States against aggression: "As the ruthless war-mongers of Europe focus their eyes on a peace-loving America ... the youth of our country heed the call to arm for defense" (Simon, "Case Number 1" 1). To do this, Captain America was provided the super-soldier serum, which enhanced his strength and agility to the peak of human perform-ance.

In the following issues, Captain America was everywhere: in the Pacific theater battling against the Japanese, in Europe raiding Hitler's bunkers, and in the United States rooting out "fifth columnists," always managing to get back to his alter ego as Private Steve Rogers just in time to miss a roll call and be sentenced to cheerfully peel potatoes. Some of the most interesting storylines are those in which he disciplines "un–American" behavior within the national borders, thereby promoting the creative staff's definitions of proper national identity.[3]

The central theme found in these stories is the normative good asso-ciated with an interventionist worldview. Heroes promote the "common sense" knowledge of the Nazi and Japanese threat while villains either oppose intervention or actively sabotage the American will to war. For example, Captain America's first enemy is the Red Skull, a Nazi agent who later turns out to be George Maxon, an American industrial magnate who was promised the title of Minister of Industry in exchange for helping the Nazis by sabotaging the American defense industry. His crime was so "un–American" that Captain America allows him to die (Simon, "Captain America and the Riddle of the Red Skull"). This rather harsh ending to a story read by millions of children is indicative of the America that Simon and Kirby wanted to promote. Their desired national identity was of an America engaged in the world's conflict, idealistic but with a dose of gritty realism.

Thus went *Captain America Comics* until the war was over, and the hero lost his raison d'être. Without Nazis and their collaborators to battle against, Captain America did not survive the overall downturn of interest in superheroes. After wandering in the desert for four years (the editors even turned the comic into *Captain America's Weird Tales* in order to adapt to the comic book market's new focus on horror stories), the comic folded in 1949. In 1953 and 1954, the comic's publisher decided to revive the char-acter with Communists in the place of the Nazis as the "other" for the America that the Captain symbolized.[4] First in a comic known as *Young Men*, then in his own comic book subtitled "Captain America ... Commie Smasher," new adventures were told in an effort to feed symbiotically on the geopolitical narrative of the new Cold War. This run of the series was exceedingly short, perhaps because it did not effectively engage in Cold War discourse: "The series offered no further discussion of Cold War issues beyond the message that Communists were evil, overweight, and poor dressers" (Wright 123). This was a brief revival, perhaps mirroring the American people's war exhaustion following World War II and the Korean War. The comic again folded, and Captain America would not return for over a decade.

DISAVOWING A DECADE

Captain America remained on the shelf for the rest of the 1950s and the early 1960s, suffering an indignity that other famous heroes from the Golden Age such as Superman and Batman never did—being mothballed. However, in 1964, Captain America came in from out of the cold—literally. In *Avengers* #4, Captain America was discovered frozen in an iceberg by a newly formed team of superheroes, and upon awakening (unharmed after being frozen for two decades because of the super-soldier serum, naturally) he told the superheroes his unique narrative. In the story woven by Stan Lee (who had been in the Timely Comics offices 24 years earlier when Simon and Kirby created Captain America), Captain America had been nearly killed in 1944 in an attack that led to the death of his teenaged sidekick, Bucky. Captain America was thrown into the waters of the North Atlantic and was chilled into a state of suspended animation.

In the pages of *Tales of Suspense* and later in his own comic, Captain America was no longer the vaguely xenophobic super soldier from World War II but was reinvented as a more liberal symbol of American values. Instead of defending America against the "other," Captain America engaged in the culture wars raging over America's internal "others." The 1960s were a traumatic time of transition in the United States, with the war in Vietnam sparking domestic debate and the civil rights debate at home flaring into further domestic discord. Further, the political views of the young comics-reading audience had changed since World War II, generally becoming more socially liberal and anti-imperialist (see also Mondello 238). Thus, the creative staff avoided the xenophobia of the 1940s and the red baiting of the 1950s incarnations of the hero. Communism was rarely discussed in the pages of *Captain America*, despite the obvious possibility of the hero's intervention in Vietnam. Indeed, Captain America only made two trips to Vietnam during the entire war, and then only to rescue captured American soldiers, a relatively depoliticized endeavor that contrasted obviously with his continual intervention in World War II. Because of Captain America's lack of engagement with Communism, the hero was in need of a foil for his "American" ideology. This was found in the Nazis who, despite their lack of real-world relevance, remained a useful "other" for Captain America. Indeed, Captain America remains in battle against the Red Skull (Hitler's #1 agent) and the aristocratic Prussian *Junkers*, Baron Zemo and Baron Strucker, to this day. These villains were locked with Captain America in a "fascism vs. freedom" dichotomy that proved useful in constructing an image of America as devoted to individual freedom and equality of opportunity.

Captain America's wartime exploits were glamorized and foregrounded in the mid–1960s, with whole issues devoted to reprinting earlier stories that contemporary readers were unlikely to have read. However, this nostalgia for the past was contextualized within a "man out of time" narrative, in which Captain America had to re-learn what America is, enabling him to expound on the ways in which America had changed since World War II. This plot uses Captain America as a stable pivot from which to view a changing America; this plot device is fallacious, however, as the 1960s writers recast Captain America himself. Indeed, the 1940s Captain America rarely commented on domestic politics or culture beyond his interest in collaborators and Nazi sympathizers. The 1960s Captain America was scripted as a New Deal Democrat, opposed to racism and discrimination, but generally in favor of the Establishment. However, he is not so linked to the Establishment that he is part of it; in contrast to the wartime Captain America, he is not an official arm of American policy implementation but rather views himself as a symbol of the American ideal or the American dream rather than the American government.

This new narration of Captain America is also a new narration of America itself. In a material sense, it ignores the continuity as told in the Captain America stories themselves—if the 1964 Captain America is to be believed, all of the stories told in *Captain America Comics* from 1944 to 1949 and then from 1953 to 1954 never occurred. This disavowal of the comics was a strategic move on the part of the creative staff, eliminating the embarrassing McCarthyite red baiting of the 1950s. Thus, the realignment of the comics' narrative effectively writes a new history of America, blotting out the stain (as viewed in 1964) of the McCarthy hearings and other aspects of American history.

However, much as nature abhors a vacuum, comic book fans abhor holes in continuity. It took nearly a decade for the writers of *Captain America* to address this one. In 1972 they introduced a new Captain America, who was identical to the original Captain America in appearance. Of course, the story begins with mass confusion as identities are confused and discord is sown among the comic's characters. Nevertheless, the "real" Captain America's friends discover the deception because the new Captain America says things like "This time I'll use my full strength—and knock him flatter than a Russkie's bankbook" (Englehart, "The Falcon Fights Alone" 5) and "Don't worry, pal. The Coloreds never bother anybody" (Englehart, "The Falcon Fights Alone" 6), which is not New Deal Captain America's traditional manner of speaking. Soon, his true identity is unveiled: the "Other" Captain America is the Captain America from the 1950s. As a boy, he was a Sentinel of Liberty (Captain America's wartime fan club) and even did his master's thesis on the adventures of Captain America.[5] He went to Germany after World War II to study the hero's exploits from the German perspective and there discovered that the Germans had stolen the super-soldier serum that was responsible for Captain America's super-strength and reflexes. He reported this to the American government but would not give them the details unless he was allowed to

The 1950s Captain America returns in the 1970s as a proxy for intolerance and bigotry in America. From page 23 of "Two Into One Won't Go!" in *Captain America*, Issue 156 (New York: Marvel Comics, 1972).

become the new Captain America, since the original had not been heard from since 1944. They agreed, and subsequently he had plastic surgery to look like Steve Rogers, the original Captain.

By the time he was ready to go into action, the Korean War was over, and the government shelved him. He became clinically paranoid, seeing Communists everywhere because he was never exposed to the "vita-rays" that the original Captain America was exposed to after receiving the super-soldier serum in 1940. He suited up and began his own McCarthyite battle against Communists in the United States (these adventures constitute the "commie-smasher" comic books of 1953–54). The government was embarrassed, so they captured him and put him into suspended animation. His sudden appearance in 1972 is explained as the product of a government worker disgruntled by Nixon's trip to China, who freed the 1950s

Captain America to steer America away from accommodation and détente. Thus, the McCarthyite anti–Communist crusade in the United States is narrativized as aberrant behavior caused by an imposter, perpetuating the national narrative of an innocent America.

Of course, superhero comic books revolve around action, and generally the physical strength to defeat enemies in combat is seen as a proxy for moral strength. These melees are accompanied by dialogue through which ideological positions are established. This battle was no different:

> *"Real" Captain America*: "You think I'm a traitor? Grow up, fella—times have changed! America's in danger from within as well as without! There's organized crime, injustice, and fascism—or wouldn't you recognize that?"
>
> *1950s Captain America*: "Are you calling me—a fascist? You mealy-mouthed rat! You're scared to face up to the commies in a war, like a real man! I'm a real man! And I'll kill you to prove it!" [Englehart, "Two Into One Won't Go" 22–23].

In this dialogue the same "freedom vs. fascism" dichotomy employed to contrast America and the Nazis (described above) is used to cast the 1950s Captain America (and America itself, by proxy) as a reactionary, masculinist enemy of social justice whose first impulse is violence. The "real" Captain America emerges victorious over the 1950s Captain America, completing the re-narrativization of both the comic book's continuity and thus, American history. An essentialized and morally pure America is left behind as the product.

In serial storytelling, the changes just described constitute a "retcon," which is a shortened version of "retroactive change in continuity." Continuity is "the term used by fans and publishers to refer to the coherence of the internal history and workings of super-hero universes including the 'biographies' of individual characters" (Locke 26). Reynolds (26) outlines three forms of continuity that operate within comic book discourse. The first, serial continuity, is the continuity of events within a serial narrative. For example, if the Red Skull dies in *Captain America* #100, he should still be dead in *Captain America* #101. The second form of continuity, hierarchical continuity, is the continuity of character's characteristics within a serial narrative (that is, Superman should not be able to fly at the speed of light in *Action Comics* #433 and only at the speed of sound in *Action Comics* #434, at least not without explanation). The third form of continuity, structural continuity, refers to the umbrella of social linkages between various serial narratives (usually between all of a company's comic books—i.e. the Marvel Universe, or the DC Universe). This last form of continuity is an attempt to weave a coherent reality out of the myriad stories told by a company's creative staff. Retroactive change in continuity refers to the shifting of established continuity into a new form, seeking coherence where perhaps there was none, or where the status quo was unacceptable. In this case, it is not just *Captain America* that is being "retconned" but it is the established national narrative of the United States. The original Captain America, representing the spirit and ideals of America, has been purified—connecting the 1960s liberal movement with the ideals of World War II, while marginalizing the perceived conservatism of America in the 1950s. In addition, it leaves ambivalent the relationship between America and communism, which for the young and liberal readership was not necessarily the biggest threat to the United States.

BEATING A DEAD HORSE

Following the defeat of the 1950s Captain America and the retconning of official history in 1972, the comic book continued to construct an American narrative that was in opposition to a particular form of conservative discourse that combined elements of racism and fascism. An early form of this can be seen in the dialogue between the two Captain Americas above. This discourse allowed a linkage to be made between the external enemies of the essentialized America, the Nazis, and those within the United States who were opposed to integration and racial equality. This elision, although often ham-handed and caricatured, effectively promoted a socially liberal America by demonizing its internal others: namely opponents of racial equality.

In 1979, this demonization harnessed the narrative device of the 1950s Captain America once again, using the character to create a connection between 1950s McCarthyism and conservative opposition to integration. In the storyline, Captain America is looking for his girlfriend, Sharon Carter, who is a secret agent for the U.S. government. She had been investigating an organization known as the National Force, a racist organization that had been holding rallies in Central Park during which members dress in white sheets with the swastika adorning their shoulders. Each rally typically includes a face-off between the National Force and a multiracial group of protesters. However, in each rally the National Force burns crosses, after which the white protesters suddenly agree with the National Force. Sharon, who is white, had been to a rally and had been converted thus to the National Force's cause. Captain America investigates, and discovers that the National Force is run by a man known as the Grand Director, who is overtly racist, as shown in this monologue from a rally: "[M]y fellow Americans, I say to you that we must act now—and act swiftly—to make our beloved country strong once more! The only way to insure [*sic*] America's strength is to make her pure! Because a white America is a strong America!" (Mackenzie, "Aftermath" 26).

Captain America makes the linkage between the racists in America and the Nazis of World War II obvious for the reader: "This is my fight. It's been my fight since the days of Auschwitz and Treblinka" (Mackenzie, "Aftermath" 31). When Captain America captures agents of the National

Force, they spontaneously burst into flames, a method of suicide that is a metaphor for the goals of the National Force, as expressed by an agent prior to his own suicide: "We have lived by the flame! And, by the flame, shall we be free! By the flame, shall our beloved America be purged ... until she is strong once more" (Mackenzie, "Flame and the Fury" 6). The pro–Captain America narrator of the story in this case inverts the flame metaphor, making the racist–Nazi connection on behalf of Captain America: "Captain America falls silent. He has seen the flames before. In Warsaw ... in Berlin ... but that was a lifetime ago. And he had defeated the hate-mongers then ... had watched as their dreams of conquest went up, quite literally, in smoke" (Mackenzie, "Flame and the Fury" 7).

The National Force is a caricature of anti-integrationist political groups such as the KKK and the neo–Nazi movement. From page 27 of "Aftermath!" in *Captain America*, Issue 231 (New York: Marvel Comics, 1979).

Captain America later discusses the National Force with the police commissioner, who tells him that although he sympathizes with the hero's disdain for the National Force, he has been told not to interfere with them by someone in a position of power in the government. This time it is the police commissioner who makes the racist–Nazi connection for the reader: "I understand completely, my boy! I know how these hate organizations work! They prey upon the Jews, the blacks, the old, the sick—anyone that they can set up as scapegoats for the ills of society! They gain the support of the gullible, the hateful, and the fearful ... and parlay that into power on a wide scale!" (Mackenzie, "Flame and the Fury" 16).

The allusion to government officials supporting the National Force sets up the understanding that while everyday Americans may not be racist, the activities of the National Force advance the agenda of at least some elites.

Meanwhile, the stage is set for a massive confrontation between the National Force and African American gangs from Harlem. As the rumble gathers steam, the Grand Director begins to have doubts, but Dr. Faustus, a villain specializing in mind control, assuages his conscience. Captain America intervenes between the National Force and the gangs, delaying the confrontation until the National Guard arrives and takes control. The gangs flee, and the National Force's agents all burst into flames, including Captain America's girlfriend, Sharon Carter. Captain America follows the Grand Director, only to discover that underneath his hood, he is the 1950s Captain America. Caught off guard, Captain America is drugged by Dr. Faustus into becoming a public face for the National Force's racist agenda:

> *Captain America:* Look at them, my fellow Americans! You can plainly see the color of our nation's greatest enemy! It does not wash off! Animals like them have turned our cities into urban jungles! Our streets into asphalt battlegrounds! They are bleeding us to death and picking their teeth with our bones! But no more! Now is the time for all honest, red-blooded Americans to unite—beneath the banner of the National Force! [Mackenzie, "Crossfire" 6].

Later, Captain America sees the newly painted swastika on his shield scrape off in battle, and he realizes he has been duped. Soon thereafter we learn that the 1950s Captain America had been freed from his mental institution by Dr. Faustus, who had worked there as a hospital administrator and that Dr. Faustus's mind-gas, concealed in the burning crosses, was responsible for the conversion of all the white people at the rallies to the National Force's cause. After the failed attempt to inspire a riot in Harlem, Dr. Faustus and the 1950s Captain America are on their way in a blimp to dispense the mind-gas over New York City, sparking race riots. However, Captain America intervenes, and when the 1950s Captain America is told by Faustus to attack the "real" Captain America, he refuses and instead triggers his suicide belt, bursting into flames. Captain America then stops the nefarious plot by physically defeating Dr. Faustus.

Through this comic book narrative, several claims about the nature of the retconned American narrative are made. The most important claim is that racism is an internal other that is a foil to real Americanism, which is multicultural and devoid of prejudice. This is accomplished through the explicit linkage made between the internal threat of white supremacy and the external threat of fascist Nazi aggression predicated on racial science. As illustrated above, the substantial differences between these two positions are elided into insignificance, as both are described as varieties of "hatemongering."

The second claim made in the story is related to the first: that racism is innately foreign to an innocent America. This is accomplished through the location of America's racist corruption within the character of Dr. Faustus, whose symbolic name identifies him as someone whose ambition has led him to the temptation of evil. Indeed, it is not clear which, if any, of the National Force actually agreed with the white supremacist ideology of the organization, or whether they were all victims of the mind-gas produced by Dr. Faustus and distributed through his burning crosses, as dramatized by Sharon Carter. This is true also of the 1950s Captain America, the erstwhile Grand Director, who dies without ever revealing whether he was a willing or unwilling ally of Dr. Faustus.

This in turn leads to the third claim made by the story about America: that true Americans, regardless of their political ideology, should ultimately put the national interest ahead of their own. This was most clearly visible in the death of the 1950s Captain America, who, presumably drugged with mind-gas and confronted with the living embodiment of the American ideal—the "real" Captain America—would rather commit suicide than raise his fists to fight.

REDEMPTION

If we accept the retcon of the narrative accomplished by the creative staff in 1972, this suicide brings the 1950s Captain America full circle. According to that retcon, the character began as a hero, motivated by real patriotism but tainted by a small character flaw (as evidenced in his blackmailing of the U.S. government to get the serum administered to himself). That patriotism became magnified by the incomplete medical treatment until the hero himself became a villain, threatening the very values that he began by fighting for (as evidenced by the red baiting of the 1953–54 run of *Captain America Comics*). The character was resurrected in 1972 as a villain, but because of his paranoia he did not realize that he was anything but the hero that he once was. Finally, in 1979, the character comes back as a villain, and indeed as a betrayer of the values that America is scripted as embodying. However, the character is brought full circle by the realization of what he has become, specifically when confronted by the vision of "real" American values, leading him to commit suicide, purifying himself with the fire that he originally wanted to use on America itself to purge the nation of outside influences.

Thus, the 1950s Captain America embodies a metanarrative of redemption within the larger American narrative. The retcon that created the character (as a separate entity from the "real" Captain America) was intended to establish the continuity of American national identity from the wartime righteousness of the 1940s directly to the liberal idealism of the 1960s, excising the red baiting McCarthyism of the 1950s from both the continuity of the Captain America character and from the overarching American national myth. Further, the character was brought back to use as a figurehead for the National Force, linking the 1950s red baiting with the anti-integration movement of the 1970s and enabling the "real" Captain America to champion the cause of a multicultural America. However, the metanarrative of redemption allows a further lesson to be drawn from the story of the character.

The overarching motivations for the 1950s Captain America have been shown to shift from patriotism (initially) to misguided patriotism (red baiting) to racism (drug-induced support for the National Force) and finally back to patriotism (suicide). The character's final purification through fire, although undesirable in real life, illustrates the possibility for redemption for every American. Given the narrative use to which the 1950s Captain America was put, this implies that ideological differences within the American political system are ultimately not critical; just because a group took an immoral and un–American position in the past does not mean that they will be outcasts forever. The door is open for the McCarthys, racists, etc. to accept the particular narrative of America that is set out in the pages of *Captain America* by the creative staff.

This, of course is not the first retcon in *Captain America* and it is not likely to be the last. Indeed, the character has recently gone through a schizophrenic episode of sorts, resulting in his "death." In the pages of many Marvel Comics titles, he was engaged in a storyline known as "Civil War." This storyline pits the Marvel superheroes against one another over the so-called "Super-human Registration Act," a comic book proxy for the controversial real-life Patriot Act. In this storyline, Captain America leads the fugitive heroes opposed to mandatory registration and deputizing of super-humans by the U.S. government. Here, he can be seen to once again be embodying a largely idealist liberal perspective in opposition to a pragmatist conservative perspective (assuming equivalence between the comic book universe's political positions and the political positions of our "real" universe). However, in a parallel continuity, known as "Marvel Ultimates," Marvel Comics has created an alternate universe that effectively ignores the established continuity of the characters. In this storyline, Captain America is frozen in the ice of the North Atlantic from World War II until the late 1990s, and upon being unfrozen he takes the lead of a superhero team known as the Ultimates, a government team opposed to terrorism. The Ultimates' Captain America is more violent than the original, and uses firearms and explosives in ways that the original Captain America would never consider. He is (again, using real-life terminology that may not map precisely to the comic book universe) more conservative in his views on politics and morality than the established Captain America.

Some comic book fans have hypothesized that Marvel Comics might eventually make the Marvel Ultimates universe the "official" continuity, disavowing the entire history of Captain America (and other heroes) in a massive retcon that makes the retcon described throughout this paper seem trivial in scope.[6] Such a retcon of Marvel's narrativization of American nationhood would have to reflect larger societal shifts in America. The lack of a hegemonic construction of American identity symbolized by the "50/50 nation" and "Red state versus Blue state" discourses (see Kaus, n.p.) makes it unlikely that such a shift is imminent. However, it certainly explains the dueling Captain Americas that Marvel is publishing.

NOTES

1. It should be noted that Superman does encounter Hitler and Stalin, but only in an "imaginary" story in which he captures them and takes them before the League of Nations. This story is not in continuity, however, and can be found in the February 27, 1940, issue of *Look* magazine.

2. It was suggested by a colleague that the seemingly out-of-place Mercury wings on Captain America's temples indicate that he is, in a way, a messenger of the gods as well; however, in this case he brings word of the American civil religion. While I have never found anything to substantiate this in the historical record of Captain America's creation, it is the best explanation I have yet heard for what is surely an odd feature of his uniform.

3. Simon and Kirby only made a few issues of *Captain America Comics* before they left in a contract dispute with Timely Comics. Kirby would later return to the comic several decades later.

4. Timely Comics became known as Atlas Comics in the 1950s and later changed its name to Marvel Comics, which it is known as today.

5. He is a notable exception to the maxim that the academic study of superheroes will not lead to a job.

6. It should be noted that there is little to no evidence to support this; it remains a hypothesis only.

WORKS CITED

Adamson, W. *Hegemony and Revolution*. Berkeley: University of California Press, 1980.

Anderson, B. *Imagined Communities: Reflections on the Origin and Spread of Nationalism*. New York: Verso, 1991.

Bhabha, H. "Introduction: Narrating the Nation." *Nation and Narration*. Ed., Bhabha, H. London: Routledge, 1990. 1–7.

Dijkink, D. *National Identity and Geopolitical Visions: Maps of Pride and Pain*. London: Routledge, 1996.

Dittmer, J. "Captain America's Empire: Reflections on Identity, Popular Culture, and Post–9/11 Geopolitics." *Annals of the Association of American Geographers* 95 (2005): 626–643.

Englehart, S. "The Falcon Fights Alone!" *Captain America* 154. New York: Marvel Comics, 1972.
_____. "Two Into One Won't Go!" *Captain America* 156. New York: Marvel Comics, 1972.

Gregory, D. *Geographical Imaginations*. Oxford: Blackwell, 1993.

Jones, G. *Men of Tomorrow: Geeks, Gangsters, and the Birth of the Comic Book*. New York: Basic Books, 2004.

Kaus, M. "Fifty-fifty Forever." *Slate Magazine* 2004. 3 October 2006. http://www.slate.com/id/2073262/.

Locke, S. "Fantastically Reasonable: Ambivalence in the Representation of Science and Technology in Super-Hero Comics." *Public Understanding of Science* 14 (2005): 25–46.

McKenzie, R. "Aftermath!" *Captain America* 231. New York: Marvel Comics, 1979.
_____. "Crossfire" *Captain America* 233. New York: Marvel Comics, 1979.
_____. "The Flame and the Fury." *Captain America* 232. New York: Marvel Comics, 1979.

Medved, M., and M. Lackner. "The Betrayal of Captain America." White paper published by the Foundation for the Defense of Democracies, 2003.

Mondello, S. "Spider-Man: Superhero in the Liberal Tradition." *Journal of Popular Culture* 10 (1976): 232–238.

Renan, E. "What is a Nation?" *Nation and Narration.* Ed. H. Bhabha. London: Routledge, 1990. 8–22.

Reynolds, R. *Superheroes: A Modern Mythology.* Jacksnon: University Press of Mississippi, 1992.

Ro, R. *Tales to Astonish: Jack Kirby, Stan Lee, and the American Comic Book Revolution.* New York: Bloomsbury, 2004.

Said, E. *Orientalism.* New York: Vintage Books, 1979.

Sharp, J. "Publishing American Identity: Popular Geopolitics, Myth, and *The Reader's Digest.*" *Political Geography* 12 (1993): 491–503.

Simon, J. "Captain America and the Riddle of the Red Skull." *Captain America Comics* 1. New York: Timely Comics, 1941. 32–45.

_____. "Case #1: Meet Captain America." *Captain America Comics* 1. New York: Timely Comics, 1941. 1–8.

Wolf-Meyer, M. "The World Ozymandias Made: Utopias in the Superhero Comic, Subculture, and the Conservation of Difference." *Journal of Popular Culture* 36 (2003): 497–517.

Wright, B. *Comic Book Nation: The Transformation of Youth Culture in America.* Baltimore: Johns Hopkins University Press, 2001.

Super-Girls and Mild Mannered Men: Gender Trouble in Metropolis

GERARD F. BERITELA

In the clichés of superhero narrative, roles of gendered power are often acted out in the scenario of the endangered, submissive woman being rescued by the super-powered man, thus bringing into play culturally sanctioned performances of masculinity and femininity. Lois Lane being rescued by Superman forms a constant and defining moment in the mythos of these iconic characters, as evidenced by its inclusion in the title credits of both *Lois and Clark* and the recent animated Superman television series. In contrast, there exist in many instances lesser-known depictions of women wielding superpowers and rescuing men. This chapter will look at a number of examples of these gender reversals, concentrating specifically on the characters in the Superman mythos in the period surrounding the 1950s.

From the time of his creation in 1938 by Jerry Siegel and Joe Shuster, Superman has become the most widely known and representative figure in the superhero genre. Rocketed as an infant to Earth moments before his home planet's destruction, his alien origin grants him "powers and abilities far beyond those of mortal men." Posing as a "mild mannered reporter," Clark Kent constantly attempts to attract the affection of the assertive reporter Lois Lane, who rebuffs him in favor of his alter ego, Superman, who, in turn, ignores her. It is this convoluted triangle of romance, deception and irony that fuels the human interest of the early stories, and it is this same triangle that significantly changes over the decades as a reflection of the gender anxieties in society.

More specifically, during the period of the fifties, the masculinity exemplified in the homosocial and heroic context of the military of World War II was rapidly being replaced with a new normative masculinity defined by heterosexual domesticity (but not without some cultural anxiety). In addition, the deployment of women in formerly male-dominated occupations made necessary by the war was giving way uneasily to an anticipated return to more rigid gender roles.

As part one of this essay will show, the presence of women with superpowers underscores the conflict between the heroic masculinity of Super-man and the pressure for that masculinity to be replaced by a domesti-cated heterosexuality. The erasure of these women and their powers preserves the heroic masculinity of Superman against the threat of domes-tication by a female equal. That this is reflective of the cultural anxiety surrounding masculinity in the '50s is made clear by a shift in the empha-sis and mood of the stories involving superwomen. The contrast between the very first story of a superpowered woman (published in 1943) and sto-ries of the '50s and early '60s will show both an increased anxiety sur-rounding the threat of domestication and an increasing discounting of the abilities of these women. Concurrently, in a number of stories, patriarchal rule is manifested by the stratagem of the teaching of "lessons."

Part two of this essay will look at the gendered power plays inherent in this stratagem and at certain ways in which the exercise of power is itself constrained and reversed. Finally, as shown in part three of this essay, the character of Supergirl comes to stand for a girl with power equal to her male counterpart. As this character is developed, issues of submission, rebellion, superiority, and victory over male domination are addressed. In addition, Supergirl allows for the bracketed expression of Superman's own compromise with the pressure to be domesticated.

PART ONE: FROM SUPERWOMAN TO SUPERWIFE

In his work, *Masked Men: Masculinity and the Movies in the Fifties*, Steven Cohan examines a number of popular films such as *The Seven Year Itch* (1955) and *The Man in the Gray Flannel Suit* (1956) to demonstrate the par-adoxical nature of hegemonic masculinity in the fifties. Domestication was simultaneously viewed as both normative and emasculating. This ambiva-lence, as enacted in film, underscores for Cohan the performative nature of masculinity and gender in general.[1] In like manner, the negotiation of heroic vs. domesticated personas, with the added level of the super-empow-ered woman in the Superman mythos, evokes and resolves the fragility of gender.

In 1943, the first story of a superpowered woman in Metropolis is pub-lished (Siegel, "Lois Lane—Superwoman" 1–12). The splash page shows Lois rescuing a bound Superman, who protests: "But you can't save me!" while Lois replies: "Oh no? Guess again!" As the story begins, Clark Kent asks Lois to "please tell me once and for all if you care for me." He is rebuffed by Lois in favor of Superman. Immediately afterward, she is involved in an accident which puts her into a coma. When told that her only hope is a far-away specialist, Clark changes into Superman, saying: "Lois—dying! Without her, life wouldn't be worth living for me. I must find this doctor." The story proceeds with Lois awaking with newfound superpowers as a result of Superman's transfusing his blood to her. As Lois goes out in search of super-adventures, the story constructs her deeds as gender-reversed echoes of the first adventure of Superman in *Action* #1. As he had intervened in a crime of "wife beating," Superwoman intervenes in a scene where a man is being pursued by his rolling-pin-bearing wife. As Superman had stopped a getaway car in which Lois was being kidnapped, she stops a getaway car in which Clark is being kidnapped. As he had whisked her away through the air and finally advised her "not to publish this little episode," she flies off with Clark and obtains his reluctant promise not to betray her identity.

The story reaches a climax when Superwoman rescues Superman and proposes to him. Without even waiting for him to answer, she says: "I accept!" and Superman acquiesces with the words "Ulp! What chance has a mere Superman got?" But just then, they discover that Clark has published the secret of Superwoman's identity. She faints, only to awaken in the hospital with the realization that it had all been a dream. The story ends with Clark, who had been waiting several hours to see her, coming in with flowers. When he asks if she is all right, she responds: "Naturally! What else would you expect of a superwoman ... er—I mean, newspaperwoman!"

The depiction of Lois here as capable, aggressive and utterly dismissive of Clark (sometimes cruelly so) is consistent throughout the 1940s. In May of 1944, a backup feature in the Superman comic begins, entitled: "Lois Lane, Girl Reporter." Many of these stories follow the same outline: Lois (sometimes explicitly in response to sexist comments) aggressively pursues a story, gets into danger, bemoans the fact that Superman isn't around to save her and then, either through luck or her own initiative, saves both herself and the day and gets an exclusive story to boot. In the 1940s, Lois' desire to wed Superman is balanced by her own adventuring (with or without superpowers), and is reciprocated by the seemingly meek and cowardly Clark's attempts to woo her.

In contrast to the earliest rendition of a woman with superpowers, a story entitled "The Girl of Steel" is published in *Action* #156 in 1951. The cover constructs the super-powered Lois as a direct threat to the hegemony of Superman. The scene is Luthor's laboratory and we see Superman crashing in through a skylight with his trademark battle cry: "This is a job for Superman!" But, in the foreground, Lois upstages him by breaking through a wall, saying: "No! This is a job for Superwoman!" The sensationalistic cover threat is neutralized by a triple move. First, the superpowers Lois receives are temporary, and known to be so from the very start. Secondly, Lois is both gullible and clumsy. She falls for the villain's story even after having noticed clues to the contrary, and the commentary points out her ineffectualness: "Working at furious superspeed, Lois struggles clumsily to control her unwieldy super-strength and complete the task in time to free Superman!" Third, Superman himself is explicitly negative toward Lois's powers, claiming that she is "a menace."

About seven years later, a second story, also entitled "The Girl of Steel," was published in 1958. Again, the cover art constructs the superpowered woman as a direct threat to Superman's primacy. Superman is shown at the bottom of the cover, standing in a river almost waist deep. He supports a railroad bridge above him. With an expression of consternation and worry, he looks at the superpowered female above him as she drags a train directly over him.[2] She says: "Superman, this feat proves I've got superpowers equal to yours! Now tell me your secret identity and I'll tell you mine!"

First of all, the mere fact that this female's powers equal Superman's is a threat. In addition, she has explicitly demanded to be treated as an equal in offering to exchange the secret of her identity in order to know his. In general, the secret identity is an indicator of power and status. Both keeping one's identity secret and knowing another's indicates a superior status. In *Feminism without Women: Culture and Criticism in a "Postfeminist" Age*, Modleski suggests that the image of "the vulnerable, finite male behind the image of omnipotent superhero" may be conceptualized as the relationship between the penis and the phallus (Modleski 109). I would add that this image also informs the relationship between superhero and secret identity. Clark is the penis, while Superman is the phallus. Referencing Lacan, Modleski reminds us that "nobody really possesses the 'phallus,' a term that refers to an idea of paternal potency and power unrealizable by any single individual, female *or* male" (91). The threat of revealing the secret identity is thus essentially the threat of revealing the mere penis behind the illusory phallus, one's vulnerability.

In addition, the relationship between Clark and Superman may be read in the light of Butler's definition of gender as "the repeated stylization of the body, a set of repeated acts ... that congeal over time to produce the appearance of substance, of a natural sort of being" (Butler 33). While the "mild-mannered" masculinity of Clark is explicitly constructed as an illusion using mask-like glasses, the persona of Superman can also be read as an appearance. An ubiquitous image of Superman shows Clark tearing open his shirt to reveal his "S." This is precisely a stylized, repeated act that creates the illusion of a natural substance, the exposure of the (not) bare chest (phallus) covered in an icon-branded second-skin.[3] Furthermore, this image may also be read in the light of Butler's discussion of drag. Clark tearing apart his weak, near-effeminate persona to reveal his manly "S" echoes the image of a drag queen at the end of a performance removing a wig, as in the film *Victor/Victoria*. Butler claims that part of the "giddiness" of drag is due to the fact that it reveals the "radical contingency" of gender. When the drag queen is revealed as a "male," the revelation that the female gender presentation was a construct infects the male gender presentation as well (137). In other words, guise will be guys. In the case of Clark/Superman, the super-male persona is further compromised by the fact that his "S" is itself an obvious (albeit skin-tight) costume and cannot even claim the essential nature of a male body as justification for its male performance. Returning to the context of this story, the threat of exchanging secret identities, and thereby becoming vulnerable to this girl with equal powers, is ironic in that the girl of steel has no secret identity to share. However, she does have a secret, as will be mentioned later.

Inspired by the banter between Lois and Superman during which Superman explains why he can't marry her, Jimmy Olsen magically creates a Super-Girl to be Superman's helper and companion. But, like Lois in the first "Girl of Steel" story, the only thing she accomplishes is to make trouble for Superman. Explicitly described as "impetuous" twice in the narrative, she reaches the apex of being a "super-nuisance" when she discovers and inadvertently reveals Superman's secret identity to Lois. After being reprimanded by Superman, Super-Girl gets a chance to redeem herself by rescuing him from kryptonite. Although she claims that it does not affect her, her secret vulnerability is that she was magically created with powers equal to Superman's which include his weakness to kryptonite. Dying, she returns to the magical limbo from which she came. However, the status quo is fully restored only when Clark proposes to Lois. Reasoning that Superman would never propose to her, Lois concludes that Clark cannot be Superman, and turns down his proposal. He thinks: "I figured she'd reject Clark! But what if she had accepted? Whew!"

These two "Girl of Steel" stories contrast sharply with the 1943 story. In neither of them is the superpowered woman portrayed as capable, much less as echoing the deeds of Superman. In addition, there is both an increasing intensity of the pressure to marry, and an ever-more monolithic negation of the possibility of domesticity, love and marriage. In 1943's "Lois Lane—Superwoman," the framing iteration of the status quo involved Clark wooing Lois only to be rebuffed by her. His love for her is affirmed by his statement that "without her, life wouldn't be worth living for me." The end of the story repeats the image of the smitten Clark, who has waited "several hours" to see her. In contrast, the framing iteration in 1958's "Girl of Steel" involves Superman explicitly resisting the pressure of marriage. In contrast to 1943, where the love of Clark for Lois was explicitly acknowledged and the possibility of marriage considered without dread; here marriage is mentioned only to be summarily dismissed or falsely and ironically invoked with Clark's insincere, manipulative proposal.

Later stories continue the trend of both increasing the pressure of domesticity and defusing both it and the powers of the women. This is done by limiting the motivation of superpowered women to obtaining Superman as a husband. In the 1943 story, Lois' wish to marry Superman was balanced by her desire for "high adventure and excitement," and she comments while battling criminals: "This is more fun than knitting socks!" By November of 1960 (Siegel, "Battle Between Super-Lois and Super-Lana" 19–28), the sole motivation of Super-Lois and her rival is to show which of them "can be a better wife for Superman." The women use their powers solely for performing domestic super-deeds such as literally cooking super-sized dinners and making themselves "super-glamorous" with the jewelry of Helen of Troy and Cleopatra. This move is reflective of an increasing discomfort with women having roles other than domestic. Where, in 1943, during the period of World War II's deployment of women in the workplace, Lois' options revolved around the axis superwoman/newspaper-woman; here both roles are collapsed into super/non-super husband-hunter. The title of the Lois-centric stories of the 1940s ("Lois Lane, Girl Reporter") is replaced in the 1950s with the title "Superman's Girl Friend Lois Lane."[4] The romantic triangle of the 1940s which saw an assertive and capable Lois caught between a seemingly cowardly but enamored Clark and a seemingly uninterested Superman is replaced in the 1950s with a marriage-obsessed Lois competing with a marriage-obsessed Lana over a truly uninterested Superman.

PART TWO: LESSONS LEARNED?

Concurrent with the stories discussed above, a number of stories are published that not only feature superpowered women but also illustrate a thinly veiled metaphor for the exercise of patriarchy (the teaching of lessons) which at the same time allows for a limited reversal of the gendered roles of submission and power. If the stories previously described reflect an increased pressure for domesticity and a discounting of female power, these stories reflect the assertion of patriarchal power over women (while at the same time allowing a limited affirmation of female agency and dignity). These stories follow the lead of the wildly popular sitcom of the mid to late fifties, "I Love Lucy," in which the woman is constantly trying to infiltrate her husband's domain, is often "taught a lesson" by him, and still at times by sheer ingenuity and resourcefulness carries the day—to the extent that it is often unclear who is really the teacher and who is the one taught.

A story that features Lois is entitled "The Superwoman of Metropolis" (Weisinger); the original introduction reads as follows:

> For years, Lois Lane has been trying to solve the mystery of Superman's secret identity! So, one day, to teach inquisitive Lois a lesson, the Man of Steel makes her a Superwoman! Then, when Super-Lois tries to protect her secret identity, the fun begins! You'll witness a keen duel of wits between Clark and Lois when she becomes ... the Superwoman of Metropolis![5]

The accompanying artwork shows Superwoman catching Clark as he falls

Lois Lane as superhero in "The Superwoman of Metropolis." From page 1 of "The Superwoman of Metropolis" in *Superman's Girlfriend Lois Lane,* Issue 8 (New York: DC Comics, 1959).

from a skyscraper. Clark's position is one of utter (feminine) passivity, with his legs spread apart and lifted high over his head. Lois says: "If you could stay away from trouble for a change, I wouldn't have to spend so much time rescuing you, Clark!" He responds: "You're not fooling me, Superwoman! Pretty soon I'll have proof that Superwoman is really Lois Lane!" Here, not only is there a reversal in rescue and rescued, the gendered power plays between the two are reversed as well. Clark is now the pest whose impetuous nature places him in situations from which Superwoman must rescue him, while he futilely attempts to negate the power differential by discovering her secret identity.

The story begins with Lois suggesting that Clark should confess his identity as Superman. Instead, he decides to turn the tables. The next day, Superman gives Lois super-powers, claiming that this will allow him to leave on a long mission, with someone "who knows his methods" filling his shoes. The rest of the story revolves around Lois protecting her identity from an inquisitive Clark. She does this successfully three times, at one point graciously protecting Superman's identity as well. A fourth trap ends in a draw. The fifth trap is successful. Lois reveals her identity to Clark. But, at that moment, her powers expire and Clark is ironically in a position where he will have to expose his identity to her in order to respond to the emergency. Clark's "long experience" enables him to find a way to act without revealing himself. As the story ends, Clark pretends not to believe that Lois was Superwoman at all. Lois then tells him to ask Superman to verify her story but thinks better of it: "hm.... On the other hand, maybe I'd better not suggest asking Superman! When he hears about it, he's liable to remind me how for years I've been the same kind of pest to him—about his identity! So maybe I'd better forget the whole thing!" While thinking this, she looks over her shoulder at Clark, who exhibits a sly glance and a knowing half-smile.

Unlike previous stories, in which the superpowered female is seen as a threat, here the gender reversal is meant to be comic in nature. As the introduction explicitly states, "the fun begins." There are a number of elements in the story that allow it to be seen as misogynistic fun. First of all, Superman is the one who bestows powers on Lois. Furthermore, his motive in doing so is explicitly to "teach her a lesson." Both of these facts serve to underscore Superman's patriarchal power over her and her powers. He is the one who gave them to her and he is the one who is secretly manipulating her and her powers for his own ends. Finally, the entire story is constructed as a "duel of wits" in which Superman risks nothing. If Lois fails to conceal her identity, that demonstrates his superior ability. If she succeeds in concealing it, she will still come away from the experience duly chastened for her inquisitiveness.

Nevertheless, there are elements in the story that open a space of dignity and power for Lois. First, Lois succeeds three times in avoiding the traps Clark sets. Each time he acknowledges that she acts "cleverly." Secondly, she surprises him by protecting his secret in an unselfish act that he did not expect. Thirdly, the commentary itself proclaims her "equal to the challenge" that Clark presents. Throughout this story she is shown to be both capable and heroic. Furthermore, in the fourth trial, Clark outwits himself by setting her a test he cannot use against her without revealing his own identity. As she will do at the end of the story, he decides to "forget" about it. While it is ostensibly Lois who learns the "lesson," Clark also learns that Lois can be both capable and gracious.

Nine months later, another story more radically reverses usual gender roles. In *Superboy* #78, readers meet "Claire Kent, alias Super-Sister!" The story begins with Superboy's adoptive mother telling him of her hunch that "something amazing will change [his] whole life today." Superboy dismisses it, ridiculing her "feminine intuition." Later, Superboy spots a "queer craft" in the sky. He is just as surprised to find that its pilot is a female, as she is surprised to find a flying boy. Superboy prevents a crash while thinking: "Just like a woman to lose control." The telepathic pilot from a matriarchal world berates Superboy for his "insulting thoughts," only to have him respond: "If you women run your world the way you run spaceships ... well, I'm glad I don't live there!" She responds: "Another insult! I'll teach you a lesson, you snippy boy!" Superboy soon discovers that he has been turned into "a ... a girl!" Rushing back to look for the spaceship, the former Superboy is dismayed to find it gone and says: "Holy cow! I ... I'll remain a girl even though I still have a boy's mind!"

The ramifications of a boy's mind in a girl's body are fleshed out as Claire Kent visits Lana Lang. When told to mix batter for a cake, Claire's thoughts are: "I'd rather be the batter in that ball game the boys are playing! But I ... I can't join them now ... *sigh*" Moments later, a mental warning goes off in Claire's mind, claiming: "Arrow Girl in danger...." Claire thinks: "It's a job for Superboy ... er ... Supergi—oh, I'm all mixed up!" After Arrow Girl (an amusement park performer) is rescued, a bystander guesses that Claire is actually Superboy's sister. As Claire flies away the bystander says: "You may not be as able as Superboy, Super-Sister! After all, super or not ... you're just a girl!" Claire responds: "Hmm ... I'll show them that Super-Sister can do as well as Superboy!"

As the story continues, Super-Sister figures out that the mental warning is her new power of super-feminine-intuition. At first Super-Sister is delighted and thinks that she has had the last laugh on the spacewoman since, "Instead of punishing me, she gave me a new super-power I never had before...." The only limitation is that it only alerts Super-Sister of *women* in danger. Super-Sister gradually accepts this limitation and gladly goes beyond the call of duty by helping the girl she saves to keep her job. At that point, Superboy is awakened by the spacewoman, who reveals that the whole experience was an illusion. Superboy responds: "Well, I learned my lesson ... I know now how it feels to be a girl and meet undeserved scorn and ridicule from men!" As the spacewoman leaves, she responds: "Good, Superboy! We always treat our men fairly on our women-ruled world! Farewell!"

It is exquisitely and ironically appropriate that the sighting of a "queer craft" sets this story in motion. While on the surface the story does little more than condemn gender-based prejudice, a closer reading yields a somewhat more radical subtext. The fact that Super-Sister retains "a boy's mind" leads to her yearning for the stereotypical pastimes of males and disdaining "girl stuff." It seems clear that the author's intent is that Claire's initial discomfort with her reassigned gender roles should be seen as a symptom of her "true," essential male gender. However, the fact that the story repeatedly states that Super-Sister has "a boy's mind" opens up at least a conceptual space where the gender assigned to one's body is not the sole determinate of one's gender identification. Conversely, Super-Sister's acceptance of her new gender (her dismay at being a girl seems to dissolve into delight when she discovers her new super-feminine-intuition) hints at the malleability of gender.

Furthermore, the entire story is driven by the spacewoman from a matriarchal planet. She is the one who is responsible for Superboy's "transformation" and has given him a new superpower for her own ends. She is the one who is manipulating him for the explicit purpose of teaching him "a lesson." In direct contrast to "The Superwoman of Metropolis," here it is the woman who exercises patriarchal power as the bestower of powers and the teacher of lessons to the male. At the end of the story, Superboy has learned the lesson she taught, as she returns to her matriarchal world with the nonsensical caveat that men there are "treated fairly."[6]

This story is unique among the "lessons" stories not only because the gender roles are reversed, but also because there is no ambiguity in the conclusion about who is the teacher and who is the taught, no muting of the patriarchal power of the teacher. The fact that a woman can exercise unambiguous patriarchal power and teach "lessons" to a male implies that there is no essential link between patriarchy and maleness, and thus no inherent right of men to exercise patriarchy over women. However, lest we assign too radical a subtext to this story, we must remember that she exercises power over SuperBOY, not SuperMAN. And even if the gendered roles of power are reversed, this story does nothing explicitly to challenge the legitimacy of one gender ruling over the other.

The "teaching of lessons" theme continues in a story centered on the character of Supergirl, who was introduced in May of 1959. In *Action* #258 (Binder 19–26), a story is published entitled "Supergirl's Farewell to Earth." The cover depicts Superman hurtling Supergirl in a transparent capsule away from Earth. She says: "Please, please, Superman—don't banish me! Give me another chance!" His reply is: "I'm sorry to end your career, but you're a failure as Supergirl! I must exile you to another world!"

Throughout this story, the theme of her obedience and submission to Superman is underscored. As Supergirl finishes one of her super-deeds, she thinks: "I've always followed Superman's orders! I've kept myself out of sight while doing super-feats!" At this point in their relationship, Superman has commanded her to keep her very existence as a super-powered girl secret during her "training period" and has not yet revealed his secret identity to her. She then sees Krypto the superdog flying and "impulsively" plays with him. When Superman encounters them, he is angry that she has "disobeyed" by revealing her existence to Krypto. He dismisses her rationale that Krypto is only a dog and says: "You must be taught a lesson!" Superman commands Supergirl to enter a transparent capsule which he hurls out into space with these words: "To an Asteroid, Supergirl! That's your punishment! I forbid you to return for one year!" The next panel claims that the reason for the capsule is to keep Krypto from following her scent and relieving her loneliness. Even Supergirl notes the harshness of Superman's reaction: "I could just fly back to Earth by myself now and ... uh ... No! I'll obey Superman, even though I think his punishment is too severe!" During her exile, Supergirl watches her friends from afar, noting that at least Superman did not forbid her that. An emergency arises, and Supergirl figures out a way to rescue her friends without leaving the asteroid, and thus, again, not disobeying Superman.

The story then takes an odd turn. Krypto arrives with a note from Superman telling her to return to Earth to avoid a drifting cloud of Kryptonite dust. The internal consistency of the story is compromised by having Krypto deliver the message since, ostensibly, the reason for having her flung there in a capsule was to avoid the possibility of Krypto finding her. The use of the capsule is thus left without justification. It seems likely that the use of the capsule serves to emphasize the submission of Supergirl. She is not leaving Earth under her own power, not even accompanied by a stern Superman. She is utterly and literally abject as Superman throws her away from Earth. This becomes even stronger on the cover, which implies that the exile is meant to be permanent since Superman speaks of "ending her career."

As Supergirl returns to Earth, her absence as Linda Lee (her secret identity) has stimulated a missing-persons search. Her story of being lost in a nearby swamp is accepted until one reporter corners her after the others have left and examines her arm for evidence of insect bites. Seeing none, he challenges her to deny that she is a hitherto unknown girl of steel. To his surprise, Linda admits her secret. The reporter (who is, of course, Clark) turns away thinking: "Linda has failed me! I see now that she could be tricked into giving away her big secret!" But Supergirl stops him in his tracks by revealing that she knows he is Superman. She explains that, as he was about to examine her, she attempted to stop him by fogging his glasses. As that attempt failed, she thought: "Wait! Nothing happened! Those are Super-lenses! Now I know who he is! Ha, ha!"

As the story concludes, Superman reveals that the entire exile was a ruse to put Supergirl in a situation where she would have to protect her secret "in the toughest situations." Superman declares that she has passed the test. When Supergirl excitedly asks if she can now be revealed to the world, Superman refuses, claiming that he needs her existence to remain secret so that she can serve as his secret emergency weapon. When asked, then, the reason for the test, Superman responds: "Well ... uh ... I figured that if you could keep your own big secret, I could trust you to know mine!" The final panel follows with Supergirl asking: "My goodness! You mean it all led up to telling me you were Clark Kent?" The expressions on Supergirl's and Krypto's faces are those of glee as Superman responds: "Uh ... yes, Supergirl! Only you ... er ... found it out by yourself! Is my face red!"

In interpreting these "lessons" stories it should be noted, as Foucault has shown, that the exercise of power is never solely repressive. Power and resistance arise together and are always in relationship with each other (Foucault 94–98; also see Jagose 80–83). Furthermore, discourse, which for Foucault transmits and produces power, also is always "polyvalent." That is, even while it reinforces power, discourse "also undermines and exposes it, renders it fragile and makes it possible to thwart it" (Foucault 100–102). The ambivalent interplay between patriarchal power and female dignity in these stories demonstrates that polyvalence.

Like the other "Lesson" stories, this story involves a delicate balance between patriarchal power and female dignity, between submission and assertiveness. Throughout the story, Supergirl's obedience is underscored, even as she considers Superman's "lesson" to be overly harsh. Neverthe-less, the story ends with her outwitting Superman and pre-empting his authority to reward her by discovering the reward for herself. He even acquiesces in his own submission by his sheepish expression in the last panel, verbally expressed by his hesitant "uh's" and "er's." Still, even her assertiveness is bounded by submission. All of her actions are within the bounds of his commands. Even her passing of the test results not in the reward she desires (a reward she could easily attain herself, were it not for her obedience to him), but in the reward he intends to give. Yet, the sta-tus quo is irrevocably changed. The power differential of the secret iden-tity is broken in a way that is both within and outside the law of the Superfather. She discovers independently what he was about to reveal. Nevertheless, she is still only allowed to be his secret weapon, his hidden appendage, his phallus. In her reading of Lacan's essay: "The Signification of the Phallus," Garber makes use of the notion that men (at least in fan-tasy) *have* the phallus while women (at least in fantasy) *are* the phallus (Garber, 1992, pg. 356). In a symbolic manner not unlike the Hindu char-acterization of the goddesses as the shakti or power of their male consorts, Supergirl is still Superman's shakti: his submissive, secret phallic power. That situation will, however, change, as discussed in part three.

PART THREE: FROM UNKNOWN SUPERGIRL TO WORLD'S GREATEST HEROINE

At her introduction in 1959 in *Action* #252 (Binder 20–28), Supergirl is both like and unlike the other super-powered women previously men-tioned. Like the sensationalistic covers of both "Girl of Steel" stories, the cover of this issue hints at a perceived threat to the super-male. The cover shows Superman landing next to a crashed rocket out of which flies Super-girl. To his assertion that what he sees "must be an illusion," she responds: "Look again, *Superman!* It's me—*Supergirl!* And I have *all* your powers!" The cover caption makes explicit the sense of threat in its proclamation: "Introducing: 'The Supergirl from Krypton!' Is She Friend or Foe?"

Despite the assertion that she has "all" Superman's powers, there are a number of plot points which defuse any question of her being an actual equal or threat. One way of defusing this threat concerns their relationship. Supergirl is Superman's younger cousin, which legitimates Superman's patriarchal rule over her. In addition, making them cousins precludes any threat of a romantic relationship developing between them. She cannot pose the same threat of domestication as other superpowered women, at least not explicitly. Another way in which the inequality between them is established concerns secret identities. As has been said earlier, the keeping of a secret identity is indicative of a power differential between characters. In this case, Superman assists Supergirl in creating one for herself, but does not reveal his own. Interestingly, he does not even tell her his Kryptonian name, which leaves her to address him by the awkward epithet "Cousin Superman." He knows both her Kryptonian name and her secret identity, while she knows neither of his names.

The final way in which the inequality between them is established is the most explicit. Superman declares that she can become the "Girl of Steel," but only after she has undergone long practice under his tutelage (and admonishes her that her very existence as a Supergirl must remain secret). That Superman's admonition is indeed received as a command that requires obedience is substantiated when Supergirl decides to fly over the town by night. Her rationale is that she will not be seen at night, and thus she is "not disobeying Superman!"

In *Action* #285 (Siegel 1–36), two years and nine months after her introduction, Supergirl's existence is revealed to the world. The subtext inherent in this coming out of Supergirl's becomes clear when taken in the context of the stories published in the months leading up to this milestone. As collected in a 1968 reprint, the overall story arc can be read as the story of Supergirl's emergence from male domination. She begins as the stereotypically invisible powerful woman (Siegel, "The Unknown Supergirl" 1–13). She can exercise power but only if it is bounded by submission to a man and is wielded in secret, "behind the throne." She ends as Superman's equal, partner, and even rescuer.

As the story begins, Superman tells her that he has decided to reveal her existence. This sets in motion the specter of her repressed desire to rebel, which is manifested in the character of Lesla Lar, an evil double of Supergirl who drains her of her power (Siegel, "Supergirl's Secret Enemy" 14–24).[7] The story is constructed in such a way that Lesla only comes to earth by trading places with Linda while Linda sleeps. For the duration of the story, even when Lesla occasionally allows Linda to resurface, submissive Linda has no superpowers. This evil twin acts out by becoming a villain's "emergency weapon" even while she plans to betray both him and Superman. The artwork consistently shows her with raised (phallic) finger which is shown more or less erect as she alternates between deceptive submission and thoughts of rebellion. When she and Superman go on a mission she purposely creates a great spectacle, even while remaining out of sight, the motive of which is, she explicitly states, to "show up Superman."

This is in direct contrast to Supergirl's behavior in the following story, where she contemplates how she would not overtake her boyfriend in a swimming race because "men enjoy feeling superior to women." Significantly, Supergirl never becomes consciously aware of her evil, traitorous and non-submissive duplicate. She does, however, ultimately disobey Superman.

As the story arc continues, the threat of Supergirl possibly surpassing her previous mentor is invoked when she (temporarily) becomes invulnerable to kryptonite. Superman wonders whether, since she is now "superior to me, maybe our relationship ought to be reversed! Perhaps I should become her assistant!" (Siegel, "The Three [six] Red K Perils" 36–52). Although this invulnerability to kryptonite does not last, the final story will explicitly refer a number of times to her saving Superman from kryptonite. As with Lois Lane in the 1943 story, Superman becomes the one rescued.

In the penultimate story of this arc (Siegel, "The World's Greatest Heroine" 53–64), Supergirl finally disobeys Superman. By this time, Supergirl has been adopted, and Superman tells her that he will meet with her and her parents at a specific time so that they will be the first to learn of her secret identity. However, before the appointed hour, Linda's parents encounter mortal danger, and Supergirl is left with no other option but to save them openly herself. After the rescue, Supergirl is alarmed that she "disobeyed Superman," and fears that he will change his mind about announcing her existence. At that point, Superman arrives and quells her fears. The specter of disobedience has been resolved. The timing of this "disobedience," along with the earlier hint that her powers were linked to her subconscious, rebellious "Lesla" side, suggests that she can only reach her potential through disobedience, however mild.

As the story progresses, while explaining her origin to her parents, Supergirl explicitly states that she has "often" saved Superman from kryptonite. Supergirl's existence is then announced to the world. The first reaction shown is from a young female whose admiration of Supergirl is exquisitely gender-stereotype bound: "She's adorable! I love her hair!" A beautiful Hollywood actress is angered that Supergirl will receive more attention than she will. A circus strongman is threatened by the ridicule he expects to receive from people who know that a young girl is stronger than he, and criminals abandon their planned crimes to avoid the shame of having "a young girl" capture them. Superman recounts to the audience a number of Supergirl's deeds, the first of which is her "saving" him by destroying a kryptonite meteor from afar. As Superman and Supergirl tour the world together, a man comments, "What a superb couple!" while a woman says: "She's terrific! Cute, too!"[8]

Their being described as "a superb couple" suggests that Supergirl represents Superman's compromise with domesticity. She is the closest he will come to a marriage partner. In addition, the next issue that shows Supergirl on the cover ("Superman's Super-Courtship" 15–27) makes this subtext even more explicit. Inspired by his statement that "if I ever did marry, it would be to someone super and lovable like ... you!," Supergirl decides to play matchmaker for Superman. Watching him embrace the otherworldly superwoman she has found, Supergirl says: "How strange that the women he is finally going to wed looks exactly as I will when I grow up!" Furthermore, even if Supergirl and Superman can never wed, she, along with the aforementioned super dog and later even a super cat, become the core of Superman's extended "Super-Family."

Returning to the story at hand, as Supergirl receives a standing ovation from the UN, Superman says: "Physically, she's the mightiest female of all time! But at heart, she's as gentle and sweet and as quick to tears—as any ordinary girl! I guess that's why everyone who meets her loves her." As the story concludes, Superman's leaving on a mission sets the stage for Supergirl's first open adventure, or, as the editorial comments construct, her "greatest test!"

The final story in this arc is entitled "The Infinite Monster." Supergirl faces a monster so gigantic that only his feet and legs are visible. Pentagon officials, learning of the threat, decide to call on Supergirl, even while one of them says: "Supergirl?! A mere girl handle a major crisis like this?!" The scoffer's doubt seems, at first, justified when Supergirl's first attempts to subdue the monster are unsuccessful. Further comments again question her ability: "Supergirl can't stop that creature! How I wish we had Superman here instead of that girl!" Overhearing these remarks, Supergirl is even more determined to prove herself. Using a bazooka-sized ray gun, she shrinks the monster into "an infinitesimal creature." The shrunken creature appears to be seven or eight inches high, judging from his size as she holds him in her hand. With the monster in hand, she replies to her critics: "Satisfied, Gentlemen?" They respond: "You're every bit as resourceful and terrific as your cousin Superman.... Congratulations!" She then takes the monster, still alive, to the "Fortress of Solitude," where it will remain imprisoned as her "fascinating trophy." A second round of accolades follows, during which Superman publicly reiterates his approval of her, and says: "From now on, we're going to be a team, she and I...." The story ends with Linda lounging on her bed in a stereotypical female pose: on her stomach, head supported by one hand, with legs raised from the knees and ankles crossed. She thinks: "I'm so happy! I'm no longer just Superman's emergency weapon! Now I'm his partner! Golly, things'll be very different from now on!"

As mentioned before, in Foucaultian terms, power and resistance arise simultaneously. Thus, the patriarchal power that limits Supergirl is also the engendering matrix in which she comes into her power. Her resistance is, at first, manifested subconsciously in the figure of Lesla Lar, and then openly, albeit in a subdued way, with her disobedience to Superman.

When the situation calls for it, Supergirl uses her big gun. From page 8 of "The Infinite Monster" in *Action*, Issue 285 (New York: DC Comics, 1962).

Her temporary superiority to him is invoked and defused; nevertheless, her ability to rescue him is repeatedly affirmed. Lastly, her shrinking of the "Infinite Monster" and keeping it as a "trophy" begs to be read as a metaphor for the taming and obtaining of phallic power. Supergirl, with her own "big gun," has shrunk the infinite phallus into something she can engulf in her hand and keep as a trophy. She goes from *being* Superman's phallus (emergency weapon) to *having* a phallus all her own.

The repeated markers of Supergirl as "female" (from her being "gentle, sweet, and quick to tears" to her pose at the end of the issue which lacks only an embroidered poodle on the skirt), when combined with her ability to tame and appropriate phallic power, suggests that Supergirl does indeed "trouble" gender, even if it is within certain limitations. She does become, after all, the world's greatest "heroine." The journey of Supergirl from secret weapon to hyper-feminine "partner" reflects the culture of the early 1960s in which women (or, at least, reassuringly feminine girls) were, again, beginning to be acknowledged in the work force. In 1961 President John F. Kennedy established a Commission on the Status of Women, with Eleanor Roosevelt as its chairperson. One of the cover features of *Life* magazine for March 23, 1962, was entitled: "How Nice to be a Pretty Girl and Work in Washington." If the comics of the fifties dealt with the threat of domestication and the specter of female power by turning a capable Girl Reporter into an obsessive, ineffectual Girl Friend; then the comics of the early Sixties embrace the power of a super (phallic) hyper-feminine Girl who becomes the focus of a muted domestication.

If Foucault is right not only about the polyvalence of discourse, but also right in asserting that resistance usually occurs not in one overarching revolt, but in multiple, imperfect points of resistance (Foucault

95–96), then the imperfections and ambivalences of these stories of super-gender reversals and their lessons learned (by whom?) both reflect the anxieties and ambivalences surrounding gender in their times and point toward further gender trouble ahead for Super-Girls and Mild Mannered Men.

NOTES

1. See especially chapter 2 of Stephen Cohan's *Masked Men: Masculinity and the Movies in the Fifties.*

2. The phallic and sexual overtones of this image enhance the gender reversal involved. The same image is used in an even more "queer" manner on the cover of *Superman's Pal: Jimmy Olsen* #45 of June 1960. In that instance, a "lad" drags the train and Superman is shown obviously enjoying his passive role in the scenario while Jimmy Olsen worries that he has been replaced as Superman's "pal." In the story itself, the "lad" has the name "Dik-Ray."

3. Revealingly, Supergirl and other women with superpowers are not depicted in the same way. Supergirl's changes typically show her removing her wig with some of her clothes draped over her arm. She does not expose her chest in the same manner. She does not reveal the phallus in the same way as he does. In "The Superwoman of Metropolis," Lois is shown in a similar exposure of the chest, however, immediately afterwards her powers expire. Steve Younis at the *Superman Homepage* writes: "To my knowledge, Clark Kent first ripped open his shirt to reveal his Superman costume underneath way back in the Superman Fleischer cartoon titled 'Electric Earthquake' in 1942. Since then Clark Kent has been seen doing this time and time again. The image has been drawn over and over again on the cover of Superman comics, with 'Action Comics #171' in 1952 being the first. This image has been used not only on comic book covers, but on merchandise from DVDs to Magnets, from Video Games to T-shirts, and from Toys to Scissors.... This familiar image has been used for the cover of *TIME* magazine, and has been the focus of statues and figurines, promotions and advertisements."

4. The first comic devoted wholly to Lois is *Showcase* #9 in 1957. It is here that the title *Superman's Girl Friend, Lois Lane* is used, and it also marks the first appearance of the adult Lana Lang, who becomes Lois' rival for Superman's attentions. And, yes, the title is Superman's "Girl Friend," not girlfriend, further distancing him from the romantic threat of Lois.

5. The sexism inherent in this introduction is acknowledged in a 1973 reprint of the story (*Superman's Girl Friend: Lois Lane* #131), in which the introduction is changed to read: "Can Lois outperform the mighty Superman himself? See for yourself in ... The Superwoman of Metropolis."

6. In 1960, it is still possible to envision a just and admirable culture that is ruled solely by a single gender. By way of contrast, in later stories involving women from matriarchal planets, the matriarchies come to an end at the stories' conclusion. In "The Girl who was Mightier than Superman" (*Superman* #180 in 1965), a natural disaster destroys the matriarchal civilization; in "The Revolt of the Girl Legionnaires" (*Adventure* #326 in 1964), the matriarchal rulers of the planet "Femnaz" (yes, they were called "Femnazis"; Rush Limbaugh isn't as original as he thinks he is) are convinced to repent of their ways; and in "The Mutiny of the Super-Heroines" (*Adventure* #368 in 1968), the matriarchal government is overthrown.

7. Lesla Lar comes from Kandor, a miniaturized city of Kryptonians kept in Superman's Fortress of Solitude. Interestingly, just as Supergirl's Kandorian double represents her repressed desire to rebel, Superman's Kandorian double, Van Zee, represents Superman's repressed desire for domesticity. Van Zee is married to an earth-born double of Lois Lane and has two charming children.

8. It is tempting to see something slightly queer in having a man comment on the two of them as a couple while a woman comments on how "cute" Supergirl is.

WORKS CITED

Binder, Otto. "Claire Kent, alias Super-Sister." *Superboy* 78. January 1960.
_____. "Supergirl's Farewell to Earth." *Action* 258. November 1959.
_____. "The Girl of Steel." *Superman* 123. August 1958.
_____. "The Supergirl from Krypton." *Action* 252. May 1959.
Butler, Judith. *Gender Trouble: Feminism and the Subversion of Identity.* New York: Routledge, 1990.
Cohan, Steven. *Masked Men: Masculinity and the Movies in the Fifties.* Bloomington: Indiana University Press, 1997.
Dorfman, Leo. "The Girl who was Mightier than Superman." *Superman* 180. October 1965.
Foucault, Michel. *The History of Sexuality Volume 1: An Introduction.* Trans., Robert Hurley. New York: Vintage Books, 1980.
Garber, Marjorie. *Vested Interests: Cross-Dressing and Cultural Anxiety.* New York: Routledge, 1992.
"The Girl of Steel." *Action* 156. May 1951.
"How Nice to be a Pretty Girl and Work in Washington." *Life* 23. March 23, 1962.
Jagose, Annamarie. *Queer Theory: An Introduction.* New York: New York University Press, 1996.
Modleski, Tania. *Feminism without Women: Culture and Criticism in a "Postfeminist" Age.* New York: Routledge, 1991.
Shooter, Jim. "The Mutiny of the Super-Heroines." *Adventure* 368. May 1968.
Siegel, Jerry. "Battle Between Super-Lois and Super-Lana." *Superman's Girl Friend, Lois Lane* 21. November 1960.
_____. "The Infinite Monster." *Action* 285. February 1962.
_____. "Lois Lane—Superwoman." *Action* 60. May 1943.
_____. "The Revolt of the Girl Legionnaires." *Adventure* 326. November 1964.
_____. "Supergirl's Secret Enemy." *Action* 279. August 1961.
_____. "Superman." *Action* 1. June 1938.
_____. "The Three (Six) Red K Perils." *Action* 283. December 1961.
_____. "Trapped in Kandor." *Action* 280. September 1961.
_____. "The Unknown Supergirl." *Action* 278. July 1961.
_____. "The World's Greatest Heroine." *Action* 285. February 1962.
"Superman's Super-Courtship." *Action* 289. June 1962.
"Tom Baker, Power Lad!" *Superman's Pal: Jimmy Olsen* 45. June 1960.
Various. *Lois Lane: Girl Reporter.* Backup feature in *Superman* #28, May 1944, to #42, October 1946.
Victor/Victoria. Dir. Blake Edwards. Metro-Goldwyn-Mayer, 1982.
Weisinger, Mort. "The Superwoman of Metropolis." *Superman's Girl Friend: Lois Lane* 8. April 1959.
Younis, Steve. "Revealing the Costume." *Superman Homepage.* 13 December 2006. http://www.supermanhomepage.com/other/other.php?topic=shirt-rip.

From Jimmy Durante to Michael Chiklis: The Thing Comes Full Circle

JEFF MCCLELLAND

Since 2002's *Spider-Man* debuted in theaters and reached astronomical financial success, Hollywood has pursued comic book properties at a frenzied pace and with renewed vigor unseen in previous decades.[1] In light of this observation, it seems obvious that the Fantastic Four, the comic book family that heralded in the so-called Silver Age of comics, would eventually make their mark on the silver screen. And in 2005 audiences around the world had the opportunity to view just that for the first time ever.[2] Movies such as this Tim Story–directed film provide the opportunity for wider exposure of previously developed yet relatively obscure characters (at least compared to contemporaries like Superman and Spider-Man) such as the Fantastic Four and specifically, as I will focus on, Ben Grimm, the craggy, cantankerous, golden-hearted Thing. Although the movie was not exactly a critical success,[3] its performance was financially solid enough[4] to merit a sequel (namely the June 2007–debuting *Fantastic Four: Rise of the Silver Surfer*), keeping these characters in the national spotlight a while longer, hopefully providing audiences with the opportunity to appreciate the history that comes along with this new interpretation.[5] As Michael Chiklis, Hollywood's newest version of the Thing, remarked on the role he was hired to undertake, "There were a handful of Marvel comics that I really loved, but the FF was my favorite, and particularly the character of Ben Grimm, the Thing. I just related to him.... I liked the fact that they were more accessible as characters, and particularly Ben" ("Interview"). It is this accessibility that drew me to the character, and it is what will propel the concept of the character onward into the future, unchanged from his 1961 inception.

When contemplating fictional characters in relation to the issue of longevity, one of the most familiar anecdotes revolves around the notion that when times change, characters that last—in the popular, commercial sense, at least—find a way to change with them, and in this paper, I don't intent to dispute that as a hard and fast rule. The intention of this chapter is to discuss the character of Marvel Comics' the Thing—the muscle behind the super hero group the "Fantastic Four"—his influences, cultural and otherwise, and ultimately, I hope to prove that this character's uniqueness in this regard comes from his unwillingness to change. His (pardon the pun) rock-solid characterization provides a foundation for the exception to the rule; even as he remains the macho, overcompensating blue-collar throwback, he refuses to fade away. I will focus on three distinct aspects of the Thing throughout this essay. First will be the early history of the Thing and the concept of the American everyman. Next, I will examine the Jewish influences on the Thing and comic books in general. Finally, I will delve into the exposure of the Thing's character in incremented measures. In many ways, the Thing's until recently unacknowledged cultural history provides the basis and consistency for his everyman characterization, his background a revelation that comes at a time when scholarly work is beginning to acknowledge the Jewish authority behind many comic book characters and much of the industry.

LEE AND KIRBY: THE THING'S BEGINNINGS

The Thing was originally created as part of Marvel Comics' first Silver Age periodical, the *Fantastic Four*, in 1961 as a response to rival DC Comics' *Justice League*[6] title. Many point to this first issue as the book that revived the comic book industry as a whole, which had, to that point, been languishing under the governmental microscope that had come from Fredric Wertham's witch-hunt of the 1950s.[7] The super hero genre in comics that had thrived throughout the Second World War had soon after withered and given way to western and romance titles with no end in sight; only perennial stalwarts like Superman and Batman remained profitable enough to enjoy unbroken publishing runs on various titles. Staff writer Stan Lee was given the task of creating something that could rival *Justice League*, DC's new hit book, and since he had planned on quitting the comic book field anyway, his wife Joan convinced him to write the story that he had always wanted to write. Thus was born a team with a very nationalistic goal—they strove to beat Communist Russia into space.

While the Fantastic Four's endeavors would give way to missions by the real-life likes of Yuri Gagarin and Alan Shepard, their book lives on, continually published for over 45 years. Longevity and recognition of this sort in the contemporary world of fiction is difficult to come by, and the lasting presence of Ben Grimm, the Thing, as a recognizable figure within America's popular culture and subculture can only be attributed to his cultural identity as the American "everyman": from the neighborhood in which he grew up to his struggles with his religious background to his psychological insecurities. Ben Grimm is, in a sense, you and me[8] in the fact that he, unlike many of his contemporaries, is not a perfect hero or a perfect human being. The Thing is not Superman and does not aspire to be;

he does not have a secret identity and cannot hide his rocky exterior, meaning that he cannot, in turn, hide his humanity. The Thing is stuck with his lot in life, and like many of his readers and others throughout the world, he does his best with the tools that he has been given.

Fantastic Four creator and father to Marvel Comics, Stan Lee has been known for many things, but among those are three peculiar traits: his exuberance in any situation, his poor memory, and his affinity for creating characters modeled after himself. He has admitted that Spider-Man was created to be him as a teenager, Reed Richards is modeled in his image as an adult, and Dr. Strange is also Lee—in a cloak ("Soapbox 3/99").[9] Lee broke the mold, then, in modeling the Thing's speech pattern after one of the most popular and certainly one of the most gregarious personalities of the 1920s into the 1960s: Jimmy Durante ("Soapbox 10/99").

Durante, an actor, singer, comedian and pianist, among other things, possessed the larger-than-life characteristics that were necessary for the more literally large Thing, and his strong working-class New York accent made a smooth transition from one character to the other. Truly, Ben Grimm possesses Durante's over the top characteristics to this day. As it was easy for audiences to admire and relate to Durante's language and mannerisms for the human, everyday qualities that his words retained, it was just as easy for comic book readers to feel a closeness to the Thing. Whereas Durante was known for his catchphrases, such as "I'm mortified!" Grimm was equally likely to spout, "What a revoltin' development!"

There is a covert prestige in speaking in forms that normally are considered nonstandard, and using a thick New York accent helped separate both Durante and the Thing from the social elite of the time. Superman, Batman, Wonder Woman and Captain Marvel (to name a few) all spoke a pristine, flawless English, which is fine, but a bit condescending. If Superman, for example, would start to speak with a noticeable dialect, his stature as a "perfect" hero would diminish. By speaking in a nonstandard version of the language—and to a certain extent being monolingual to Superman's vast multi-lingualism—the Thing appeals more to those known as the "common man" and therefore raises his own popularity with them. By using phonetic text on a page, Stan Lee was able to make the Thing flawed and perfect at the same time.

With deference to Lee, the most crucial influence to Ben Grimm's identity and exposure is Jack Kirby, a widely imitated, yet sometimes undervalued and underappreciated comic book artist responsible for creating or co-creating the Fantastic Four, the X-Men, the Hulk, Captain America, the New Gods[10] and scores of other titles and characters for and apart from Marvel. Kirby collaborated with Lee on the first 102 consecutive issues of the Fantastic Four title—a record streak for mainstream comics until recently[11]—but this feat and Kirby's influence is perhaps overshadowed by Lee, whose natural zeal is markedly opposite Kirby's more diffident personality. In addition, Kirby died in 1994 while Lee continues to be a marketable, recognizable face for Marvel Comics and its characters, the textbook definition of a "company man" (even after, amazingly enough, his lawsuit with Marvel regarding the Spider-Man movie). Kirby projected his own self-image onto his creation of the Thing, a strong, often irritable, hard-working individual, and nowhere is that more evident than in a 1978 issue of *What If … ?*

Marvel's *What If … ?* title allowed creators and readers alike look into the realm of what could have been within the Marvel Universe, and tales generally centered around a divergence from an important moment in comic book continuity. This particular issue put original Marvel creators (and a secretary Flo Steinberg) in the role of the Fantastic Four. Although Jack Kirby wrote this issue along with penciling it, he still placed Stan Lee

Jack Kirby portrays himself as the Thing. From page 21 of "What If the Fantastic Four Were the Original Marvel Bullpen?" in *What If …?*, Volume 1, Issue 1 (New York: Marvel Comics, 1978).

in the role of Mr. Fantastic, leader of the team, while he gave himself the role of the Thing. In the issue, Kirby portrays himself as a quiet but stubborn artist, hiding his identity and tired of living in the shadow of others.

JEWISH INFLUENCE

As it turns out, Kirby lent the Thing more than just some of his personality traits; in July of 2002, Manhattan's Cosmic Comics hung a (somewhat crass) sign on its front window, asking the question: "How do you circumcise an orange brick?" Now in its third volume and at a time when the editorial policy at Marvel Comics promoted a more "realistic" image for its characters—where Spider-Man would reveal his secret identity to his Aunt May and Captain America and Iron Man would let the whole world know their faces—the Thing came out as a member of the Jewish faith[12] in the 56th issue of the series. This revelation was something that had always been assumed around the Marvel offices but never overtly presented in the comic book sense, at least according to some.

In an interview with the *Jewish Journal* of Greater Los Angeles, Marvel editor Tom Brevoort noted that "When Karl [Kesel, writer of the issue in question] sent me the [story], my reaction wasn't, 'Wait! That's a new Thing.' My reaction was, 'Oh, of course'" (Aushenker). In a separate interview, Brevoort divulged that "Jack Kirby, the Thing's co-creator, was Jewish and apparently, at least in his eyes, from all available information, he believed that the character was Jewish as well. He had done a drawing of the Thing that apparently was over his hearth that had the Thing in a yarmulke, holding the Torah and so forth" ("Shape").

The Thing's middle name, Jacob, could easily be seen as a nod to Kirby, whose given name was Jacob Kurtzberg, but that would require writer Stan Lee to be at most in tune with Kirby's presumed wishes and at least open to suggestion. In reality, the name may be just a coincidence, but if so, it remains quite a coincidence at that.

While both the evidence and conjecture presented to this point hopefully lead to a better understanding of the Thing, an outsider's view will only take one so far. The comic book community is both wide-ranging and closely knit, and the following three creators, each part of his own medium but all participating in the same overall community, have their own unique view on Ben Grimm as a character. Michael San Giacomo, Peter David, and Sean Kleefeld weighed in with their thoughts on the Thing, Jewish culture, and the secret to long-lasting success.

Michael San Giacomo is a reporter for the *Cleveland Plain Dealer* newspaper and has been an outspoken proponent for the creation of a Superman museum in the city that birthed the icon. He recently waded into the comic book industry with his five-issue *Phantom Jack* series, published through Image Comics, and is currently looking to extend his character's existence beyond those five issues. While the reporter, who also writes the online column "Journey into Comics," notes the marked similarities between Jack Kirby and the Thing ("He's a lot like Jack. He's irascible; a grouch"), San Giacomo notes the distinction of what *is* and what *might be* the idea that Kirby was projecting onto his co-creation. "The Thing is what Jack would have liked to have been," he explained. "Jack Kirby was shy and kept to himself—maybe he was able to express himself when he was drawing the Thing." San Giacomo also expressed doubts that the Thing's religious preferences were "understood," as the story goes throughout Marvel lore. "No one ever assumed that [the Thing] was Jewish," he surmised. "No one ever thought about it." Whether this is true or not depends on personal opinion, but San Giacomo offered his take on the situation: he believed that Peter David, comic book writer and member of the Jewish faith, first suggested the idea.

David is a comic book mainstay, employed for decades by numerous companies with lengthy appointments on many of the industry's top titles. David is perhaps best known for reinvigorating Marvel's sagging *Incredible Hulk* franchise that he wrote from 1987 through 1998, although he reached greatest commercial success with *Spider-Man 2099*, also from Marvel. (The writer is prolific outside of the comic book industry, too, as his credits include a line of Star Trek novels and the Nickelodeon television series "Space Cases.") While David denies being the inspiration behind the Thing's newly revealed religious preferences, he is responsible for establishing that Doc Samson, green-haired supporting character in the *Incredible Hulk* title, is Jewish. According to the writer, when one steps back to take a broader look at the four-color characters, we may find that these fictional beings are more blank slates than many would like to admit. "When you get right down to it," David explained, "all of the characters are generally the same. Never confuse change with the illusion of change" (email, 15 February 2006). Taking Spider-Man for example, David stated that even though he married his longtime love interest Mary Jane Watson in 1987's *Amazing Spider-Man* annual, "he's still the same old Spidey."

David further delves into the psyche of super heroes and their significant others by taking into consideration the character of Lois Lane, "Superman's Girlfriend" (as her 1958 title proclaimed). Since the 1930s, Lois Lane's character has been the epitome of what a strong female was supposed to be, but by today's standards, her early representation depicts anything but strength. "Let's face it, Lois never had much character outside of her relationship to Superman," David explained:

> She was a snoopy reporter whose entire reason for being was to show how much more clever Superman was than her. Which, when you're dealing with a medium aimed at ten year olds, makes sense. Superman, in tandem with Batman, were the four-color equivalent of the Little Rascals "He-Man Woman-Hater's club," back-patting each other over their cleverness in outwitting Lois yet again. Boys rule, girls drool. Considering the target audience, that's the only appropriate attitude. But the combination of women's lib, socially conscious editors and an aging readership demanded that Lois be given a brand new character. She's still a reporter, she's still Superman's significant other, but she's now much more of a partner ... a change that was pretty much seamless since the old characterization it was supplanting just didn't work for the newer audiences [email, 16 February 2006].

Sean Kleefeld is a fan who has put his habits to use within the field. After producing exhaustive archival work for his Fantastic Four-themed website, Kleefeld has managed to contribute that knowledge to the comic book industry, as he was included in a special historical section of *Fantastic Four*, issue 500 (the "director's cut" edition, which contained more peripheral material than the regular edition, as the title returned to its first volume numbering), and contributed to the Fantastic Four DVD release. In addition, he writes the regular column "Incidental Iconography" for the *Jack Kirby Collector* publication. To Kleefeld, the revelation that the Thing is Jewish is nothing to be surprised about. For those who, for whatever reason, didn't know about the character's religious background, according to Kleefeld, "it can add a dimension to the character that they hadn't previously seen. Given that he's not a devout Jew, however, it's something that can be fairly easily overlooked and someone who starts reading about the character today might not ever learn what sort of spirituality drives him."

As for the idea that the Thing is really Jack Kirby in disguise, Kleefeld allows that Kirby left a piece of himself in all of the characters he created, whether that be the Thing, Captain America, or even the villainous Dark-seid. "Personally," Kleefeld adds, "I see more of Jack—well, Jack circa the 1960s—in the Thing than in any other character, but I see enough differences there that I wouldn't say that the Thing was just Jack's avatar. If nothing else, the Thing had a better memory!"

The Thing isn't the only comic book character to be influenced by Jewish culture or Jewish creators. Comic books, and especially comics from the time of the first super hero explosion following the 1938 appearance of Superman, were overwhelmingly created and produced by Jews in New York, a focal point for both comic book publishing and Jewish immigration. The comic book medium, explains Al Jaffee, a comic creator whose works appear in early issues of *MAD Magazine*, was considered unrespectable at the time, offering those of Jewish heritage (a representation of roughly two percent of the American population) their only opportunity to work in a design-related field. "We couldn't get into newspaper strips or advertising; ad agencies wouldn't hire a Jew," said Jaffee. "One of the reasons we Jews drifted into the comic-book business is that most of the comic-book publishers were Jewish. So there was no discrimination there" (Kaplan).

Gerald Jones's *Men of Tomorrow*, an intricate, meticulous account of the early days of comic book publishing, speaks extensively of the Jewish influence on popular culture. Jones, a former comic book writer himself (perhaps best known for his run on *Green Lantern*), writes of the pride Jews took in this influence:

> Jews ran the movie studios and wrote the songs—and not the pampered children of rich German families but old shtetl fur peddlers and Delancey Street spielers. Benny Goodman was the sound of sex. There were Jewish movie stars, not only clowns like Eddie Cantor but Paul Muni, Sylvia Sydney, even Ricardo Cortez. Jewish dads made sure their gangster-crazy kids knew who Edward G. Robinson and John Garfield were behind their goyish screen names. "Did you read Walter Winchell today?" they'd say. "He's Jewish, you know." Those dads had grown up viewing American culture through the eyes of outsiders, but the kids knew it was their culture, theirs to take and theirs to remake [128].

When the character is viewed in that religious and cultural context, there are obvious parallels, one being the idea of the Thing as an interpretation of the Golem of Jewish lore, a magic, half-demon protector made of clay from the Moldau River. (Recently, Michael Chabon's *The Amazing Adventures of Kavalier and Clay* used the Golem extensively in the book inspired by Superman's creators). And in the 22nd issue of the title *Mar-*

vel Knights 4, the Thing meets a version of the mythical Golem. In this issue, the Golem is terrorizing the neighborhood in which Ben Grimm grew up, even though its intention was to protect it; the Thing eventually convinces the monster to destroy itself (as it has become obsolete), prompting him to wonder, then, how long it would be "before his time is up" (Aguirre-Sacasa 22).

EXPOSURE

The question then returns to the idea of popularity and longevity. Has the Thing remained in the cultural foreground in spite of or because of his obvious deficiencies? San Giacomo, David and Kleefeld had their own thoughts on the matter. While David refers back to earlier comments about all characters being basically the same, Kleefeld and San Giacomo both take note of the Thing as a tragic character. According to Kleefeld:

> [The Thing is] this normal guy, who's suddenly trapped in a body that alienates him from the rest of the world. He can't go where normal people can, he can't use things the way normal people use them, he doesn't even look like anyone else any more. He's permanently set apart from society and is in a constant struggle to fit in. So you have this tragedy—his loss of humanity—combined with this notion of alienation that everyone seems to experience periodically, and you're quickly tapping into some very powerful stuff emotionally.

Added San Giacomo: "[This was] the first time, in 1961, that we ever had a hero who was not handsome. His exterior was clearly meant to show that he had a heart of gold. Here's a guy who's just a guy; there's instant appeal to that."

The Thing's history, then, is that of an outsider, and his supposed deficiencies lend themselves to that: his physical deformities, his nonstandard English, his struggles with self-confidence and a short temper. His popularity, almost inversely, stems from this notion that he is not Superman and that he is not Batman. Ben Grimm was not brought to earth in a rocket ship to serve as a messianic figure[13]; he was not born with immediate wealth and a butler at his disposal; the Thing was born in a tough neighborhood where he had to fend for himself. Whatever Grimm made of his life, he did it on his own merit and in spite of the social barriers set up in place against a man in his position. Growing up and fending for himself on Yancy Street, a hyperbolic representation of the seedy side of New York City, Grimm idolized his brother Daniel, the leader of the local gang. Ben would ultimately assume leadership of the Yancy Street Gang before being placed in the custody of his aunt and uncle due to his parents' (and subsequently Daniel's) deaths. He epitomized the vaunted "American Dream" by becoming greater than the sum of his parts; Grimm left the slums for a better life and a college degree by way of a football scholarship, becoming a pilot in the United States Air Force,[14] and using those applications to segue into test piloting and astronaut training. Cosmic rays (chosen for their unknown quality in the 1960s) gave Ben Grimm his super-human persona, but what he did before molded him as a very real, very human being.

If we look at his four-color contemporaries, it is easy to see how the Thing, in regards to longevity and characterization, holds his status as the exception to the rule that those who wish to stay active must change with changing times. In his earliest printed inception, Superman was not the planet-moving paradigm that he is portrayed as today; he was often shown as someone who fought against social injustices rather than super villains, someone who stood up to corrupt businessmen and wife beaters. In the third issue of *Action Comics*, Superman confronts a greedy mine owner who places worker safety below profit. Superman threatens to bring "the entire roof down" on the owner to prove his point about the unsafe conditions. Reed Richards, the Thing's fictional best friend and Fantastic Four team-mate, was a far cry in early issues from the loving spouse that he is shown to be in more recent comic books, as he would coddle his wife and force her to conform to traditional gender roles of the time, something that would be seen as oppressive and sexist today.

When the Thing was created in 1961, he was clearly created to be a part of a larger concept. Whereas most superhero comic books published in the previous 20-plus years featured a solo character with the abilities needed to tackle nearly any problem, Ben Grimm was just one cog in the machine that was a team-centered book. He was one-fourth of the Fantas-tic Four, and as such, he would obviously receive less "face time" than would his solo counterparts. There were, after all, three other characters in the book, and each would conceivably be allotted equal representation. The Thing's adventures remained limited to the monthly Fantastic Four title, with a few notable interruptions, until the mid 1970s. Shortly after the Fantastic Four's inception, the Thing shared a number of issues with the Human Torch and Dr. Strange in Marvel's revamped *Strange Tales* series, but the Thing was finally allowed to take center stage as the pri-mary character in the September 1973 issue of *Marvel Feature*. This 11th issue gave readers another chapter of the many classic Thing-Hulk con-frontations, but it represented so much more for the characterization of the former: the Thing was finally being spotlighted in his own series. After a second issue under its new direction, *Marvel Feature* quickly evolved into *Marvel Two-in-One*, which remained in print for 100 issues and seven annu-als. The book was, in many ways, a guided tour through the Marvel uni-verse, with the Thing leading the way. Each month (the title ran bi-monthly until issue 15), the Thing would meet with another from the vast library of available Marvel characters, and the plot of each issue would be fairly predictable; the two heroes spotlighted in a particular issue would team up to combat a challenge that, supposedly, neither would be able to handle on his or her own. Unfortunately, many issues would seemingly serve only as marketing opportunities for new characters or those who were not as recognizable to the average reader (one only has to see the cover to *Marvel Two-in-One* #79, featuring the forgettable Blue Diamond, to understand). But despite the revolving door co-stars that writers had to work into the issues, the Thing began to see his character deepen in a way that might not have been possible in the main Fantastic Four title. Ben Grimm saw his own regular supporting cast grow with the likes of Wundarr and Bill Forrester, a new Goliath. More importantly, writers began to delve more deeply into Grimm's past for clues as to why he was who he was, and the examples they conjured only strengthen the character's position as the classic everyman.

The sixth issue of *Marvel Two-in-One*, with a cover date of November 1974, featured the Thing and fellow *Strange Tales* co-star Dr. Strange in a story that would later be re-imagined in 2005's *Tales of the Thing* #1. The story itself was somewhat bizarre in that it featured, among other things, a mystical harmonica, but it helped lead into an amazing moment of character development—or perhaps character reinforcement—for the Thing. While the Thing had long since discussed his urban upbringing, the characters who would make recurring appearances from Grimm's past would usually be limited to the Yancy Street Gang, and their involvement would nearly always be represented in a farcical manner with shadowy figures throwing rotten fruit or other garbage as the Thing walked by.

In this issue, though, we see Ben Grimm as a member of a larger community, as a man concerned with the welfare of those he left behind when he gained his semi-celebrity status as a member of the Fantastic Four. Members of a crowd who witness a young girl's tragic death are, as part of this story, each affected in different (and often ironic) ways. One observer happens to be from Grimm's old neighborhood, and when his paranoia gets the better of him, it is the teenager's grandmother who calls in a favor from the Thing. Over the course of their subsequent conversation (and with the help of introspective thought bubbles that only comic books can provide), we come to see Ben Grimm as a man grateful for his status, for his education and for the care that came from members of his former community. On his way to visit the elderly Mrs. Coogan in order to help her grandson, the Thing lets the reader in on his feelings: "When I think o' whut I owe that gal! Shucks, she wuz practically a second mother ta me! If not fer the way she looked after me as a kid—whut with both my folks workin' to keep us eatin'—heck, I'd prob'ly spent my life shootin' pool an' brawlin' in th' streets, 'stead o' goin' ta college an' gettin' ejjicated!" (Gerber 11).

Phonetics and all, the underlying feeling is clear: in this instant, and many others just like it, Ben Grimm is transformed from a static four-color character into, if just for a moment, a very real human being. While he had used his newfound status to escape the slums of New York City, the Thing never forgot where he came from, and more importantly, he would use his abilities to help those in his former community. Ben Grimm played the role of the hometown hero, leaving to find greater fame but returning to help others reach beyond their own complacency.

Marvel Two-in-One ended its run in June 1983 with its 100th issue, but this was merely a lead-in to July of '83's *The Thing*, the title character's first self-titled ongoing series, where he shed the need for a co-star just as he soon relinquished his membership in the Fantastic Four (as with many things in comics, the separation was not permanent). This venture lasted three years and 36 issues before finally losing steam and the character was relegated again to his supporting role, without much interruption, for the next 20 years. Finally, in November of 2005 (with a cover date of January 2006), the Thing returned to his own series in a second volume. Surprisingly, but not completely without precedent, the series only reached its eighth issue before being cancelled due to low sales, though it is interesting to mention that *The Thing* #8 was still selling several thousand units above some other, still-ongoing Marvel books. The reasons for the book's cancellation were many, but much of the blame could be placed on the proliferation of Fantastic Four books available to the direct market at the time. As the eighth issue of the character's book shipped to comic shops around the country, there were five other books with the words "Fantastic Four" in their titles.

The Thing reconnects with his past on Yancy Street. From page 6 of "Death Song of Destiny!" in *Marvel Two-In-One*, Issue 6 (New York: Marvel Comics, 1974).

Regardless of the reasons behind the title's demise, writer Dan Slott made the most of his eight issues, strengthening Ben Grimm's status as a member of the Jewish community. In 2002s *Fantastic Four* #56, the elderly and obstinate Hiram Sheckerberg was introduced as a character from

After decades of hinting at his heritage, the Thing finally has his Bar Mitzvah. From page 18 of "Last Hand" in *The Thing***, Volume 2, Issue 8 (New York: Marvel Comics, 2006).**

Grimm's past, and that remained his only appearance until the second *Thing* series. In the title's final issue, the Thing, previously hesitant to embrace his religious background, took advantage of a technical loophole to celebrate his bar mitzvah. It was in this issue where readers learn that in the fictional Marvel Universe Ben Grimm has been the Thing for thirteen years, and after rationalizing that Grimm's transformation could be seen as a rebirth of sorts, Sheckerberg and a rabbi convince the hero to celebrate his heritage. After forty years of "real" time, the Thing took a leap of faith, taking the opportunity to compare his own tragic life to the Biblical story of Job (Slott 18). Tom Bondurant, author of the online column *Grumpy Old Fan*, reflected on the short-lived series and its impact: "The last issue of Dan Slott's The Thing is a touching sendoff to the short-lived series, bittersweet even though we know the character isn't going anywhere. Indeed, Ben Grimm is the quintessential Marvel hero, cursed for decades to be alienated from polite society even while forced into the superheroic spotlight. Nevertheless, he has persevered, gradually learning to make the best out of his situation."

Whereas some characters are constantly revised to conform to the times, Ben Grimm, on the other hand, stays the same as time changes around him. For better or for worse, the Thing is who he is, providing stability that takes strength from the real, flawed aspects of his character and all of his cultural intricacies which shape him into the pop culture icon that he is today. Ben Grimm is an everyman in every sense of the word; he can be whatever the situation or storyline calls for, but somehow he never loses his core identity that was crafted by Stan Lee and Jack Kirby. Revealing the underlying influences of Judaism just serves to strengthen this concept, and the Thing becomes more real as a Jewish kid from the streets of New York than he otherwise might have been. In a sense, Ben Grimm becomes more like us as a society because of his obvious differences (some distinctions subtler than others), and his minority status meshes seamlessly with the concept of America as a "melting pot"—not in the sense that he will ever truly assimilate into a society where his differences disappear, but in a sense that the dissimilarities he shares with others now become a common uniter. The Thing cannot lose his cultural distinctiveness; in many ways he now joins an immigrant culture that takes pride in the differences that set them apart from what society considers to be normal.

As the *Fantastic Four* sequel makes its way into theaters, one can't expect the Thing's Jewish heritage to come to the forefront, at least not in the revelatory manner it did in the pages of the comic book. As those working on the first motion picture undoubtedly found out, trying to squeeze over 40 years of history into a 90-minute film leaves little time for character nuances, as obvious or subtle as they may be. Whether it occurs in the first sequel or second or third (assuming the movie franchise survives that long) is inconsequential; Ben Grimm's characterization does not revolve around religious heritage—it is merely enhanced by it. The character of the Thing has survived intact in every series, in every medium he has appeared in, and it will continue to do so as long as creators continue to respect the obvious attraction that such an approachable character provides.

Twenty years separated *The Thing* volume one from *The Thing* volume two. A publishing gap that large might signal drastic changes for a fictional character, but not surprisingly, the first issue of the first volume reads much like the first issue of the second volume,[15] and chances are that the third volume (an inevitability in the cyclical nature of the comic book industry) will take many of its cues from its predecessors as well—and for those that follow the character, that's just the way it should be.

NOTES

1. I choose *Spider-Man* over 2000's *X-Men* simply because of the former's incredible box office take. While *X-Men* is generally seen as the film that brought comic books back to the attention of Hollywood after 1997's genre-killing *Batman and Robin*, I see *Spider-Man* as the dam-bursting event. After grossing over $400 million at the domestic box office and matching that figure worldwide ("Spider-Man Daily Box Office") it would spur a proliferation of comic book-based movies that is perhaps unmatched in any era of cinema.

2. Roger Corman directed a live-action Fantastic Four film a decade earlier, but it was never released. Bootlegged versions do exist, allowing fans to understand just *why* the film was squelched.

3. The movie was lambasted by many critics, but Roger Ebert's *Chicago Sun Times* review was one of the most scathing and certainly one of the most influential reviews of the 20th Century–Fox would-be tent-pole: "It's all setup and demonstration, and naming and discussing and demonstrating, and it never digests the complications of the Fantastic Four

and gets on to telling the story. Sure, there's a nice sequence where the Thing keeps a fire truck from falling off a bridge, but you see one fire truck saved from falling off a bridge, you've see them all. The Fantastic Four are, in short, underwhelming ... [a]nd really good superhero movies ... leave 'Fantastic Four' so far behind that the movie should almost be ashamed to show itself in the same theater" (43). In defense of the film, its intended audience was undoubtedly much younger than, for example, that of the movie *Batman Begins*, and probably even *Spider-Man*. Even so, the superhero group has survived poor media representation before, as those who have seen the outlandish 1979 cartoon "Fred and Barney Meet the Thing" can attest to.

4. With a production budget of around $100 million, *Fantastic Four* has grossed roughly $155 million domestically and another $175 million worldwide throughout its in-theater run ("Fantastic Four Daily Box Office").

5. The Disney/Pixar film *The Incredibles*, more financially successful than *Fantastic Four*, takes a great deal of inspiration from the Marvel comic book, clearly in the fact that the story focuses on the super-hero family. *The Incredibles* preceded *Fantastic Four* in movie theaters.

6. Publisher Martin Goodwin put it aptly in a conversation with writer-creator Stan Lee: "If The *Justice League* is selling, why don't we put out a comic book that features a team of superheroes?" As Lee said, "His logic was irrefutable" (Lee, *Origins* 16). While Lee's later concept, *The Avengers*, more snugly fit the Justice League model, *Fantastic Four* proved enough of a success to guarantee the company's new publishing direction would move toward the super hero.

7. In 1954 Wertham published *Seduction of the Innocent*, in which the child psychologist claimed that "in the lives of some of these children who are overwhelmed by temptations the pattern is one of stealing, gangs, addiction, comic books and violence" (26). Comic book historian Les Daniels writes, "The fact that a phrase like 'Coca-Cola' could be substituted for 'comic books' in that sentence is indicative of the nature of Wertham's attack, which was largely based on guilt by association" (114). Wertham blamed everything from juvenile delinquency to homosexuality on comic books, and the outcry reached all the way to the United States Senate. As a result, the Comics Code Authority, a device for self-regulation, was adopted by the comic book industry. The code was only recently dropped from Marvel comic books (DC and others still carry it).

8. Stan Lee always had big plans for the Thing; in his unabashedly nigh-ostentatious publication *Origins of Marvel Comics* (the primary purpose of which appears to be to provide readers with reprints of the earliest Silver Age Marvel Comics, such as the first issues of *Fantastic Four* and *Hulk*), Lee gives his readers some insight on the creation of each member of the quartet: "Anyway, I felt there should be one more member of our still-nameless ménage," he wrote, "one character who was to be included for drama, for pathos, for color, and for the sheer offbeat quality he could provide. He'd be the most unlikely hero of all— ugly, morose, and totally antisocial—possessed of brute strength and a hair-trigger temper. He just had to become the most popular one of all" (17–18).

9. Not all of Lee's creations were modeled after himself: Charles Xavier, "Professor X" of the X-Men, was based at least partially on actor Yul Brynner. "I may have visualized known actors," Lee admitted to a question about character conceptualization, "but I usually ended up with my own personal favorite—and I'll give you three guesses who that is!" ("Soapbox 3/99").

10. The legend purports that Kirby intended his New Gods concept to supercede Marvel's *Thor* publication, with the loose Norse interpretation reaching its conclusion with the foretold Ragnarock. When Marvel balked at the idea of killing a popular character in Thor, Kirby took the idea to rival DC Comics and created both the New Gods and the entire "Fourth World" concept.

11. Brian Michael Bendis and Mark Bagley have since surpassed Lee and Kirby's feat, setting the new mark at 110 issues with their *Ultimate Spider-Man* title, also from Marvel. Their consecutive streak concludes in 2007.

12. The story concludes with a nod to readers: Powderkeg, the issue's throwaway villain and one facilitator for the religious-cultural revelation, waits to be taken into custody while tied to (and with) a lamppost: "And you're really Jewish?" he questions the irascible Thing, who answers with a confrontational "There a problem with that?" "No!" responds the criminal. "No, it's just ... you don't *look* Jewish."

13. I say "messianic" because of the obvious Christian allegory that the idea of Superman conjures, made even more poignant by his "death" and subsequent resurrection in the early 1990s; however, originally, Superman and Clark Kent were very much the product of Jewish history, from the story of Moses as a child to the concept of Diaspora and cultural assimilation. Superman's creators, Jerry Siegel and Joe Shuster, were both Jews from the Cleveland area.

14. Originally, both Ben Grimm and future teammate Reed Richards were participants in World War II, but as time passed, that military service became less and less plausible. In 1996 it was revealed that Grimm fought in the original Gulf War, and more recently his military experience has been generalized into nondescript service.

15. Series writer Dan Slott remarked: "He's one of those *perfect* characters [who doesn't] need to be reinterpreted or reinvented. You just stand back, let him go, and try to tell good stories with him" (Brady).

WORKS CITED

Aguirre-Sacasa, Roberto. "The Yancy Street Golem." *Marvel Knights 4* 22. November 2005.
Aushenker, Michael. "Funny, He Doesn't Look Jewish." *The Jewish Journal of Greater Los Angeles.* 10 November 2002. 3 December 2005. http://www.jewishjournal.com/home/print.php?id=9419.
Bondurant, Tom. "This Monster, This Man." *Grumpy Old Fan.* 13 July 2006. 15 July 2006. http://blog.newsarama.com/2006/07/13/this-monster-this-man.
Brady, Matt. "It's a Thing Thang with Dan Slott." *Newsarama.* 14 July 2005. 15 July 2005. http://www.newsarama.com/forums/showthread.php?s=&threadid=38129.
Chabon, Michael. *The Amazing Adventures of Kavalier and Clay.* New York: Random House, 2000.
Daniels, Les. *DC Comics: Sixty Years of the World's Favorite Comic Book Heroes.* New York: Bulfinch Press, 1995.
David, Peter. "Re: the Thing and Jewish culture." E-mail to the author. 15 February 2006.
_____. "Re: the Thing and Jewish culture." E-mail to the author. 16 February 2006.
Ebert, Roger. "'Fantastic' Flop: Underwhelming Collection of Superheroes Does Nothing Interesting with Powers." *Chicago Sun-Times* 7 July 2005: 43.
"Fantastic Four (2005): Daily Box Office." *Box Office Mojo.* 10 January 2006. http://www.boxofficemojo.com/movies/?page=daily&id=fantasticfour.htm.
Gerber, Steve. "Death-Song of Destiny!" *Marvel Two-In-One* 6. November 1974.
"Interview with Michael Chiklis." *PS2 Fantastic Four.* 5 July 2005. Activision Games. 6 July 2005.
Jones, Gerald. *Men of Tomorrow: Geeks, Gangsters and the Birth of the Comic Book.* New York: Basic Books, 2005.
Kaplan, Arie. "How Jews Created the Comic Book Industry." *Reform Judaism* 32 (2003).
Kesel, Karl. "Remembrance of Things Past." *Fantastic Four* 3 (56). August 2002.
Kirby, Jack. "What If the Fantastic Four Were the Original Marvel Bullpen?" *What If ... ?* 11. October 1978.
Kleefeld, Sean. "Re: questions on comics." E-mail to the author. 16 February 2006.
Lee, Stan. *Origins of Marvel Comics.* New York: Simon and Schuster, 1974.
_____. "Stan's Soapbox." *Spider-Girl* 6. March 1999: 11–12.
_____. "Stan's Soapbox." *Wild Thing* 1. October 1999: 14–15.
San Giacomo, Michael. Telephone interview. 15 February 2006.
"The Shape of Things to Come." *Orthodox Union.* 30 November 2005. http://www.ou.org/ncsy/projects/kp/5763/kpwint63/thing.htm.
Slott, Dan. "Last Hand." *The Thing* 2 (8). August 2006.
"Spider-Man (2002): Daily Box Office." *Box Office Mojo.* 18 November 2006. http://www.boxofficemojo.com/movies/?id=spiderman.htm.
Wertham, Fredric. *Seduction of the Innocent.* New York: Rinehart, 1954.

PART II
SUPERHEROES IN THE MODERN AGE

Frank Miller Strikes Again and Batman Becomes a Postmodern Anti-Hero: The Tragi(Comic) Reformulation of the Dark Knight

TERRENCE R. WANDTKE

"Jews created comic books, as best as I can tell. Two Jews created Superman. Another created Batman ... well, don't get me started."—Frank Miller (Eisner/Miller 3)

The regard for Frank Miller by comic book creators, critics, and fans is unparalleled. Simultaneously held in high esteem by superhero fanboys (who laud works like *Daredevil: Born Again* as revisionist landmarks) and art comic snobs (who praise *Sin City* novels as clear defiance of the "big two" superhero comic publishers), Miller bridges the cavernous divide between these seemingly irreconcilable camps. In addition, Miller has culled favor with the public at large and mainstream publications have regularly lauded him as a writer of graphic novels who transcends the juvenile subject matter regularly associated with the American comic book industry.[1]

However, he has still managed to draw some negative criticism over the years and this criticism has only intensified in recent years. Supposedly, his work is riddled with clichés based on a sexist worldview gentrified by the novelists such as Raymond Chandler; concomitantly, his work is adult not so much as a result of his aesthetic choices as his decision to regularly portray sex and graphic violence.[2] Several easy explanations could be and sometimes have been offered to explain this turn against Miller. Some lay the blame on the critics as fickle consumers who have grown tired of the late twentieth century fad that labeled comic books as a mature art form. Others have suggested that the critics have shifted their standards and are judging Miller fairly; once part of a revolutionary era in comic books, Miller has now peaked and finds himself out of step with contemporary times. While each explanation has some merit, neither fully represents the complexity of Miller and his place within the American comic book industry. Due to his iconic status as passionate devotee of Batman on one hand and angry advocate of creator owned-properties on the other, gauging the development of his artistic vision provides a means of understanding the strange tensions within the twenty-first century superhero comic book industry.

In many ways, Miller is the contemporary comic book industry as it regards and portrays itself: a determined purveyor of urban mythology, speaking with the voice of the undervalued outsider (this being the way both the superhero comic book industry and the art comic industry has described itself). Despite being an accurate summary of Miller's sense of self, this does not describe him holistically and it certainly does not acknowledge the contradictions that have become more pronounced within his character. In order to explain the growing tension within the work that offers what are arguably the most significant revisions to the superhero genre, Miller's two most famous series will be analyzed and compared.

The Dark Knight Returns started a new era of superhero comics dubbed as "grim and gritty," a treatment of Batman that made him more realistic and less subject to the concerns of the moral majority. *The Dark Knight Strikes Again* would be its sequel but one that many claimed was a sequel in name and not content. Fifteen years after the publication of the first series, the sequel departed notably from the first series in a way potentially caricaturing Miller's own work; furthermore, the narrative flattened characters that he had once made complex in what seemed like parody. The immediate differences between these two series would seem to signal Miller's growing disappointment with the superhero comic book industry, serving as a critique of a field that misunderstood and misappropriated *The Dark Knight Returns.* And the 9/11 terrorist attacks made Miller's depiction of superheroism more strident and uncompromising.

However, if *The Dark Knight Returns* deconstructed Batman (as so many critics claim), it is the more broadly satirical *The Dark Knight Strikes Again* that takes Batman squarely into post-modern territory and exposes Batman's identity as a flat cultural construction capable of containing contradictory meanings. Despite this apparently hateful treatment of the genre, Miller made statements about *The Dark Knight Strikes Again* that indicated he was just as interested in superheroes as before and perhaps even more hopeful for the mainstream comic book industry. (This has played out further with his return to DC in 2005 with *All Star Batman and Robin.*)

Through a critical reading of these texts aided by a psychoanalytic perspective encouraged by his work, the mixture of love and hate for superheroes which now propels Miller's work (and many contemporary superhero narratives) will become clearer. Like Miller, the superhero of the twenty-first century occupies a place that is neither insider nor out-sider and the diffuse identity presents itself in ways that represent increas-ing anxieties about the politics of American hero-worship.

THE JEW AS THE "OTHER" AND THE JEW AS (THE ORIGIN OF) MILLER'S SUPERHERO

When Miller first came to New York as a teenager and fell under the tutelage of Neal Adams, he brought with him comic book sequences based on the hard-boiled fiction of film noir.[3] With its concerns about male iden-tity formation and fear of the uncontrollable woman (the femme fatale), noir narratives reconstruct Cold War anxieties as a type of gender conflict popularized by psychoanalytic theory.[4] The basic dynamics of noir narra-tives have been with Miller from the start, his first wildly popular original creation being Elektra (who played the role of femme fatale in *Daredevil*). In years to come, the most prominent recommendation on the back cover of the trade paperback version of *The Dark Knight Returns* would be from Mickey Spillane, one of the most well-known authors of hard-boiled detec-tive fiction. And with *Sin City* generally known as "comics noir," it hardly need be argued that these ideas have persisted. However, while Sigmund Freud may be the source from whom early film noir indirectly draws its worldview, Jacques Lacan seems the one who most clearly describes Miller's social critiques. Always a faithful depicter of the individual oppressed by society (and rarely to be reconciled with society), Miller has extended his works to deal more fully with what he considers the nature of social psy-chology.

In "The Agency of the Letter or Reason Since Freud," Lacan elabo-rates on Freud's description of the ego as an unstable, ever-changing entity. Lacan reveals that the unity in a signifier-signified relationship between one's sense of self and one's ego is structured around a fiction, the fan-tasy that the individual can reunite with the pre-symbolic real. The indi-vidual designs objects of desire from signifiers that facilitate some sort of satisfaction for a desire impossible to satisfy. However, as objects of desire continue to change, individual personality remains in a state of flux that the individual refuses to acknowledge.[5]

The significance of these ideas to Miller's work becomes clearer by describing the way Slavoj Zizek has elaborated upon those ideas and used them within his analysis of the "Other" in society. In *The Sublime Object of Ideology*, Slavoj Zizek redefines the Hegelian idealism of Marxist political theorists so that the Hegelian dialectic becomes a process that will not end in unity with the real. Instead, a society's consciousness will always be unhappy because the unconscious desire for unity can never be satisfied. "Instead of the linear, immanent, necessary progression according to which meaning unfolds itself from some initial kernel, we have a radically contingent process of retroactive production of meaning" (Zizek 102). Therefore, the "transcendent" truths that an individual uncovers about the self are actually a convenient fantasy used to retroactively mask the contradictions within the self; by consistently fixing upon certain objects of desire, these fantasy truths about the self have a greater appearance of the truth.

Zizek's brand of Lacanian Hegelianism suggests objects are formed when the individual interprets the identity of society. When the individual asks the question, "How can I be the way I think I should be," the individual creates a fantasy of personal unity. The follow-up question for the individual then becomes, "How do I maintain my fantasy?" The fantasy is maintained through the manufacturing of objects *against which* the individual can define the self: symptoms that maintain fantasy and therefore, provide pleasure. Society explains the conflicts within itself by constructing an object (an outsider like the Jew) against which to define it. "In short, 'Jew' is a fetish which simultaneously denies and embodies the structural impossibility of 'Society.' … In other words, *fantasy is a means for ideology to take its own failure into account in advance*" (Zizek 126). The truth of society is only created retroactively through the existence of the outsider. Paradoxically, the outsider is the thing which society says society is not, but is also the greatest object of desire because it maintains the "self" of society. That desire is the result of the hidden knowledge that the best understanding that the individual or society can achieve is an understanding of the self gained only through the other.

If society, like the self, is a fiction, the only way to know society more completely is to understand it as a whole and take into account the contradictions formed through its neurotic fixations, the symptoms developed as a consequence of an impossible desire. According to Zizek, "we must in the same move identify with the symptom: we must recognize in the properties attributed to 'Jew' the necessary product of our very social system; we must recognize in the 'excesses' attributed to 'Jews' the truth about ourselves" (Zizek 128).

In both *The Dark Knight Returns* and *The Dark Knight Strikes Again*, Miller operates with something like this formulation very much in mind. However, despite the importance of using Lacan's (and in turn, Zizek's) ideas as a model to represent Miller's "societies," it is necessary to remember Freud's perspective of psychoanalysis; the contrast between Freud and Lacan marks the two parts of Miller's career represented respectively by *The Dark Knight Returns* and *The Dark Knight Strikes Again*. While Freud's case studies generally end with the patient brought back in line with the social order (a modernist belief), Lacan supposes the goal of psychoanalysis as the analysand's realization that s/he will never be justified by the perceived real world (a postmodernist belief). The shift between the two works should be understood as a shift from social study enacted with Freud's modernism versus one enacted with Lacan's postmodernism.

THE NEW ORIGIN OF THE DARK KNIGHT OR
HOW BATMAN BECAME THE MAN OF TOMORROW

Since *The Dark Knight Returns* has been frequently identified as a land-mark and its innovations often discussed, its narrative and visual aspects have the unique distinction of being clearly revolutionary and yet now too familiar. Miller is generally credited for introducing a Gotham City founded on gritty realism in which Batman lives as a profoundly obsessive, anti-establishment moralist. This interpretation of Batman has stuck and Mike Gold has identified this version of the Dark Knight (among others such as World War II patriotism and TV camp) as having had the greatest longevity (Gold 16). Some have suggested that this version of Batman returns him to the vision held by Bob Kane, Batman's creator. However, with clear acknowledgement paid to Kane's expressionist and film noir inspirations, the world of Miller's Batman is far darker. From the urban decay of the city to the anguished psychology of its protagonist to its critique of media and society, Miller's series stood alongside Alan Moore's *Watchmen* as a self-conscious unmaking of the mythos of superhero comic books. (Yet, in Miller's own very correct estimation, his treatment was much more sentimental and affectionate while Moore's was much more ironic and bitter.[6])

When it first appeared, several features of *The Dark Knight Returns* separated it from Batman comics that had preceded it and deserve to be reiterated for the sake of this study. In Miller's vision and overall narrative arc, Gotham City lacked its Technicolor benevolence, Batman became more anti-hero than hero, and society would never allow Batman to emerge triumphant. Under pressure from public interest groups campaigning against vigilantes, Bruce Wayne had retired from his career as a super-hero; he had aged and without Batman in his life (to whom Wayne often referred as another person), he became suicidal with his state of mind reflected in the decay of Gotham City, now more crime-ridden than ever before. Several standard aspects of superhero stories are thus violated from the start. Batman was no longer an agent of the state, as he had been since his mythology had been solidified during the politically conservative era of World War II. Moreover, he had done things not permitted within most superhero stories: to give up the mask and to age. Long standing conceits of the genre require all who hear the call to heroism to wear a form fitting costume, generally never considering life without an alter ego; and the superheroic figures must remain young even as history continues to unfold. Miller portrays the city as truly Gothic in appearance and the series is colored in a way that accentuates the bleak desperation.

In the opening pages of *The Dark Knight Returns*, a mustached Bruce Wayne walks the streets of Gotham, surrounded by otherworldly vagrants bearing signs that read "we are damned" (Miller, *The Dark Knight Returns*

In *The Dark Knight Returns*, Gotham City is robbed of its Technicolor benevolence
and a resigned Bruce Wayne participates in its bleak, fatalistic atmosphere. From
page 12 of *The Dark Knight Returns* (New York: DC Comics, 1996).

12). Miller's style of drawing is reminiscent of his early work under the
influence of artists such as John Romita and Neal Adams. However, while
he maintains a certain amount of realism, his style becomes slightly more
abstract, allowing him to render the vagrants more iconographically, like
gargoyles, with simple lines. Within the same series of panels, the garish
primary colors traditionally seen in comic books are conspicuously absent,
the scenes layered largely with a series of gray tones.

Media outlets are depicted within the series as unwittingly supporting the move away from concepts such as good and evil, central to heroic
narratives. Miller replaces conventional comic book panels with representations of television screens: news and talk shows that pathologize, sympa-

thize, and then celebrate serial killers such as the Joker. They have a confining effect on the reader: "Miller's unprecedented 16-panel grid works cinematically to produce a dark, claustrophobic world. The use of the confining screen also reveals Miller's view of the TV generation: they can be convinced of anything with ease. The regular, unbreakable grid is a symbol of how ordered and small the lives of the people are" (Blackmore 43).

Superman's Smallville sweetheart, Lana Lang, is a television news personality, represented not only as older but also considerably less shapely (in a television debate, she is called the "fat lady"). One of Batman's few defenders, she fights the overwhelming tide that turned against superheroes long before Batman's return to action as an aged crime fighter. Miller's position relative to this debate seems quite clear; within the text, media, political, and social situations that turn the superhero into a demoralizing force are satirized. Miller renders with a Hitleresque moustache Dr. Bartholomew Wolper, a psychologist who argues that Batman is the root cause of the psychopathology of Batman's rogues' gallery in Arkham Asylum.

As the narrative expands to demonstrate the systemic nature of the problem that Batman has fought on the lowest level (small time thieves, rapists, and murderers), Miller casts our gaze to the White House. The Ronald Reagan figure who wants to take credit for all the good work in the free world is a doddering father without a family. Ignoring the way in which the basic social fabric is deteriorating, the president masks the conflict between the disenfranchised and corrupt power-brokers by employing America's folksy sense of self on the frontier: "I like to think I learned everything I know about running this county on my ranch.... I know it's corny but I like to think it" (Miller, *The Dark Knight Returns* 84).

In order to maintain hegemonic control, the United States maintains an enemy conveniently outside its own border in the evil empire of the Cold War. In a public address, the president states: "American tr—Excuse me ... Heroic American troops are now engaged in direct combat with Soviet forces.... Now, there's been a lot of loose talk these days about nuclear war.... Well, let me tell you nobody's running off half-cocked, no sir ... but we sure as shootin' aren't running away, either. We've got to secure our—ahem—stand up for the cause of freedom" (119).

Demonstrating with his slight gaffs the contradictions within American foreign policy, the president's willful ignorance of domestic problems not only causes domestic problems to grow; the president's attempt to cover those problems by waging war ultimately imposes the self-destructiveness of the United States on the world. The actions which the president tries to justify in the above quotation causes the Soviets to launch a nuclear strike on the country.

When Wayne takes on the mantle of Batman again, he quite clearly operates outside the law in his hyper-violent confrontations with criminals, but Miller claims that this interpretation is tied to his romantic notions of Batman's heroism. As an orphan trying forever to avenge the murder of his parents, Batman must be an outsider to a world that would allow that loss to occur. In one of his first depicted confrontations with thugs, he growls, becoming more clearly the "other" thing which strikes fear. However, even though Batman lives in a morally ambiguous world (as indicated by the gray used to color the text representing his thoughts), he upholds higher standards, acting pragmatically and not cruelly. "There are seven working defenses from this position. Three of them disarm with minimal contact. Three of them kill. The other—" which Batman applies in the next panel "—hurts." An extension of a system that makes and ignores criminals, the police officer who appears on the scene yells to Batman, "You're under arrest, mister. You've crippled that man!" Batman explains himself only by saying, "He's young. He'll probably walk again. But he'll stay scared" (39). Batman finds he must continue to distance himself from those in authority positions around him:

> His new outlaw position caused him to reappraise his analysis of the social order and ultimately to ally with elements of the underclass he had initially struggled to contain. Significantly, however, this alliance took the form of protecting property as the Batman, at the head of the mutant gangs, prevents middle-class rioters from looting a supermarket. *The Dark Knight Returns* problematizes the Batman's role within a dominant political order depicted as irredeemably corrupt and bankrupt, and challenges a political system which could continually re-elect Reagan president while outlawing Batman, but reaffirms the Batman's role as lone vigilante striving for a higher justice [Uricchio 209].

The Dark Knight Returns works as a social commentary about a society that won't acknowledge its own shortcomings and inconsistencies. Consequently, Batman (the hero who exposes the dirt beneath the surface) is not recognized as a coping mechanism but as the ultimate criminal; in psychoanalytic terms, he is the symptom blamed for wide-spread feelings of unease. According to Frank Miller, "A function of tribes ... is that they must pick their scapegoat—and often without reason, without logic. In this hidden Zeitgeist a scapegoat is chosen" (*Eisner/Miller* 99). At the beginning of the series, Wayne refers to his Batman identity in the third person, a result of being co-opted by society at large. As the series progresses, he spends less and less time as Wayne, until Batman's secret identity is revealed and Wayne "dies" of a heart attack. Ultimately, the fantasy of Wayne is forsaken for the deeper truth of Batman: a creation of trauma, insidious and reassuring, sinister and righteous.

Similar to the way he extrapolates Batman's neurotic state from Batman's origin, Miller follows Superman to a logical end, making him a flag-waving patriot, blinded to national corruption; an alien grateful to be welcomed into the heartland of a country that he believes made him strong, he pledges allegiance to "the American way." In a now famous series of eight panels, the red and white stripes of a White House American flag blowing in the wind morph into the red and yellow lines of the emblem meant to represent the "S" on Superman's chest. This metamorphosis becomes quite sinister as it is accompanied by dialogue between the president, a corrupt and condescending leader, and Superman, an upright but accommodating follower (Miller, *The Dark Knight Returns* 84). At this point, the president asks Superman to tame Batman (who is publicly embarrassing the president by bringing the decay of Gotham and in turn, the president's misguided domestic policy, to light). As is revealed later in the series, the president will use Superman as his foremost weapon in an equally questionable fight against the Soviets.

In conventional terms, Superman is understood as the fantasy of the ninety-pound weakling, the greater self hidden behind the disguise of bumbling humanity. In psychoanalytic terms, Superman is the fantasy of *The Dark Knight Returns*, the unreal self and idea of unity that represents society, masking over the sickness buried underneath it all. Quite significantly (and in pseudo-contrast to Wayne), Superman seems to have lost the trappings of his alter ego, the humble reporter Clark Kent, who had hidden his strength behind an impenetrable disguise of ineptitude. When the two heroes meet and are portrayed in a pastoral setting outside the darkness of Batman's city, Kent is barrel-chested, a comfortable part of the rural landscape filled with flowers and a colorful butterfly. At odds with the vibrancy of this Disney-like representation of the world, Wayne is minimized by standing in the background of this scene, in stark relief with a wolf-like dog at his side. Wayne thinks, "There's just the sun and the sky and him, like he's the only reason it's all here" (118). In some ways, by the virtue of the dream logic of fantasy, Wayne is right, but due to his unique position within society, he can't abide by that logic. Almost inevitably, the series ends with a confrontation between the two heroes (a battle that Batman nearly wins with careful strategy, a mechanical exoskeleton, and some kryptonite).

Despite its excesses in terms of Batman's righteous violence, *The Dark Knight Returns* doesn't clearly call for the rejection of a patriotic Superman and a vigilante Batman. In the course of the story, it becomes apparent Batman works with a very definite and conservative moral code that requires him to inflict the least damage on his opponents and absolutely prevents him from committing murder. While he opposes society, that opposition is for the sake of the greater good and not a self-satisfying end in itself. And although Miller sets up a moral universe in which confrontation becomes necessary, Miller identifies ways in which Batman's presence may threaten to undo the good he does. Once Batman resurfaces and his battle with street thugs is reported on television, the Joker awakes from a catatonic state which he maintained since Batman's retirement. Apparently, the existence of superheroes results in the existence of supervillains. In addition, *The Dark Knight Returns* features "vigilantes" who emulate Batman, often for the wrong reasons and with mixed results. Typical among those inspired is Iron Man Vasquez, a delusional wrestler who appears dressed as Batman to signify his graduation from violence done with a baseball bat to violence done with a gun. Perhaps more notably, considering Miller's qualified sympathy with the motivation of Bernhard Goetz (*Frank Miller* 33), is his satiric treatment of a Goetz-like character who pushes a man on crutches into the path of an oncoming subway (with no apparent motivation except his own paranoia). And most importantly, Miller doesn't wholly reject Superman and his perspective. Since his lack of superpowers limits Batman's attention to Gotham City, he has the luxury of some moral absolutism that Superman does not have. Operating on a global scale with global concerns, Superman has to parcel out his responsibility to his country in the midst of Cold War tensions. Superman's collusion with the powers-that-be is not portrayed simply as moral blindness but a choice that acknowledges the shortcomings of the people he chooses to represent.

> I have walked the razor's edge for so long.... They'll kill us if they can, Bruce. Every year they grow smaller. Every year they hate us more. We must not remind them that heroes walk the earth.... You were the one they used against us Bruce. The one who played it rough.... They were considering their options and you were probably still laughing when we came to terms. I gave them my obedience and my invisibility. They gave me a license and let us live. No, I don't like it. But I get to save lives ... and the media stays quiet. But now the storm is growing again—they'll hunt us down again—because of you [Miller, *The Dark Knight Returns* 120, 129–130, 135, 139].

The superheroes are even paralleled in semi-comic moments such as Batman's correction of a young boy's "You got to kick his—" with his "Watch your language, son" (146) and Superman's discovery of Batman's Robin put in harm's way: "Isn't tonight a school night?" (189). Ultimately, Superman rediscovers his nobility and colludes with Batman, the man the president sends Superman to kill. Beginning with Superman's protecting Batman's "dead" body from the soldiers who come to claim it, he later discovers that Batman used drugs to fake his heart attack during their battle; with a wink at the new Robin, he keeps his silence and allows Batman to falsify his own death in order to avoid government persecution. In psychoanalytic terms, society becomes reconciled to its symptom as Superman, the ultimate insider, allows Batman to live and secretly continue his war.[7] It must be noted that this reworks Lacan's idea that society is nothing but a fiction and the only thing true that exists is the symptom. In this case, ideals are not so much false as desperately in need of the integrity the symptom provides; the ideal of the superhero is forced to recognized the dirty work of the symptom and is better for it.

GRIM AND GRITTY: THE GRIT AND GRISTLE
IN THE AFTERMATH OF THE DARK KNIGHT

With the success of *The Dark Knight Returns*, the debate about the place of comic books and the superhero in world culture was invigorated. Many comic books began to reflect a new and supposedly more mature sensibility toward its subject matter. Mainstream publishers such as Marvel and DC created alternative adult lines and independent publishers intent on pushing the envelope flourished. With Miller's vision serving as the basis for Tim Burton's Batman film, comic buying no longer was a hobby for fantasy-prone weakling boys but a collectable investment opportunity for adults. However, the matter of what constituted "adult content" seemed to elude many comic book publishers, who quickly put out comics with R-rated levels of sex and violence but whose stories remained largely the same as previous stories in the superhero-dominated medium. If anything changed in narrative terms in the general trends of this new wave of adult comics, it was the superhero who was now more violent and at odds with society. The newly revamped Wolverine and Punisher and the newly created Lobo and Spawn represented heroes who were not just outside conventional morality but heroes who were also notably nihilistic. All of the major Batman titles also took this new approach and supposedly followed Miller's lead. In terms of sales, votes were being cast in favor of this new brand of superhero and against the old-fashioned outdated do-gooders such as Superman.

During the 1990s, as characters like the Punisher and Spawn grew in popularity and comics seemed to be falling short of their adult potential, Miller retreated to work with original characters through the independent publisher Dark Horse. Foremost among his work from this period is *Sin City*, indebted to crime novelists such as Mickey Spillane. While innovative graphically, the series progressively moves toward film noir conventions such as anti-institutional tirades, hyper-masculinity, and misogyny. Miller seems to be exploring how far his readers will follow a discourse clearly stylized, constructed, and flat.[8] What kind of cultural baggage do comic book fanboys bring with them that would allow them to still call *Sin City* innovative and deep? This is exactly the question that Miller asks in his return to his Batman with *The Dark Knight Strikes Again*. In 2001, the anxious rumors long circulated among comic book fanboys were confirmed by the industry and the artist: after years away from the superhero genre, Frank Miller would once again write and draw Batman. This news was greeted with great enthusiasm because many fans, critics, and industry executives never expected Miller to return. Throughout the 1990s, Miller had stayed away from superheroes and the "big two" in a way that was loud and concerted.

Perhaps the most notable aspect of the news was that Miller would be returning to the version of Batman that in 1986 had made him famous to the public at large and more clearly than any other work brought gritty realism to the superhero genre. Frank Miller would be producing a sequel to *The Dark Knight Returns*, the dark future vision of a 50-year-old Batman. Despite Miller's anti-institutional attitudes (which he made ever more public since he began working with independent publishers), DC Comics (a subsidiary of Warner Bros.) welcomed Miller back into the fold. Certainly not inconsequential to this welcome was the simple fact that the boom period in comic book sales in the 1990s (caused by *The Dark Knight Returns* along with Alan Moore's *Watchmen* and other "adult" comic books) had completely disappeared. Sales were now lower than before the boom period and according to many critics such as Scott McCloud (114), comic books had barely moved beyond the standard superhero power fantasy that had long characterized the medium. Disregarding the DC Comics' PR claim that lightning would strike twice, many questions remained about the sequel. Who would read this sequel now that readership had shrunk so dramatically? What could an orthodox sequel do other than remind the public that comic books had not realized the new promise made in 1986? And if this were to be an unorthodox sequel, what could be done to push comic books further toward realizing their potential as serious art? These concerns did not dampen (and perhaps encouraged) pre-sales from direct sales comic stores; the pre-sales numbers quadrupled the standard sales of comic books regularly ranked number one. Published in prestige format, the three issue series would sell for a whopping $7.95 each. When it arrived in comic stores, it would be called *The Dark Knight Strikes Again* and be read primarily by eyes reshaped by the 9/11 terrorist attacks. Unlike the wholly enthusiastic reviews that accompanied *The Dark Knight Returns* (from fanboys, fan magazines, art comic journals, and mainstream media outlets), the reviews of *The Dark Knight Strikes Again* were mixed. From the beginning of the first issue, it became readily apparent that Miller's sequel was a sequel only in name.

THE SHOCK OF THE "NEW" IN THE SAME OLD BLUE AND GREY DISGUISE

While the characters in *The Dark Knight Strikes Back* still included Batman, Superman, and other DC icons and the setting was roughly the same, the characters themselves had changed in ways inconsistent with the first series. Taking place roughly three years after the events in *The Dark Knight Returns*, the new series violates many of the conventions established in the first series and the maxims about superheroes Miller developed in interviews in the 1980s. While the first series had been often credited with examining the complexity of the superheroes as icons *and* characters in a real world, this series seemed to essentialize the heroes and villains, creating flat characters and making everyone generally unsympathetic. At one level, this treatment of the fallen world of the Batman (which Miller made sacred for comic books fans) seems shocking, especially if Miller is taken at his word that he intended this sequel from the time he ended *The Dark Knight Returns*: "The sequel I had in mind was as preposterous as the original. [Batman] would be much more direct in his actions, much more willing to mess with the order of things. He wouldn't be going after the poor bastards who are muggers. He'd be going after the people who make them muggers.... The key recognition would be that he's no longer part of the authority" (Sharrett 39).

However, Miller seems to take principles operating in his later *Sin City* collections and apply them to this series. The narrative no longer sets Batman as a loner vigilante but as an organizer of all the superheroes of the world; where the first series would be readily accessible to the common reader, its sequel not only required a knowledge of the original but also a fanboy's intricate knowledge of the DC universe. With his enterprise to fight crime taken outside the confines of Gotham City, Batman becomes a fascist bully and with a cast of characters that includes the entire DC pantheon, Batman's presence is often central only in implicit and symbolic terms.

Rather than be guided by a moral code based on larger principles, Batman is guided by the utilitarian notions of what effectively realizes his goals. Rather significantly, his goals are shaped by an ambiguous desire to be free of tyranny of others (only made possible by the imposition of his own brand of tyranny). When the Flash complains that Batman is allowing innocent people to be killed in a government attack designed to flush out the vigilante superheroes, Batman replies: "This is my show! My war! We will follow my strategy! ... Just look at you! Look at Clark! He used to be good for something! Now look at him! Look at what he let them do to you! ... You want to fight me? Then fight me damn you! But don't tell me to compromise!" (Miller, *The Dark Knight Strikes Again* 145).

As leader of this superhero team, Batman flouts his position as a dictator would, the excesses of his mono-maniacal perspective clearly at odds with Miller's description of Batman in *The Dark Knight Returns*. Miller stated, "Anyone who professes an absolute ideological point of view is a would-be tyrant. Batman doesn't do this. Heroes have to work in the society around them, and Batman works best in a society that's gone to hell" (Sharrett 44). Together with figures such as the Flash, the Atom, Green Arrow, and Green Lantern, Batman will defeat Lex Luthor and Brainiac, the supervillains behind the sham government led by a computer-generated Ronald Reagan (a character with whom Superman physically interacted in the first series). In *The Dark Knight Strikes Again*, Superman seems to be well aware that he works for his arch-enemy, held as an ideological hostage because Luthor has possession of the bottle city of Kandor (the only surviving remnant of Superman's home planet).

Eventually, Batman revels in the power he gains over Superman as he positions himself as a dictator without a moral limit; Superman must capitulate because Luthor is the only other option. After revealing Superman has worked for Luthor to save Kandor, Batman replies: "Well, then. We'll just have to steal her back. Kandor. Ten million Kryptonians, at last count. It'll be a bitch if we screw this up. Good thing we won't. Let's get this much straight, Clark. From here on out, we don't debate a damn thing. We don't discuss a damn thing. You tell me what I want to know and you do what I tell you to do" (Miller, *The Dark Knight Strikes Again* 195).

Miller depicts Batman oversimplifying the hostage situation in a painfully obvious way that doesn't even create suspense by the standards of comic books aimed at a juvenile audience. In addition, while being steeped in comic book mythology only known to the most devoted of fans, Miller makes his characters overly simple, brought into conflict by fantasy situations (such as Luthor with Kandor) rather than a difference of perspective on real world social issues. Even speech patterns are oversimplified with characters practically indistinguishable from each other, both Batman and Superman using colloquialisms, slang, and curses clearly out of character for the Batman and Superman from the first series; Superman delivers silly lines such as "Bruce. You and me, we're gonna have us a talk" (79). The disparity between the introduction of Lex Luthor as a "genius" and his language use is glaring. Usually portrayed as a learned scientist and businessman, Luthor talks like a street thug lacking even the bombastic flair of his earliest appearances. Of course, Luthor is introduced as an "evil genius," which in itself has become a laughable cliché reserved for one-dimensional villains in action stories.[9] Ultimately, it becomes impossible to root for Batman because he is not the outsider, the symptom who exposes society's ills. Instead, he seems to ideologically collude with the bullies of society at large. Even though he makes the claim that superheroes will "strike like lightning and melt into the night like ghosts" (183), he forces his compatriots to share his views and believe that one will can unify a world.

Miller produces art that signals this radical change. Moving away from the first series' realistic style colored by blacks and greys, *The Dark Knight Strikes Again* represents characters in a block-like, emblematic style colored by an extensive array of brilliant hues in line with the camp of the 1960s Batman television series (that Miller hates). When Carrie Kelley, the new Robin from *The Dark Knight Returns*, is reintroduced, she no longer wears the costume of Batman's sidekick; she wears the even more outlandish, skin-tight cheetah patterned leotard and calls herself Catwoman. While Batman and Superman retain their traditional costumes, Miller turns them into childish fantasy representations of superheroes with enormous hands and feet and action-figure accessories. In his first significant appearance, Batman wears kryptonite boxing gloves. In the first series, splash pages were used judiciously to further the narrative or make clear symbolic points—such as the ironic interplay between an image of Superman with a Soviet tank held above his head and the text which represents his thoughts: "We must not remind them that giants walk the earth" (Miller, *The Dark Knight Returns* 130). In *The Dark Knight Strikes Again*, splash pages do little to further the narrative or make symbolic points and even fall short of the "wide-screen" action toted by series such as *The Authority*. Instead, these pages look like promotional posters, isolating key figures in a dramatic pose and rendering backgrounds ambiguous with carefully designed, vibrantly colored abstract designs. In Catwoman's first appearance, she rescues the Atom from his Petri dish prison and escapes by jumping from the roof of a building. A clear testament to the irrelevance of the splash page that follows is that it features no text and represents her in a position dissimilar from that in the preceding panel *and* the one that follows (Miller, *The Dark Knight Strikes Again* 30–32).

This decontextualization of characters within the story reveals itself to be quite intentional and suits well the greater sense of anxiety that pervades the work. Where Gotham was the microcosm that Batman used to anchor his sense of self in *The Dark Knight Returns*, that "realistic" sense of place remains completely absent in the sequel. Where the thoughts of superheroes once served as a contrast to the superficial world of mass media, the artifice of mass media now is superimposed upon the superheroes. When Batman and Superman first appear, they appear as shadowy figures that fill up entire pages but who are covered with panels that represent television screens. While this potentially reads as a set-up for the superheroes breaking through the static of mass media, the conclusion of the work belies this interpretation. The "triumph" of Batman's forces are significant largely because it frees the Superchix (scantily-clad, publicity hungry superhero groupies) from a presidential ban. Rather than replace the mindlessness of a media culture that allows for a computer generated president to be accepted, superheroes begin to participate in the culture; the Flash makes "rabbit ears" behind the televised images of Donald Rumsfeld and John Ashcroft and the liberal-communist Green Arrow loudly debates the conservative-libertarian Question on Chris Matthews' ribald talk show.[10] At this point, the artwork leans further from the realism (which gives the characters some integrity) through a clear move toward caricature (which makes them more ridiculous). Apparently, heroes are not relevant for the "heroic" work they do but are made relevant by entering and sustaining our mediated fantasy world. Concomitantly and as mentioned earlier, Miller appeals less to the common reader and more to the fanboy with his cast of characters but also bitterly exposes the fanboy hang-ups for the ridiculous ideas that they are. Lana Lang is still reporting the news in the sequel but looks much younger and is quite shapely, something completely inconsistent with the first series but likely to be unquestioned

In *The Dark Knight Strikes Again,* Frank Miller moves away from the style that characterized *The Dark Knight Returns*; figures are essentialized and unrealistic, and he accentuates "action figure" accessories such as Kryptonite boxing gloves. From page 90 of *The Dark Knight Strikes Again* (New York: DC Comics, 2002).

in the superhero comic world in which women are impossibly shaped in order to appeal to heterosexual male desire.

Batman and Superman again enter into a physical contest with one another, a strangely irrelevant replay of the contest from the first series. Perhaps satisfying to fanboys who regretted that the fight was cut short by Batman's self-inflicted heart attack the first time around, Miller seems to portray the growing opposition between Batman fans and Superman fans since 1986. (This developed from the interaction of Batman and Superman in *The Dark Knight Returns*, despite the fact that the series' narrative resolution brings them closer together.) After the battle which Bat-

Rather than offer a viable alternative to problematic leadership, the Flash makes rabbit ears behind a caricatured Donald Rumsfeld; thus, superheroes in *The Dark Knight Strikes Again* participate in the mindlessness of a media fantasy world. From page 245 of *The Dark Knight Strikes Again* (New York: DC Comics, 2002).

man decisively wins, Superman is only rejuvenated through a sexual encounter with Wonder Woman (a long-standing fanboy fantasy). By essentializing Wonder Woman as a feminine force of rejuvenation, Miller exposes a standard and stereotypical construction of women in comics that he long favored but has only taken to such extremes in the misogynistic film noir world of *Sin City*.[11] The distance from the first series (which gave a new integrity to superhero stories) is represented in the absurd rallying cry Batman gives to a youth culture infatuated with the image of the superhero: "Children, pull on your tights—and give them hell" (170). Clearly, Miller implements comic book tropes and accentuates them to the point of breaking. *The Dark Knight Strikes Again* works as a satire of some of the same media, political, and social situations seen in *The Dark Knight Returns*. However, disappointed with the development of superhero comic books since 1986, Miller produces a work which criticizes the industry's and consumer's incipient understanding of his own intentions.

> Since *Dark Knight*, very cynical editors have hired artists to trace off pages of *Dark Knight*, and they've hired writers to repeat what they think they understand about *Dark Knight*, which essentially is that it is very brutal, and that it includes little TV panels. Of course, all this misses the point of the whole thing, so what we're seeing is a lot of third-rate imitations. I don't like saying this really. It's pretty embarrassing. The same publisher that bought Superman

and Batman and totally corrupted them got a shot in the arm with *Dark Knight*
and *Watchmen* and a few other things. And look what they've done with it
[Sharrett 35].

In a self-referential move that identifies his unintended detrimental
influence, Miller limits Lex Luthor by representing him simply as a crime
boss clone of the Kingpin (the Daredevil villain that Miller made famous).
Since Batman functions more as an unstoppable force than a human being
capable of failure, one lone point of drama that remains is Batman's failing heart, but his monologue at this point echoes that of similarly weak-
hearted Hartigan in Miller's *Sin City: That Yellow Bastard*. The Batman of
The Dark Knight Strikes Again seems to inhabit a world of over-used and
bankrupt ideas. In contrast to the romantic attachment to the heroism of
Batman he expressed over and over in the 1980s, Miller has recently stated
that with superhero comic books "you've got to realize you're doing something intensely silly" (*Frank Miller* 107–108). Miller ends this series with
Batman destroying the Batcave and all the traditional trappings of Batman's history and thus reveals (through Batman's perspective of himself)
the bankruptcy that Miller finds with the superhero in contemporary culture. As Uricchio and Pearson suggest:

> The years since the publication of Miller's *The Dark Knight Returns* have seen
> the greatest array of character transmutations and violations of heretofore
> sacrosanct canonicity.... This moment in the last decade of the twentieth cen-
> tury, then, represents the most divergent set of refractions of the Batman
> character. Whereas broad shifts in emphasis had occurred since 1939, these
> changes had been, for the most part, consensual. Now, newly created Batmen,
> existing simultaneously with the older Batman of the television series and
> comic reprints and back issues, all struggled for recognition and a share of
> the market. But the contradictions amongst them may threaten both the
> integrity of the commodity and the coherence of the fans' lived experience of
> the character necessary to the Batman's continued success [Uricchio 184].

STRIKING TERROR IN NEW YORK AND IN GOTHAM: (ANTI-)HEROISM UNDER SIEGE

Written and drawn largely before the 9/11 terrorist attacks, *The Dark
Knight Strikes Again* was at press at that time.[12] Concerned about several
scenes and bits of dialogue such as Batman's statement "Striking Terror.
Best part of the job" (Miller, *The Dark Knight Strikes Again* 110),[13] DC
approached Miller to see whether he'd like to change anything in that
politically sensitive time. While Miller did take advantage of the opportunity, he did not change anything that the publisher had in mind (such as
the Batplane flying into a government structure or Batman's above mentioned line).

> I couldn't keep going without addressing it. So I had to stop the story and
> make it take a darker tone. Somehow, I found that in a certain way, dramati-

cally, the darker you get the funnier you get, because after a while you have to laugh. Then the visual idea pops out, like the idea of Batman with three teeth. I couldn't resist doing that. Also, all of the stuff that's implicit with super-heroes, the idea of there being mightier creatures around.... It's kind of Teu-tonic, which is funny since the superhero is a supremely Jewish creation [*Frank Miller* 110].

Instead, Miller added Superman finding Lois Lane's locket in the rubble of a government attack on Metropolis. As Superman aids Batman in his global quest for "freedom," Batman is excessively violent with no clear moral guide aside from imposing his own will on others; he cheers the new Hawkman and Hawkgirl as they decapitate Lex Luthor.

Tim Blackmore's critique of *The Dark Knight Returns* tends to overstate the ideas of the 1986 text but seems well-suited to *The Dark Knight Strikes Again*, which does not feature Batman as a savior and suggests no place outside the crushing influence of society: "Alexis de Toqueville's primary fear ... is that democracy will transmute itself into authoritarianism; Frank Miller's *Batman: The Dark Knight Returns* depicts this event. Both authors trace the same path: from the decay of democracy and the birth of the authoritarian state to the loss of individual rights, the rise of the charis-matic leader, the mass which follows him, and the future of the state" (Blackmore 37).

The reason that this applies more directly to the sequel is not only due to the fact that these criticisms have been leveled at George W. Bush in a post–9/11 USA; these criticisms apply to the society portrayed in *The Dark Knight Strikes Again* and also the "hero" portrayed therein. With Miller claim-ing all his work in the near future would be a response to 9/11, this use of 9/11 events makes the story more strident in its criticism of the recent treat-ment of superheroes by folding together Batman's agenda with Miller's quickly developed satire of the Bush administration.[14] While retaliation for past wrongs seems to be Batman's standard m.o., here the retaliation is the sham government's response to Batman's attack (Batman's attack is the past wrong). Moreover, after defeating Lex Luthor and Brainiac, the super-heroes seem only to be pranksters with no leadership strategies to offer as an alternative to the new Rumsfeld/Ashcroft approach. In fact, the only clear leader for the free world might be the new Superman, strangely in line with the former government's domineering attitudes. Rejecting the American idealism of his adoptive parents, Superman figuratively speaks with them and takes on the mantle of the overman to whom no moral stan-dards apply: "You were wrong. I am not one of them. I am not human.... And I am no man's servant. I am no man's slave. I will not be ruled by the laws of men" (Miller, *The Dark Knight Strikes Again* 220). When Superman hovers above the earth with his newly rediscovered daughter Lara, he asks, "What exactly shall we do with our planet?" (247).

This statement simultaneously serves as a criticism of and perhaps connection between the moral bankruptcy in the authoritarian power fantasy structure of most comic book narratives (a structure which has only become more pronounced since 1986) and what Miller perceives as the ineffective, unilateral stand of the Bush administration. In the process of a fascist Batman teaching the dumb lug Superman "how to be a man," *The Dark Knight Strikes Again* accentuates the unfortunate aspects of escapist comic book entertainment (with only one male superhero capable of righting all wrongs). Predicated on a notably singular and one-dimensional perspective and flaunting its excessive use of genre conventions, *The Dark Knight Strikes Again* functions as a postmodern narrative aware of its own hyper-masculine construction. Throughout the course of the narrative, the fate of the world is never in question, as the superheroes always have the greatest power and win in comic books (although there is a significant question of whether the world will be better for their winning); the only thing that creates dramatic tension at the conclusion is the question of the new Joker's identity. As Batman has known from the start (impossibly intelligent in the sequel only because everyone else is so stupid), the new Joker is Dick Grayson (the first ward of Bruce Wayne and therefore the first Robin).

More clearly in violation of the first series than anything else (in which Batman constantly laments not having Grayson at his side), this conflict takes shape as something even more contrived than the Batman-Superman rivalry (at this point Batman claims to have fired Robin because he couldn't cut it).[15] The only "reality" is the sham story created to ensure reader interest; truth is created retroactively.[16] Unlike the first series in which characters represented components of the Lacanian model (with Superman as society and Batman as its symptom), every character acts in a way that makes the self subservient to the system. However, with its conflict entirely contrived and its workings exposed (by revealing the weaknesses of the narratives of the superhero and society which it employs), the narrative itself acts a symptom of the culture critiqued in *The Dark Knight Returns*— but the narrative only gives the reader a greater sense of culture when recognized as such.

FINDING ONE'S CHARACTER AND LOSING ONE'S SELF: WHO WATCHES FRANK MILLER

The motivation for Miller's revision of his hallmark work resides with his disappointment with the industry's appropriation of *The Dark Knight Returns*. With this in mind, it could be said that Miller exercises his celebrity status as power over industry that at one time told him he'd never make it with his crime drama approach. Using the industry to criticize the industry, he could be seen as a one-time fanboy relishing the fact that he has become the superhero he always dreamed he could be (and now is punishing the bully for the bully's former abuse of the 90-pound weakling). Perhaps imagining himself as the "outsider" who now has fantastic control over the mainstream, his work as a writer is not terribly unlike that of his refashioned Dark Knight, the new bully who shows society who the real man is. As the readership for comic books has shrunk since the bust of the late nineties, editors at the "big two" have again ascended to a former position of power and are making more conservative choices, which Miller resents:

> It seems now, because sales are down, it's harder to get published, it's harder to get work off the ground unless you're really established. So editors are powerful again. They were very powerful when I first came into comics, because there was very little work to be had. They got steadily weaker as we inmates took over the asylum. But now they've steadily become as powerful as they were before. Now if you're a *Batman* editor or a *Superman* editor, you simply sit down at a convention and a line of people want to buy you drink and beg you for work! [*Eisner/Miller* 296].

However, this reading is complicated by comments that Miller has made about *The Dark Knight Strikes Again*. Rather than clearly acknowledge a distaste for the genre much more virulent than Alan Moore's *Watchmen* (the supposedly more bitter counterpoint to *The Dark Knight Returns*), Miller expresses a love of the superhero narrative and a hope for the future of the genre. Miller seems almost giddy with the machinations of his sequel; responding to the question of why he would return to writing superhero stories, he states, "I've always loved the superhero stuff. It just felt to me like a lot of the stuff that was coming out was getting a little too full of itself and wasn't enjoying the sweet absurdity of superheroes" (*Frank Miller* 107).

In fact, the statements he made during his creation of *The Dark Knight Returns* in 1985 seem more well-suited to the tone of *The Dark Knight Strikes Again*: "Superheroes have lost their human context. That's precisely why the comics have gotten so weak, and the stories seem so pointless and so irrelevant.... Now, modern superhero comics have reached the point where there are so damn many superheroes and so damn much superpower flying around that there's no room left for anything human.... Just look at how many characters are being killed these days. It's as if all there is left of them is the pathological thrill of a snuff film" (*Frank Miller* 34).

The cynical reader of Miller's more recent statements might conclude that he was manufacturing industry-friendly sound bites to maintain his relationship with the industry. However, that would not take into consideration Miller's long-standing vocal opposition to creative restrictions exercised by the "big two" and the simple fact is that the industry now needs Frank Miller more than Frank Miller needs the industry. The essence of his new position seems to be the desire to embrace the "sweet absurdity" of the superhero and perhaps of his position as someone who is simultaneously an insider and outsider. He states that *The Dark Knight Strikes Again* is not a satire: "No.... Near parody is fair, because I think that it kind of slides in and out of it. I just let that happen because that's what felt right with the story. Because I felt that, every once in a while, you've got to take a deep breath and realize that you're doing something intensely silly, and then go back to the operatic. For me, it's the juggling of the two that creates a nice kind of tension. I think that I was reacting to the over-reverential tone of so many modern comics" (*Frank Miller* 107–108).

While *The Dark Knight Returns* works more as a quintessential modernist text with dialectic tension resolved and a new truth found within the text, *The Dark Knight Strikes Again* works more as a quintessential postmodernist text with dialectic tension never resolved and truth, at best, found outside the text (but then again, postmodernists often suggest that everything is a text and there is nothing outside the text). Unlike the trade paperback version of *The Dark Knight Returns*, which begins with an introduction by Frank Miller that recounts his life at the time of the book's creation, the trade paperback version of *The Dark Knight Strikes Again* begins with an "introduction" by Frank Miller which presents a newspaper article by Vicki Vale, a long-standing character in Batman's world. Unlike the first introduction, which suggests that Miller can objectively come to know himself and his work, the second introduction shows Miller staying within his subjective perspective, the comic book world of his choice. While modernist texts tend to present truth with certainty, post-modernist texts tend to present truth only so far as they can stretch the uncertain limits of the texts themselves.[17] With this new found approach to superhero stories which reads as a bitter indictment, Miller seems to have discovered a new sense of liberty. Often referred to as a representative of the integrity of traditional superheroes and the new aesthetics of art comics in the same breath, Miller has defined a margin for himself, a fixed space outside the main text that allows him to appreciate the ridiculous tradition he formerly eschewed. Acknowledging that he is neither wholly implicated or wholly separate from that industry, Miller in this way represents the place of comic books within society much better than my playful speculation about his motives at the beginning of this section.

Rather than make a frontal assault which validates the regime to be attacked, Miller chooses to discredit the institution through his laughter. Rather than continue to make the argument for the relevance of comic books (much less superhero comic books), Miller now forgoes that argument and relishes the dubious respectability afforded by culture at large to comic books. Therefore, the charge that superhero comic books have become even more insular and self-referential in the 21st century doesn't bear the sting it might. For Miller, there seems to be no better place from which to launch serious criticism of society than from a position that he acknowledges society should not respect. Far from discrediting his criticism, it gives new credence to his work, as he fashions an identity for himself built not on a singular position but on irresolvable tension (like society itself). Miller revels in the absurd joy that he will never be reconciled to society and thereby his "outsider" voice becomes more potent than ever before.

> *"I think comics are at their best when they are provocative, and their outlaw nature is what I want to seek out in them.... We don't need to keep rationalizing our existence. Now I think we're on the offensive, culturally"—Frank Miller* (Eisner/Miller 178).

NOTES

1. Along with Alan Moore, Frank Miller would instrumentally shape the new sense of superheroes seen in the boom period of the late 1980s and early 1990s. Although Moore is often cited by critics as the superior craftsman (*Watchmen* is the only graphic novel included in *Time*'s list of the 100 greatest novels since 1923), Miller seems to have more staying power as the comic book creator who straddles the fence between artistic innovations and popular interests. (Celebrities such as Ben Affleck sing his praises as a great artist at awards ceremonies.) And since the comic book bubble burst in the 1990s, any of the "big" names in comic books that have been established subsequently (Grant Morrison, Warren Ellis, and even Neil Gaiman) have yet to displace him.

2. In *Reinventing Comics*, Scott McCloud recounts his Ray Suarez's take on *Sin City*: "Many of these books are filled with adolescent guy power trips, sexual fantasies, borderline occult stories, mythological characters, and in many cases, blood, blood, blood" (81).

3. The first two chapters of Fantagraphics' interview collection, *Frank Miller*, address the influence of noir stylings on Miller's art from the beginning of his career.

4. According to Alain Silver, this "indigenous American" art form suggests not only "a dark mood in American society, but equally, almost empirically, as a black slate on which the culture could inscribe its ills and in the process produce a catharsis to help relieve them" (Silver and Ward 1). As indicated by the notion of catharsis, a healing through self-exposure, this concern with control over the self is shaped by the Western world's attachment to Freud's psychoanalytic theory. When that theory becomes narrative, general anxiety is male anxiety and the variable to be subjected to male power is woman; the woman stands for a society potentially out of control. Women, in general, represent a problem as an idea contrary to the identity clearly delineated by a Freudian narrative. The femme fatale refuses to participate in Freud's male need for meaning and identity, the only meaning in film noir; she is, in the most extreme sense, nothingness. According to Mary Ann Doane, "The femme fatale is an articulation of fears surrounding the loss of stability and centrality of the self, the 'I'" (Doane 2). If men give in to their sexual desire for the femme fatale, they have committed themselves to sexual abandon and a loss of control, and control, of course, serves as the fundamental basis for identity.

5. He extends this idea that the fundamental desire of human beings is the unity of one's identity in "Of the Gaze as Objet Petit a." The individual, as we've come to understand it, wants to be the pre-symbolic self, the self completely body (the signified). Since a return to the pre-symbolic is impossible, the individual feels inadequate before the interpolated gaze of everyone else, the gaze of the Other. Just as the individual may perceive others as objects to satisfy desire, the individual perceives the self as the object of the Other. That interpolated gaze is the individual's own but nevertheless functions as an external pressure. In an attempt to satisfy the impossible desire and counteract feelings of inadequacy, the individual uses the *objet petit a* (the signifier) as a stand-in for the true object of desire: a unity that can never be achieved.

6. "Alan was eviscerating the entire notion [of the superhero]. I was very sentimentally celebrating it" (*Frank Miller* 105).

7. Miller has expressed an admiration for the early vision of Superman which should be read as desire to reclaim (and not destroy) Superman: "Batman is as good and pure a superhero as you can find.... True, he has his roots in the pulp magazines, particularly *The Shadow*, but that material and at least part of the Batman come from somebody's reaction to real life, which puts him closer to artistic legitimacy than almost any other superhero, with the exception of Superman" (*Frank Miller* 34).

8. Scott McCloud refers to *Sin City* as "ironic": "Miller's *Sin City* is a tongue-in-cheek, over-the-top hyper-noir send-up" (81).

9. In the trade paperback version of *The Dark Knight Strikes Again*, Miller provides an "introduction" that is a newspaper article written by Vicki Vale, Bruce Wayne's sometime reporter girlfriend. Likewise, she uses language that would never make it to print, including a generous sprinkling of profanity, and it sounds very similar to other characters in the sequel's noir-ish universe.

10. This pastiche approach to representing media reality at the end also includes Batmite, a fanciful character hated by the fans devoted to the grim and gritty Batman.

11. Another nod to the faddish commercialization of superheroes (which further violated any integrity Wonder Woman might be thought to have as a character) was the image of Wonder Woman on the cover of issue 2; clearly Superman's "woman," she wore replicas of Superman's famous S-shaped chest shield as earrings.

12. More specifically, Miller had completely finished issues 1 and 2, and issue 3 (the concluding issue) was yet to be completed. Miller's retooling of the final issue caused it to be delayed and many speculated that DC had delayed due to concerns over its content.

13. "I long ago determined that a character like Batman can only be defined as a terrorist if his motto is striking terror. I don't want to dodge it and also, I wanted Batman to creep you out. That I wanted from the start. I don't want you to like this guy" (*Frank Miller* 110).

14. Miller's criticism of the comic book industry should be read largely as a criticism of the larger political situation in the country; with Miller's view of interlocking systems of corruption, the comic book industry would simply be a microcosmic version of the U.S. administration.

15. Other elements of the sequel which can be considered logical impossibilities within the narrative of the first series include the revelations of the long-standing relationship between Superman and Wonder Woman and Lara, the daughter they produced (now a teenager).

16. Miller opens up the possibility that the story itself is nothing but Batman's power fantasy, formed retroactively by Batman's dying mind. "Lex Luthor. Evil Genius. Archfiend. Headed for a fall. That's unless I'm as crazy as everybody thinks I am. Hell. Maybe I am Nuts. Maybe I'm still lying on the cave floor, clutching my chest...." (Miller, *The Dark Knight Strikes Again*, p. 217). This takes place as Lex Luthor beats Batman, which is, of course, all part of Batman's plan.

17. With Miller's claim that his post–9/11 work will be propaganda, he seems to be working beyond the modernist idea that propaganda is bad art and within the post-modernist idea that all art is propaganda; the important thing for a post-modernist would be to be aware that all art is propaganda.

WORKS CITED

Blackmore, Tim. "The Dark Knight of Democracy: Tocqueville and Miller Cast Some Light on the Subject." *Journal of American Culture* 14. 1 (1991): 37–56.

Doane, Mary Ann. *Femmes Fatales*. New York: Routledge, 1991.

Eisner/Miller. Ed., Charles Brownstein. Milwaukie: Dark Horse, 2005.

Frank Miller: The Interviews: 1981–2003. Ed., Milo George. Seattle: Fantagraphics, 2003.

Gold, Mike. "Our Darkest Knight." *The Greatest Batman Stories Ever Told*. New York: DC Comics, 1988. 12–16.

Lacan, Jacques. "The Agency of the Letter in the Unconscious or Reason Since Freud." *Ecrits*. Trans., Alan Sheridan. New York: W.W. Norton, 1977: 1–7.

_____. "Of the Gaze as Object Petit a." *The Four Fundamental Concepts of Psychoanalysis*. Trans., Alan Sheridan. New York: W.W. Norton, 1981. 67–119.

McCloud, Scott. *Reinventing Comics*. New York: HarperCollins, 2000.
Miller, Frank. *Daredevil: Born Again*. New York: Marvel Comics, 2001.
_____. *The Dark Knight Returns*. New York: DC Comics, 1996.
_____. *The Dark Knight Strikes Again*. New York: DC Comics, 2004.
_____. *Sin City*. Milwaukie: Dark Horse, 1993.
_____. *Sin City: That Yellow Bastard*. Milwaukie: Dark Horse, 1997.
Sharrett, Christopher. "Batman and the Twilight of the Idols: An Interview with Frank Miller." *The Many Lives of Batman: Critical Approaches to a Superhero and His Media*. Eds., Roberta E. Pearson and William Uricchio. New York: Routledge, 1991. 32–46.
Silver, Alain and Elizabeth Ward. *Film Noir*. New York: Overlook, 1992.
"*Time* Critics Lev Grossman and Richard Lacayo Pick the 100 Best English-Language Novels Since 1923." *Time*. 2005. *Time.com*. 22 November 2006 http://www.time.com/time/2005/100books/the_complete_list.html.
Uricchio, William, and Roberta E. Pearson. "'I'm Not Fooled By That Cheap Disguise.'" *The Many Lives of Batman: Critical Approaches to a Superhero and His Media*. Eds., Roberta E. Pearson and William Uricchio. New York: Routledge, 1991. 182–211.
Zizek, Slavoj. *The Sublime Object of Ideology*. New York: Verso, 1997.

The "Transcreation" of a Mediated Myth: Spider-Man in India

DAN O'ROURKE AND PRAVIN A. RODRIGUES

"Comics are becoming the new pop art. The new pop communication. The new drug. This is not just comics, but a breathtaking new multi-media format. Comics are the new culture"
—*Shekar Kapur, Gotham Entertainment Group (Weiland 1)*

The initial drawing that accompanied the press release was certainly eye-catching: Spider-Man in a *dhoti?* Indeed, the familiar red and blue costume of "our friendly neighborhood Spider-Man" was augmented by the traditional, simple cloth wrapped around the waist and draped over the legs. This animated blending of Western and Eastern cultures symbolized the joint venture of Marvel Enterprises and Gotham Entertainment Group to "transcreate," as they called it, the story of the web-slinging superhero within Indian culture. Following the success of the movie *Spider-Man* in India, the two companies offered a four-part retelling of the hero's origin with an Indian lead character, sites, and cultural themes from that country. Thus the exploits of Peter Parker in New York became the adventures of Pavitr Prabhakar in Mumbai.

This essay explores the cultural adaptation of the Spider-Man story as a form of mass-mediated mythology. The authors of this analysis believe that the unique rhetorical form of the comic book and its predominantly youth-oriented market present an interesting opportunity to explore the synthesis of cultural narratives and myths across geographic boundaries. In *The Hero With a Thousand Faces*, Joseph Campbell observes, "The community today is the planet, not the bounded nation" (Campbell 388). Campbell invokes Carl Jung's archetypal image to assert that monomyths of heroic action link the unconscious fears and hopes of individuals with the conscious desires of the collective. Jung acknowledges that elements of the archetypal image can be found in the essays of Plato as well as Nietzsche. For his part, Campbell extends this theory beyond Western thought and adds that in Hindu and Buddhist philosophy the process is called *vivecka*, or discrimination (Campbell 11–19). This conception of the uni-

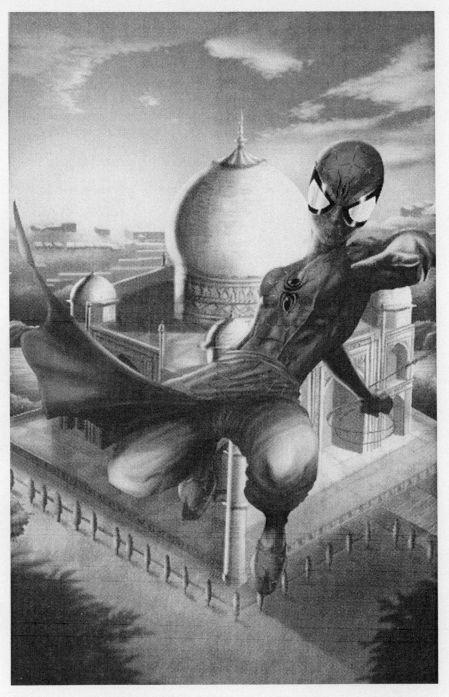

The unusual sight of Spiderman in a dhoti: *Spiderman: India.* From page 50 of *Spiderman India: Limited Collector Edition* (New Jersey: Gotham Entertainment Group, 2004).

versality of mythic images and stories enables the authors of this essay to assert that the "transcreation" of the Spider-Man narrative from Western to Eastern culture is an example of a modern monomyth found in the form of a comic book.

To critique the tale of Pavitr Prabhakar as a cultural "transcreation," it is necessary to know something of the narrative form and history of comic books in America. Over time, comic books have been forced to compete with alternative media. The fluidity of form among superhero stories in films, on television, in video games, and on the internet allowed these narratives to adapt from genre to genre. Still, the speed and cost of the production of comic books have made this medium the most accessible to the blending of cultural myths and superheroes.

A Brief History of Comic Books

Communication scholars have previously examined comic strips and editorial cartoons as rhetorical artifacts (for examples see Bostdorff 43–59; Morrison 252–60; Medhurst and DeSousa 197–236; Turner 24–35) but relatively little has been written about comic books. In his highly insightful history of the medium, Bradford W. Wright observes that the first comic books were little more than a collection of daily comic strips (Wright 2–4). In May 1934, the comic book business was born with the publication of *Famous Funnies* (Andelman 37). Pulp magazines featuring science fiction stories were in decline and publishers soon exhausted the supply of daily comics trying to meet the demand for comic books. Early publishers solicited new stories under the generic themes of "Detective Comics" or "Planet Stories" (Andelman 41; Pustz 26). At this point, the audience for comic books shifted. Comic strips and political cartoons were part of the larger forum of a newspaper. The newspaper attracted a wide range of readers and made the comic strip a small part of its offering. On the other hand, the comic book attracted primarily young people and created a whole new category of consumer: the youth audience. A 1943 Market Research Company survey reported that 95 percent of all 8 to 11 year olds as well as 84 percent of 12 to 17 year olds read comic books (Pustz 27). More than a decade before rock-n-roll revolutionized American marketing and tapped into the values of the baby boom generation, comic books offered inexpensive entertainment for young consumers. Elvis and the Beatles were on the horizon, but Superman was the first king of popular youth culture.

In 1938 Jerry Siegel and Joel Shuster sold the story of Superman to DC Comics for one hundred and thirty dollars (Wright 8–9). By the seventh issue of *Action Comics,* the saga of the superhero from the planet Krypton was selling 500,000 issues a month (Wright 8–9). This mythic story of a "hero from a foreign land" gave birth to the modern comic book. The drama of a superhero battling for "Truth, Justice, and the American Way" was the answer for a generation of youth who dreamed of better days. America was mired in an economic depression and war was looming in Europe. Superheroes were vigilantes who operated outside the law and government restrictions to always get results. The success of Superman spawned many followers, including Batman, Captain America, and the Green Lantern. These heroes conquered all foes, including Hitler. The first issue of *Captain America Action Comics* had the Super Soldier hitting the Fuhrer in the face one year before America declared war on Germany (Wright 30). America went to war grudgingly but sympathetic immigrant writers and illustrators took the youth of the country to battle much earlier.

The Golden Era of Comics coincided with the uncertainty of World War II. In 1942, *Business Week* estimated that 15 million comic books were sold each month while the publishers added that each book had a "pass-along" value of five additional readers (Wright 31). In 1943 twenty-five million comic books were sold each month (Pustz 27) with gross retail sales reaching 30 million dollars a year (Wright 31). The *New York Times* reported that twenty-five percent of all books sent overseas to soldiers were comic books, including 35,000 copies of *Superman* every month (Wright 31). *Yank,* the U.S. Army newspaper, reported that PXs—military supply stores—sold ten times as many comic books as copies of the *Saturday Evening Post* and *Readers' Digest* (Wright 56–57). To show that soldiers were no different than the rest of the country, *Yank* also cited a report from the Market Research Company of America that estimated that 70 million Americans, about half the population at the time, read comic books (Wright 57).

This is not to suggest that comic books were universally accepted. Like most forms of popular culture, social elites were quick to criticize this form of light entertainment. In 1940 a columnist for the *Chicago Tribune* characterized comic books as "graphic insanity" (Wright 27). Parents, educators, and social leaders worried about the potentially harmful effects of depictions of sex and violence in comic books and their impact on young readers (Wright 86–108). After the war, superheroes lacked the opposition of the Axis powers and were replaced by crime comics. Graphic depictions of violence and sexual themes increased, as did the protests. Dr. Fredric Wertham, a New York psychiatrist, asserted that aberrant behavior in children could be attributed to the violent and graphic messages in comic books (Jones 270–277; Wright 92–108). By October 1948, fifty American cities had banned or placed restrictions on the sale of comic books (Wright 98). Critics also worried about the perceived subtext of homoerotic themes. Tales of millionaire bachelors and their young wards donning skin-tight costumes to fight crime did not resonate with the puritanical tastes of social reformers. One critic wrote that the glorification of superheroes was akin to a primitive religion and could undermine prevailing social values (Wright 29). In the 1950s, America's fear of the corrupting social influence of comic books was so great that the Senate Subcommittee on Juvenile Delinquency held hearings on the matter at about the same time that Senator McCarthy's "Red Scare" began the search for Communists (Pustz 41). From violence to blasphemy with a touch of sex to boot, comic books were an easy target for conservative authority figures.

One issue of particular relevance to this study was the criticism of "jungle comics." Young artists and writers invoked cultural stereotypes to create superheroes that sought to preserve or improve the social order. Wright observes that these urban storytellers were acting as "Super New Dealers" to protect and promote the programs of President Roosevelt. Domestically, superheroes in the 1930s and 1940s battled for the rights of coal miners, assailed child labor, attacked political corruption, and even fought for product safety (Wright 23–24). Interest in European issues led the immigrant artists, many of whom were Jewish, to take their superheroes to war against Germany and the Axis powers. Characterizations of Asian, African, and South American people also invoked stereotypical and ethnocentric treatment. "Jungle comics" were usually stories of a white hero paternalistically rescuing the simple native people from an assault by a foreign agitator. In comic books, Tarzan was an example of a Caucasian who protected indigenous African tribes. One of the first heroes created by legendary cartoonist Will Eisner was "Sheena, Queen of the Jungle" for Fiction Houses' *Jungle Stories* (Andelman 40). A typical "jungle comic" would be the story of Captain Desmo, American aviator, who helped the British Empire crush a native rebellion of Indian workers. A foreign agent by the name of Von Stern had been stirring up the natives to create a destabilizing insurgency (Wright 36). After Pearl Harbor, the Japanese were particularly targeted for stereotypical propaganda. Racist titles such as "The Terror of the Slimy Japs" or "The Slant Eye of Satan" referred to the enemy as "yellow apes," "yellow devils," or "little yellow doggies" (Wright 45). Skin color was only half of the message of such racial slurs; the sneak attack of December 7, 1941, led comic book writers to invoke "yellow themes" as messages of cowardice and deception. It was clear in the Golden Age of Comics that the popularity of the medium was built upon strong images of heroes and villains that invoked cultural values and stereotypes. The comic books of the 1940s were not global enterprises.

After the war, the popularity of comic books slowly eroded. The advent of television in the 1950s can be directly related to the reduction of comic publishers by half in the 1960s (Wright 182). In the second half of the twentieth century, comic books suffered the same problems of diversification, amalgamation, and competition as most media. The rise of Marvel Comics as a competitive force, the growth of underground and alternative comics, the economics of collecting, and the corporate consolidation of media forced publishers to compete more vigorously for a smaller share of an increasingly competitive market (Andelman 183–192, 229–238; Pustz 61–109). Surveys in the 1980s revealed that only twenty-nine percent of Americans between the ages of seven and twenty-four still read comic books. Today, the average American consumer of comic books is twenty years old and spends twenty dollars a month on the product. (Wright 280–283). In the contemporary media market, the chief source of revenue from comic books comes not from readers, but from viewers and players.

The marketing of comic art and licensed products has always been an issue for the corporations that hold the rights to comic characters. Superman made millions for DC Comics and its parent company, Time-Warner Communications, through radio, television, motion pictures, and the myriad products bearing the Superman logo. However, Siegel and Shuster fought for years to receive commensurate compensation and credit for their creation (Jones, *Men of Tomorrow*). Today, the companies that produce comic books generate more from licensing revenues to alternative media, including movies and video games, than from sales (Wright 259). New, interactive technologies such as computer games have replaced comic books as the most popular form of youth entertainment. In the Age of Information, media conglomerates are now looking beyond American shores to identify new markets for their "super products." Global initiatives for American comic books are not limited to India but extend to the Middle East and France ("Marvel Invades"; *Fantastic Four*). The intent of these media giants seems to be to replicate the American experience by gaining entrance to new international markets through the more receptive youth culture. This corporate initiative utilizing comic books as a wedge into new cultures and media markets merits investigation.

MYTH AND THE RHETORICAL FORM OF COMIC BOOKS

Joseph Campbell writes that "dream is the personalized myth, myth the depersonalized dream" (Campbell 19). Since before the dawn of symbol use, humans have used myths to communicate their individual dreams and collective stories. Pre-symbolic humans "acted out" dramas as a way of sharing their perceptions of the world. Stories about dangers in the natural world, great hunting adventures, or the accomplishments of ancestors were presented from generation to generation for the education of the tribe. These were stories of identity—Who are we? Where did our tribe come from? What are the keys to our continued survival? Our primitive ancestors lived in a world defined for them by the dramatic presentation of myths.

As primitive people became more adept at symbol use, words moved to the forefront of the narrative while dramatic presentations became supplemental clarifications and traditions of tribal lore. The advance of reason led to the development of scientific inquiry that soon relegated myth to the realm of fantasy. No longer could a simple story explain the complexity of the world. Still, myths persisted as stories of identity and purpose. Science could theorize about the origin of the world and how the human body functioned, but it could not define a human's purpose or place in the world. The myths that survived offered moral lessons of heroic ideals and the shortcomings of our ancestors. These stories became sacred truths of our families and communities because they identified the hopes to which future generations could aspire, as well as warnings about recurring circumstances in the drama of our daily lives.

In the modern world, myths persist as lessons for members of the community. Many myths are associated with the history and traditions of religious institutions. However, secular tales of bravery, courage, or villainy may arise as cultural lessons. The tale of John Henry is a classic American myth that pits man against machine. Similarly, tales of athletic achievement or individuals overcoming adversity can become mythic lessons in the hands of a talented writer. Danny Fingeroth, longtime writer for Marvel Comics and author of *Superman on The Couch*, suggests that the secular nature of comic books makes them perfect for a religiously diverse culture such as the United States (Fingeroth 23). The god-like qualities of many superheroes enable them to defeat evil and instruct young readers across religious demographics in appropriate social behavior. But just as early myths had to compete with the advance of scientific narratives, modern myths must compete with alternative messages in the mass media.

Wright states, "Just as each generation writes its own history, each reads its own comic books" (Wright 23). One might interpret this statement to observe that the topics of comic books change for each generation, just as other forms of popular culture adapt to changing market tastes. However, Fingeroth goes even further to suggest, "[W]hen you think of Superman, you most likely think of the Superman that was in vogue when *you* were a child. There's been a Superman for every decade since the character was created, as there have been Batmen, Wonder Women, and Spider-Men" (Fingeroth 20). The first Superman did not possess heat vision, invulnerability, or the power of flight; those powers grew over time. Moreover, writers and illustrators have stretched stories and images to alter the character and his appearance to fit their image of the superhero. The first Spider-Man drawn by Steve Ditko was less muscular and more lithe, a theme returned to in the motion picture with the casting of a smaller actor, Tobey McGuire. Each artist has tried to create his own distinctive portrait of the character, from John Romita, Sr.'s powerful image of the superhero to Todd McFarlane's 1990 images of the lean, graceful youth in the red and blue costume. To truly appreciate the evolution of an iconic comic book character such as Spider-Man, you must not only read the stories but see the physical transformations of the art as well.

Marvel Comics has further demonstrated the malleability of comic narratives in its Ultimate series. The Ultimate versions of Spider-Man, the Fantastic Four, and the X-Men are reinterpretations of the 1960s comics for comic book readers of today. For example, in the *Ultimate Spider-Man*, the scientific experiments that created the radioactive spider that bit Peter Parker are no longer legitimate university experiments. Illicit corporate experiments in human growth potential are the source of the radioactive arachnid. In the *Ultimate Fantastic Four*, Reed Richards and his colleagues do not travel into space to be bombarded by cosmic rays. These young scientists are transported into another dimension where their bodies are transformed into another state of being. In what might be considered an extension of "string theory," Reed theorizes that their bodies now exist in another evolved form of their former selves. The advance of science over four generations and the aging of the average comic reader have given license to comic writers to increase the sophistication of the stories. The Ultimate series is evidence of how comic books are adapting to reach out to a new audience in the highly competitive mass mediated age.

A further piece of evidence of how comic books adapt is the awareness of publishers to competing superhero narratives. Once comic books held nearly exclusive rights to the province of the superhero. But as other communication outlets evolved, the popular myths of superheroes proved highly attractive to alternative media. Superman was the first to leap off the pages into radio and then television. Today, competing superhero narratives may be seen in multiple monthly magazines, television, movies, video games, and on the Internet. The stories in these various media are not always consistent and may even be directed at different segments of the youth market. The Spider-Man of the movies organically generates webs, whereas his comic book counterpart invented a device to shoot a web-like, biodegradable substance. Superboy did not meet Lois Lane until he moved to Metropolis in the comic books. In the television show, *Smallville*, Lois Lane moves to the small farm town to meet her future love. Marketing and the improved media literacy of the audience allow publishers and producers to segment portions of the population. Comic books, like movies, offer ratings on their covers to suggest an appropriate age range for the prospective reader. Movies, however, are expensive and take time to produce, thus only one motion picture can be offered to all viewers. Comic book publishers, on the other hand, offer several versions of Spider-Man comic books to appeal to young and older readers every month. Those who would cross genres to read another comic book, see a movie, or play a video game are far more likely to be able to differentiate stories than generations past. Still, successful television shows like *Smallville* or movies like *Spider-Man* can influence comic book writers to reshape their stories to "tie-in" to the success of another mediated narrative. In the highly competitive youth market, comic books must do everything possible to challenge the more interactive forms of media.

Finally, we must acknowledge that most comic book readers follow the stories passionately for a period of time and then move on to other forms of popular culture. This allows comic writers and illustrators the creativity to "reinvent" heroes and villains for each generation of reader without fear of repercussions from long-term traditionalists. Thus the mythic quality of a comic book must maintain a narrative continuity with its origins but artistic vision, competing media representations, corporate pressures to succeed, and the recognition of an ever changing audience make comic books a malleable form of mediated myth.

THE "TRANSCREATION" OF SPIDER-MAN

Most Americans know the story of Spider-Man. In 1962, Stan Lee envisioned a new kind of superhero. Peter Parker was a bookish high school student who was shy and reserved. He lived with his Uncle Ben and Aunt May after the death of his parents. On a science field trip to a university laboratory, a radioactive spider bit Peter and the young man soon discovered that he had acquired the proportionate strength, speed, wall-climbing ability, and heightened senses of the spider. Peter's first instinct was to use this newfound power to make some money to support himself and his aging aunt and uncle. He did this by appearing as a "masked marvel" at a local wrestling match. He easily defeated his opponent but soon discovered that "masked marvels" cannot cash checks. One evening when he was leaving the arena, a man being chased by the police ran by him. The man escaped, to the chagrin of the officers, who asked Peter why he had not stopped him. Peter quickly explained that it was not his job and that he would not stick his neck out for anyone. Later that evening, Peter discovered that his beloved Uncle Ben had been killed in a robbery attempt. In a fit of anger, Peter tracked down the killer only to discover that it was the same criminal he could have stopped earlier that evening. The guilt over his inaction coupled with the lesson that his uncle had preached, "Those who have been given great power assume great responsibility," motivated him to become the crime-fighting superhero Spider-Man (www.marvel.com/universe/Spiderman).

The story of Spider-Man was steeped in the American culture of the 1960s and became an instant success. In the midst of the Cold War and on the heels of the Cuban Missile Crisis, this country was threatened by the prospect of nuclear annihilation at the hands of the Soviet Union. The military industrial complex was in full swing as America slipped into the quagmire of Vietnam. The assassination of John Kennedy had devastated the country and now the nation sought new, vibrant heroes. A British rock group named The Beatles arrived on the shores of America and young people quickly took to their message. Soon the country would see young and old divided, hawk debating dove, and black confronting white authority. America's traditional heroes seemed out of step with the times. Citizens challenged the leadership of presidents and traditional icons. The comic book heroes of World War II such as Superman and Captain America found themselves draped in a flag that many mistrusted. Changing times called for new heroes and new myths.

Spider-Man voiced the laconic spirit of the young baby boom generation; all the while he was driven by the guilt of his past failings. Stan Lee tapped into the public's simultaneous hope for and fear of science with the irradiation of Peter Parker. Spider-Man was a hero empowered by a radioactive accident, yet the teenager tried to deny his fate. Fortunately, Parker's desire for wealth and comfort was subsumed by the larger responsibility of pressing social issues. Spider-Man was a reluctant hero who came to relish his powers despite attempts by newspaper publisher J. Jonah Jamieson to brand him a menace. Guilt, moral ambiguity, public admonishment, humor—clearly, Spider-Man was not your parents' superhero.

For Joseph Campbell, the story of Spider-Man would be a classic monomyth. He writes, "A hero ventures forth from the world of common day into a region of supernatural wonder: fabulous forces are there encountered and a decisive victory is won: the hero comes back from his mysterious adventure with the power to bestow boons on his fellow man" (Campbell 30). In twentieth century America, secular science replaced the pantheon of the gods as the world of wonder. *Spider-Man* followed the comic book formula of *The Hulk* and *The Fantastic Four* to become a reluctant hero, a victim of science destined to aid his fellow man. Prometheus sought fire; Jason searched the world for the Golden Fleece (Campbell 30). In every generation across every corner of the globe, the hero is tested before he may serve the people.

If Peter Parker attempts to balance the themes of ancient myths and modern science, Pavitr Prabhakar swings right into the role of the mythic hero. In his introduction to *Spider-Man India,* Sharad Devarajan, president and CEO of Gotham Entertainment Group, writes: "We always believed that the superhero relates to a universal psyche already firmly established in India through centuries of mythological stories depicting gods and heroes with supernatural abilities. This project is the true culmination of such a synthesis allowing us to interweave the ethnic & mythological themes of India into Spider-Man's very origins and powers" (Kang 4).

The transcreation of Spider-Man immerses the character in the mythology of India. It is ironic that Spider-Man was one of the first superheroes to be identified with the city of New York. Superman fought crime in metaphorical Metropolis while Batman roamed the streets of Gotham City. Yet it was the teenage crime fighter who was transported to the city of Mumbai.

Gotham Enterprises realized that India is currently undergoing a transformation in the global economic sector and seized this moment to offer its "transcreation" monomyth. In the past few years, fueled by the software and tech boom, India has become one of the world's fastest growing economies. Fareed Zakaria, offering a cover story on India's growth in *Newsweek*, notes, "Over the past 15 years, India has been the second fastest-growing country in the world—after China—averaging about 6 percent growth per year. Growth accelerated to 7.5 percent last year and will probably hold at the same pace next year. Many observers believe that India could well expand at this high rate for the next decade." More important, Zakaria draws attention to the Pew Global Attitudes Survey, released in June 2005, which found that 71 percent of Indians had a favorable impression of the United States, marking that "only Americans had a more favorable view of America (83 percent)." Based on the survey, Zakaria concludes, "Indians are extremely comfortable with, and well disposed toward, America." He also surmises that "Americans also find India understandable." Couple this with the phenomenal rise in consumerism in India— "Personal consumption makes up a staggering 67 percent of GDP in India, much higher than China (42 percent) or any other country" (Zakaria 37) and one can see why the CEO of Gotham India thought "the time was right" to offer a "transcreation" of Spider-Man to American and Indian markets.

"The concept of comics in India is quite recent compared to the European, American and Japanese industries, but is nevertheless almost 50 years old" (Wikipedia). American comic book characters still dominate the Indian market, but a popular series of indigenous comics, the Ramayana, Mahabharata, and the Amar Chitra Katha, has arisen. These series first began publication in the sixties and are steeped in Indian mythology, drawing largely from the Hindu scriptures. Mythology is a strong undercurrent in Indian culture. Joe Forty notes in his sweeping visual volume of mythologies of the world, "India blurs the borders between gods and men.... Myth in India has remained archaic; a collective heritage which even today continues to refashion and reshape what is one of the most complex living cultures in the world." Mythology is integrated into the Indian experience and is best explained by Rabindranath Tagore, the Indian poet and Nobel laureate of literature who is also credited with coining the words of the national anthem of India, "To man the figure of a myth is as real as a figure of history. The point is not which is the more reliable fact, but which is the more enjoyable fiction."

To analyze myths across cultural boundaries, Joseph Campbell observes that the monomyth traditionally portrays three stages in the journey of the hero: separation—initiation—return (Campbell 30). The four-issue transcreation of *Spider-Man India* is a redefinition of the origin of the superhero; therefore we may examine the comic book series as the separation of Pavitr Prabhakar from his human community to become a superhuman hero. Campbell offers five steps in the process of separation: (1) the Call to Adventure; (2) Refusal of the Call; (3) Supernatural Aid; (4) the Crossing of the First Threshold; and (5) the Belly of the Whale (Campbell 36).

The opening page of *Spider-Man India* is a composite of three drawings: First, at the top of the page, a tearful young boy is seen clutching an older male while the name "Pavitr Prabhakar" appears in a word balloon. Second, a yogi with flaming white hair and a spider tattoo on his forehead holds an illuminated image of a spider and states: "Your destiny awaits you...." Finally, at the bottom of the page a monstrous green face with glowing yellow eyes screams, "Pavitr!" On page two, the teenage Pavitr awakens yelling. Uncle Bhim calls from the next room to ask if he is all right and wonders if it is the recurring nightmare (*Spider-Man India* 1). The Call to Adventure has been sounded.

The selection of Pavitr as Spider-Man India is presented more as an act of karma than the accidental initiation of Peter Parker into the world of superheroes. Pavitr is a teenage boy who has come to live with his Uncle Bhim and Aunt Maya after the death of his parents. He is a bright young boy who has won a partial scholarship to a top school in Mumbai. Money is tight but the social adjustment is Pavitr's greatest fear. He is taunted by his classmates and called "dhoti boy" and "desi" (*Spider-Man India* 1). All of the other students are depicted in Western dress; only Pavitr remains in the traditional Indian dhoti.

It is important to reflect on the strategic decision of the Indian artist, Jevan Kang, to drape Pavitr/Spider-Man India in a dhoti. Wikipedia defines the dhoti as "a rectangular piece of unstitched cloth wrapped about the waist and the legs.... The dhoti is the traditional male garment of India" (http://en.wikipedia.org/wiki/Dhoti). The dhoti has been symbolic as an indigenous garment, reasserting a distinct Indian identity coupled with a belief in simplicity and honesty. The garment can be traced back for centuries in India's history but its symbolic meaning was reaffirmed and intensified through the images of the spiritual and political leader Mahatma Gandhi. Gandhi always was draped in a dhoti and insisted on the attire even when he met the Queen of England. Critics have noted that the symbolism of this attire has been exploited by contemporary Indian politicians and cultural icons to promote personal agendas. Wikipedia explains that "the garment has become something of a mascot of cultural assertion, being greatly favored by politicians and cultural icons such as classical musicians, poets and litterateurs. Thus, the 'dhoti' for many has taken on a more cultural nuance while the 'suit-and-tie' or, in less formal occasions, the ubiquitous shirt and pants, are seen as standard formal and semi-formal wear" (http://en.wikipedia.org/wiki/Dhoti).

The symbolism and identification for the Indian reader achieved through the strategic choice of the attire does not end with Pavitr. One young woman, Meera Jain, befriends him and expresses some empathy for his "unfashionable" traditional clothing. She tells Pavitr that she also knows what it is like not to "fit in."

Pavitr's nightmares initiate the Call to Adventure but Campbell's second stage of separation is the Refusal of the Call. One day when school bullies are harassing Pavitr, the yogi of his dreams appears before him and grants him "the power of the spider" to battle an evil that has been unleashed upon the world. Campbell notes that as early as primitive cave drawings, women were portrayed naturally because they possess the power of birth. To transform a male, a costume or form of adornment is required (Campbell, *Myths To Live By* 36). The yogi adorns Spider-Man India in a red and blue costume with a dhoti and transports him to the tallest building in Mumbai. Here, Spider-Man India discovers his powers and announces that he "can't wait to show the kids at school what I can do now" (*Spider-Man India* 1). In his excitement he passes over a robbery attempt but decides to let the police handle it. On the other hand, Uncle Bhim protects the young victim. When Pavitr hears a familiar cry, he returns to the scene only to discover his dead uncle. Like his American counterpart, Spider-Man India put personal interests before civic responsibility. Now his guilt becomes the motivation to accept his destiny.

Campbell's third stage is Crossing the Threshold. The evil that the avatar spoke of has taken the form of the Green Goblin. Wealthy industrialist Nalin Oberoi (his American counterpart is Norman Osborn) has acquired an amulet said to possess great power. Acquisition of this sacred gem has taken a decade of searching and caused the destruction of Pavitr's home village. The demon Rakshasa, a green horned behemoth, is unleashed in a ritual ceremony and it takes possession of Oberoi's body. This too is an act of fate. Rakshasa explains that his task is to unleash a host of demons upon the earth. This battle between good and evil was waged before when a great hero arose to lead the humans into battle, captured the demons, and banished them. Rakshasa knows this history and accepts his *dharma*, or duty (*Spider-Man India* 2).

The monster becomes aware of Pavitr and dispatches a minion to study and test Spider-Man India. Rakshasa transforms an employee of the Oberoi Corporation into a six-armed monster with fangs and horns. This Indian counterpart of "Doctor Octopus" must challenge Spider-Man India to win back his humanity. In the third book, Spider-Man confronts Doctor Octopus, survives, and "Crosses the Threshold" into the realm of the hero.

Campbell's final stage in the separation cycle is "The Belly of the Whale." The hero appears to die in this phase of the narrative, often consumed or seemingly defeated by a great creature or force. Yet it soon becomes apparent that the real battle is taking place not between the hero and the perceived enemy but within the hero himself. Campbell writes, "Popular tales represent the heroic action to be physical; the higher religions show the deed to be moral" (Campbell, *Hero* 38). Peter Parker battled his guilt and sense of responsibility to assume the role of Spider-Man and battle criminals. Pavitr accepts his heroic fate to fight for all humanity. In the fourth installment of the series, Spider-Man India rushes to the Oberoi building to rescue his aunt from the monster Rakshasa. He angrily assaults security guards and employees only to discover that Rakshasa has taken the woman to an offshore refinery. As he rushes to save Aunt Maya, Spider-Man India recognizes the consequences of his anger and vows never again to succumb to such rage.

Once at the refinery the physical and moral battle begins in earnest. Rakshasa has captured not only Aunt Maya but Meera Jain as well. Rakshasa taunts Spider-Man India by dangling the women before him and announcing that it is "time for your innocence to die.... This is the *gift* I bring you little spider—the gift of pain ... and from pain—strength!" (*Spider-Man* 4). Spider-Man India rescues his aunt but fails to reach Meera. Surprisingly, his former nemesis, Doctor Octopus, intervenes to save the girl and plead with Rakshasa for the salvation of humanity. Rakshasa quickly destroys his former employee and then invites Spider-Man India to join him in the power of the amulet. Spider-Man India attacks and battles Rakshasa while the monster enjoins him to embrace his anger and give in to the power of the amulet as he has done.

The artist depicts the struggle within Pavitr by drawing him as half human and half monster. Memories flood the young hero's mind until finally he hears Uncle Bhim's voice state, "(W)ith great talent, with great power ... there must also come great responsibility" (*Spider-Man India* 4). Spider-Man India then assumes the same position as the yogi who granted him the power of the spider in book one of the series. He casts off the evil and grabs the amulet from Nalin Oberoi's neck, thus destroying Rakshasa. The amulet is quickly thrown into the sea and humanity is saved. However, the authors of the Spider-Man India offer an epilogue from the *Bhagavad Gita* which reads, "The demonic and the divine are the two kinds of men in this world. The divine I have told you about. Now ... learn about the demonic" (*Spider-Man India* 4). It seems that though the Spider-Man India series has come to a close, the mythic battle for good and evil in the world continues.

CONCLUSION

The commercial potential of the *Spider-Man India* series is not yet known. Sales in America were modest but Gotham Comics published five million copies in several languages to be sold in India (Devarajan). One thing is certain: the Indian people love Spider-Man movies. The movie

Spider-Man was the top-grossing import film in the history of India, earning 53 million rupees (Bhayani). However, in 2004, *Spider-Man II* obliterated that record and earned 78 million rupees, 46.5 percent more than its predecessor (Bhayani). The film was released on 303 prints in several languages—170 in Hindi, 60 in Tamil, and 55 translated into Telugu (Bhayani).

The potential success of *Spider-Man India* lies in its ability to integrate American comic book narratives with Indian mythology. Japanese artists have proved that American youth can accept new concepts and heroes. Anime and Manga sales rose from 60 million dollars in 2002 to 110 million in 2003 (Gustines). The hope for the creators of *Spider-Man India* is that this series will introduce American audiences to a new taste in Asian storytelling.

The comic book is an interesting choice as the medium to introduce Indian culture to America. Sharad Devarajan, president and CEO of Gotham Entertainment, has said, "We truly believe that in the years ahead India will become a leading global cultural exporter.... Today's Western world has an increasingly global appetite, regardless of its cultural affiliation" (Singh 1). Gautam Chopra, partner in Gotham Studios Asia, adds, "Comic books are fun! They are inexpensive to produce (at least that's our formula) and they are inexpensive to buy" (Singh 6). These inroads into the accessible youth market, however, are only the beginning. Chopra also notes that comic books afford great creativity at a minimal cost. In today's market, he notes, more and more motion picture directors and video game programmers are turning to comic books for scripts (Singh 6). In the future, licensing rights for stories and commercial products based on comic book characters could prove as profitable in India as they are in America.

Spider-Man India is an attempt to open another door between India and the U.S. We live in a global society in which McDonald's serves the world and dhotis are sold on the Internet. The attempt of Gotham Enterprises to introduce Americans to Indian culture through a comic book narrative is both clever and calculated. Perhaps no form of American media is more adaptable than the comic book. It is difficult to imagine an Indian television program succeeding in America or transforming an Indian actor into a stereotypically "John Wayne" role. However, the "trans-creation" of Spider-Man utilized the creative potential of comic books to successfully blend East and West. The image of Spider-Man in a dhoti is no more far-fetched than a man scaling walls or a woman flying through the air. Young readers of comic books are more open to the possibility of change and are less culturally grounded than their elders. Moreover, comic books are inexpensive sources for future television, motion picture, and video game productions. It is possible that we are witnessing a mediated transformation of the modern comic book hero myth that will cross cultures and potentially produce great profit. To adapt the Spider-Man axiom, "With great stories come great opportunities."

As critics, however, we must be aware that this opportunity for profit should be viewed with the possible cultural implications of such corporate "transcreations." If comics, as stated by Shekar Kapur, are the "new drug," we must ask, what is being sold and to whose advantage? The focus of Gotham executives in their interviews seems to be the introduction of Indian popular culture to the American market. However, on the other side, Indian readers are being introduced to a powerful form of pre-packaged American culture. The tension exemplified by Pavitr's struggle with the blending of Indian traditions and Western fashion is, on a small scale, emblematic of the difficulties of "transcreating" cultural narratives. This tension increases with the possible perception that American comic books communicating modern Western scientific themes are forms of cultural imperialism—imposing their superior worldview on the ancient mythologies of developing countries. Global communication conglomerates must be aware of the history of American "jungle comics" and seek to avoid the paternalistic attitudes and Western ethnocentrism of past comic books.

The integration of American and Indian mythology into a truly global narrative has the potential to teach international readers more about our shared humanity. The authors of this essay hope that in the future, American readers and viewers will have the opportunity to learn more about bravery, courage, and overcoming adversity from an Indian hero drawn from Eastern mythology. In today's complicated and conflicted world, we need to hear from a diverse range of heroic voices that truly represent the global perspective. As Campbell wrote, "The community today is the planet" (Campbell 388). This international community has many barriers to effective intercultural communication. The hope is that the iconic images and words of comic books may prove to be a source that effectively employs ancient and modern myths to help us bridge those chasms.

WORKS CITED

Andelman, Bob. *Will Eisner: A Spirited Life.* Milwaukie, Ore.: M Press, 1995.
Bendis, Brian Michael, Mark Millar, Warren Ellis, and Stuart Immonen. *Ultimate Fantastic Four, Vol. 1.* Marvel Comics. June 2005.
Bhayani, Viral. "*Spider-Man 2* Creates Box Office Record in India." *Glamsham Enfotainment .Com.* 28 July 2004. 2 February 2005. http://www.glamsham.com/movies/scoops /04/jul/28spiderman.asp.
Bostdorff, Denise M. "Making Light of James Watt: A Burkean Approach to the Form and Attitude of Political Cartoons." *Quarterly Journal of Speech* 73 (1987): 43–59.
Campbell, Joseph. *The Hero with a Thousand Faces.* New Jersey: Princeton University Press, 1949.
_____. *Myths to Live By.* New York: Viking Penguin, 1972.
Devarajan, Sharad. E-mail to the author. 30 August 2005.
"Dhoti." *Wikipedia, the Free Encyclopedia.* 25 October 2006. http://en.wikipedia.org/wiki/ Dhoti.
Fantastic Four. 23 September 2005. http://www.comicbooksources.com/news/newsitem.cg i?id=4279.

Forty, Jo. *Mythology: A Visual Encyclopedia.* New York: Sterling, 2001: 120–136.

Fingeroth, Danny. *Superman on the Couch.* New York: Continuum International, 2004.

Gustines, George G. "Girl Power Fuels Manga Boom in U.S." *New York Times.* 28 Dec. 2004. 28 Dec. 2004. http://www.nytimes.com/2004/12/28/books.

"Indian_comics." *Wikipedia, the Free Encyclopedia.* 25 October 2006. http:en.wikipedia.org/wiki/Category: Indian_comics.

Jemas, Bill, Mark Bagley, and Brian Michael Bendis. *Ultimate Spider-Man Vol. 1: Power and Responsibility.* New York: Marvel Comics, 2002.

Jones, Gerard. *Men of Tomorrow: Geeks, Gangsters, and the Birth of The Comic Book.* Cambridge, Mass.: Basic Books, 2004.

Kang, Jevan J. *Spider-Man India: Limited Collector Edition.* New Jersey: Gotham Entertainment, 2004.

"Marvel Invades Middle East." *The Beat.* 21 October 2005. 8 November 2005. http://209. 198.111.165/the beat/archives/2005/10marvel_invades.html.

Medhurst, Martin J. and Michael A. DeSousa. "Political Cartoons as Rhetorical Form: A Taxonomy of Graphic Discourse." *Communication Monographs* 48 (September 1981): 197–236.

Morrison, Matthew C. "The Role of the Political cartoonist in Image Making," *Central States Speech Journal* 20 (Winter 1969): 252–60.

Pustz, Matthew. *Comic Book Culture: Fanboys and True Believers.* Jackson: University Press of Mississippi, 1999.

Singh, Arun. *A Brave New World: Gotham Studios Asia Talks New Launches.* 3 December 2004. 3 December 2004. http://www.comicbooksources.com/news/newsitem.cgi?id=4500.

"Spider-Man." 25 October 2006. http://www.marvel.com/universe/Spider-Man.

"Spider-Man India." 25 October 2006. http://www.gothamcomics.com/spiderman_india/.

Spider-Man India 1. Marvel Comics. January 2005.

Spider-Man India 2. Marvel Comics. February 2005.

Spider-Man India 3. Marvel Comics. March 2005.

Spider-Man India 4. Marvel Comics. April 2005.

Tagore, Rabindranath. "Tell Me A Story." In *A Treasury of Modern Asian Stories.* Eds., Milton Daniel and William Clifford. New York: Mentor Books, 1961. 15–16.

Turner, Kathleen J. "Comic Strips: A Rhetorical Perspective," *Central States Speech Journal* 28 (Spring 1977): 24–35.

Weiland, Jonah. *Deepak Chopra Starts Comic Book Company.* 29 November 2004. 30 November 2004. http://www.comicbooksources.com/news/newsitem.cgi?id=4474.

Wright, Bradford W. *Comic Book Nation.* Baltimore: John Hopkins University Press, 2001.

Zakaria, Fareed. "India Rising" *Newsweek.* 6 March 2006: 34–42.

Warren Ellis Is the Future of Superhero Comics: How to Write Superhero Stories That Aren't Superhero Stories

BRENDAN RILEY

As the hyperbolic title suggests, this essay explores the path of the superhero genre with a wry grin. In navigating the critical passageways that follow, it became clear that my own experience had shaped not only my understanding of the material (as it inevitably must), but also my expectations about what the genre was and could be. The archaeology of the genre surrounding the argument below springs irrevocably from my history as a comic reader. From this critical milieu, I suggest that Warren Ellis' comic book work pushes superhero comics in new directions by using and abusing the conventions of the genre made explicit during the "revisionist" period following *The Watchmen* and *Dark Knight Returns*.

INTRODUCTION

I came late to comic books. During a graduate course in comics and animation, a fellow graduate student gave me some independent comics to read, Brian Michael Bendis' hilarious *Fortune and Glory* among them. By the next week, I was ready to buy some comics for myself, so I sought my friend's advice and bought several single issues and two trade paperbacks: *The Dark Knight Returns* and *Watchmen*. Up to that point, the Batman in my head came from movies: he was Tim Burton's dark ninja, a gloomy guy with a nifty car who lurked in shadows. Ignorant of Frank Miller's influence on Burton, I was pleased to find that Batman worked like I thought he should. Alan Moore's writing in *Watchmen*, at the same time, captured me with its complex treatment of superheroes.

In the years since that first trip to the comic store, I have devoured numerous comics and become acquainted with comics that preceded these texts. At the time, however, I had no idea that I had started with two of the seminal comics of the modern age. Despite this auspicious start, my favorite comic was another one I bought that day, a new series about police detectives in a world of superheroes by the author of that indie comic my friend had given me—Brian Michael Bendis' *Powers.*

At first glance, *Powers* seems to be a superhero comic. Michael Avon Oeming's angular art lends itself to this sort of reading. The protagonist, Christian Walker, has enormously broad shoulders and the gait of a superhero; in fact, he's a "fallen" superhero, someone who *used* to have superpowers. There are godlike men and women whizzing about in capes, and there are nasty supervillains. At the same time, the story focuses on the character development of average people in the superhero world. The relationship between Walker and his new partner, Deena Pilgrim, becomes the centerpoint of the comic for the first several story arcs.[1] In effect, Bendis hijacks the superhero genre in favor of the police procedural.[2] What made *Powers* interesting to me was its disregard of the traditional superhero tropes, its world that explored the moments after the super-battles were over, that suggested a life for regular people in a world of superheroes.

In a sense, all new comic readers encounter superheroes the same way I did—backwards. The readily available comics are the newest ones—they sit prominently on the most visible shelves and they can be ordered ahead of time. Back issues, though more available since trade paperbacks became common, are still an iffy game, demanding patience and perseverance from readers hoping to acquire a full storyline or a run of a specific title. Thus, for most readers, superheroes *are* their present selves. Batman of the 1950s is inevitably encountered after present day Batman, and thus the former seems hopelessly hokey. However, these corny back issues still play an important role, haunting the present comics, influencing both narratives and form.

As with most literary movements, the mainstream superhero genre has undergone several large-scale shifts in focus. Many scholars suggest that *Dark Knight Returns* and *Watchmen* began the genre's revisionist era. Revisionist texts re-consider the basic tenets of their genre. In *Mystery, Violence, and Popular Culture,* John Cawelti describes four stages in genre revision, each of which we can see in the evolution of the superhero genre. The four modes—burlesque, nostalgia, nostalgic demystification, and reaffirmation—emerge in varying orders, sometimes simultaneously, sometimes individually (201–209). *Watchmen,* for instance, seems to work in the nostalgic and reaffirming modes, its stylized art and explicit genre exploration evoking comic history and crafting a new superhero text. *Dark Knight Returns* uses its nostalgia to demystify its genre (more on this demystification below).

Moore's and Miller's texts mark the beginning of an onslaught of "dark" superheroes. These ham-handed revisionist texts featured antiheroes who killed too often and brooded too much. In doing so, they seemed to sound the death knell of the genre as it currently stood. Cawelti suggests that revisionist movements sometimes signal the end of the genre in its current form, though later artists often find new ways to use the genre (209). As the smoke from revisionist comics has cleared, the comic book industry seems to be making tentative inroads into the space opened up by the movement, namely the space to reconsider what the genre is and how it will function (as opposed to focusing on fulfilling the antithesis of the genre). Of course the old heroes march on, but alongside them new stories are emerging that challenge the traditional modes of the superhero comic, that operate in conversation with the genre but push it in new directions (stories like *Powers*).

One of the premier authors pushing this change is Warren Ellis, author of *The Authority, Planetary, Transmetropolitan,* and many other comics. Ellis, along with a few other progressive comic writers, has written texts that challenge the superhero monomyth in a few key ways. Ellis' recent comics—particularly *The Authority, Transmetropolitan, Global Frequency,* and the Apparat Comics Singles Group—embody the shift taking place in superhero comics. These four comics show how writers might take advantage of the end of the revisionist era, and describe potential arcs the genre might take in the future; they are the avant-garde of the superhero market. Already the market has begun following.

My approach to this piece requires two caveats. First, I construct my argument about the superhero genre on the meta-textual level. In doing so, I focus mostly on the narrative and semiotic components of these stories. While discussions of the art do arise occasionally, they play little explicit part in the argument here. The absence of specific commentary about panels and layout should not be taken as denial of their importance, but rather as a matter of space restrictions and rhetorical convenience. Second, the text below makes a strong case that Warren Ellis' work is emblematic of the future of superhero comics. Ellis serves here as a particularly strong example of the potential for superhero comics and the medium as a whole, rather than as the only creator producing such work. Absence of references to other comics performing these operations are indicative of, again, space restrictions and rhetorical convenience.

THE AUTHORITY

In *How to Read Superhero Comics and Why,* Geoff Klock reads the revisionist comic scene since *Dark Knight Returns* and *Watchmen,* arguing that comics evolve along the lines that previous literature has evolved, namely, under the "anxiety of influence." In suggesting that Miller and Ellis bookend a revisionist period operating under Harold Bloom's schema, Klock provides an essential springboard for my argument. In essence, I suggest that the space cleared by the revisionist movement becomes fertile ground for the kind of work Ellis has produced in the last few years—comics that challenge readers to rethink their very notions of what superhero comics can be.

Bloom suggests, as Klock explains, that authors operate in constant conversation with their predecessors. Bloom writes:

Influence, as I conceive it, means that there are *no* texts but only relationships *between* texts. These relationships depend on a critical act, a misreading or misprision, that one poet performs upon another, and that does not differ in kind from the necessary critical acts performed by every strong reader upon every text he encounters. The influence-relation governs reading as it governs writing, and reading is therefore a miswriting just as writing is a misreading. As literary history lengthens, all poetry necessarily becomes verse-criticism, just as all criticism becomes prose-poetry [qtd in Klock 13].

In other words, for Bloom, all authors re-interpret texts that came before them. Works are (to borrow a phrase) always already in a critical relationship with their ancestry. Klock makes the convincing argument that "superhero comic books are an especially good place to witness the structure of misprision, because as a serial narrative that has been running for more than sixty years, reinterpretation becomes part of its survival code" (13). Comics operate within limited parameters, so creators must constantly reinterpret comic history as they write.

With the rise of revisionist superhero comics (a period noted for the *Dark Knight*'s shallow imitators), the ramification of this anxiety comes full circle as authors clear the ground for their own work by psychologically "killing" the work of their predecessors in an Oedipal bloodbath. Klock describes this aspect of Miller's work: "*The Dark Knight Returns* becomes the *fons et origo* (the fountainhead and the origin) of the revisionary superhero narrative. Miller himself has gone into Batman's fictional history and selected elements for use in his work, taking many elements ... and making them his own.... Batman's (and Miller's) struggle is not to control any villain but to master preceding visions of himself and his tradition" (47–8).

Miller engages with the Batman mythos by highlighting some key contradictions in the superhero genre. For example, Miller notes the soft treatment of violence prevalent in the industry by means of a small inset showing Batman's batarangs imbedded in a thug's forearm. This simple element contrasts strongly with the traditional batarang, which disarmed criminals in the manner of an old west deadeye shooting guns out of hands. The logical batarang, Miller suggests (via Klock), works more like a throwing star—it isn't lethal, necessarily, but certainly causes wounds.

Miller's take on the Batman/Joker conflagration highlights even more strongly the gaps in Batman's backstory logic. The Dark Knight comes to realize the folly of capturing Joker alive, tallying up each murder as a strike against himself for failing to kill Joker earlier. The final confrontation, in which Batman seems prepared to kill the Joker, highlights the grim reality that *should* haunt Batman, himself a vigilante. Klock explains that these touches of realism demolish and envelop the previous Batman mythos, opening new spaces from which to proceed. He also suggests that such ground clearing counteracts the hazy nature of past events in superhero narratives (as described by Umberto Eco[3]). Having done so, the way is opened for the genre to expand beyond the limits imposed by the accumulated strictures of tradition.

Klock's argument bookends Richard Reynolds' chapters on *Batman: The Dark Knight Returns* and *Watchmen*, comics that Reynolds anticipated were the beginning of a revisionist trend that would open new doors for the superhero genre. Klock suggests the end of that revisionist trend arrives with Warren Ellis' *The Authority* and *Planetary*, in whose pages doppelgangers for golden and silver age comics are revisited and disposed of. In particular, *Planetary*'s snowflake—a technological embodiment of a multitude of universes—comes to embody the history of comics, and the defeat of the enemies held within.

In *The Authority*, Klock argues, Ellis explores the ramifications of the revisionist model from the other side, working not to destroy the back history of comics, but rather pulling the current trends to their foregone conclusion. Where *Dark Knight Returns* suggested replacing a restrictive government with the fascist politics of its vigilante hero, *The Authority* actually does so. Its story tells of superheroes who go from cleaning up after the messes people make (as one might say Superman does) to becoming an international policing agency acting on its own authority. "*The Authority* gleefully embraces the questionable politics entailed by the terms of the superhero narrative.... The Authority accepts, along with their almost sublime levels of power, the responsibility to change the world and carry humanity where they believe humanity should go.... *The Authority* is the zenith of the superhero qua power fantasy, and the degree to which readers enjoy the title is the degree to which they participate in the genre for precisely this reason" (136–7).

Klock argues that *The Authority* draws out the ramifications of superpowered humans in much the same way that *Dark Knight Returns* drew out the ramifications of the Batman myth—elaborating on details and premises with an eye toward realism. Thus, while the supercharged antics of the Authority satisfy the stereotypical fanboy desire for machismo, the implications of these decisions complicate the superhero tradition.[4] Gone are the "moral constraints" of the traditional superhero story (139); the line between villain and hero vanishes and leaves the reader to his "obscene enjoyment."

For instance, the first storyline in the series rejects the traditional notion that superheroes must be beholden to human society. Issue one begins with an army of super villains destroying Moscow, killing thousands of people while the directors of the old superhero group, Stormwatch, look on helplessly. When Jenny Sparks (a woman with electric powers embodying the spirit of the 20th century) shows up to offer her help,

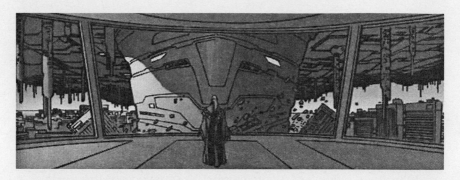

The Midnighter crushes Gamorra's headquarters with the Authority's giant spaceship. The pithy dialogue (Kaizen Gamorra's "I only wanted to have some fun" and the Midnighter's "I love being me") underscores the way Ellis brought "obscene enjoyment" to an apex. From *The Authority: Relentless* **(New York: DC/Wildstorm, 2000).**

another character asks, "Who's going to stop them, Jenny?" She answers, with the pith of an action-movie star, "A higher authority." Later, in the final confrontation with the head villain, Gamorrah (a Ming-the-Mercilous doppelganger), the action sequence rings with that same revelry in power. The Midnighter—Ellis' answer to Batman—brings an enormous spaceship down to crush Gamorrah's headquarters; two side-by-side panels maximize the reader's revelry, showing Gamorrah watching his doom approach and then showing the Midnighter's quip, "I love being me" (*The Authority* 4).

At the same time that Ellis' heroes revel in their power, they also become active in defending humanity in ways other superheroes have rarely done. In Mark Millar's first issues of the comic, for instance, the team stops a genocide being perpetrated by a third-world dictator, and they use their giant spaceship to perform rescue operations. The Engineer, a cyborg member of the team, says, "If towns are being butchered, we can stop it. If people need political asylum, we've got a ship that's fifty miles wide. God, I know this is going to sound pathetic, but I've never felt more like a super-hero in my entire life" (*The Authority*, issue 12). As such, the Authority claims to be a moral arbiter in a way that has always been a subtle part of the superhero genre, but has never been overt.

Klock suggests that *The Authority*, in its hyperbolic enjoyment of power and its traumatic origin, breaks with the old tradition, hinting at the possibilities to come in superhero comics. I suggest that in *The Authority*, Ellis also reaches the apex of the revisionist trend. The comic violates every restraint or generic limit and in doing so, ultimately seeks a different kind of superhero story—it becomes something else, as Cawelti might say. In examining Ellis' contemporary and continuing work, it becomes clear that *The Authority* was the first in a salvo of texts designed to begin landscaping the new space available in the post-revisionist era.

MODERN MYTHOLOGY AND SCIENCE FICTION

One way to begin understanding the changes Ellis proposes to super-hero comics is to examine their place in the larger landscape of literary genres. Richard Reynolds' influential *Superheroes: A Modern Mythology* suggests that superheroes represent a modern incarnation of the traditional mythical hero; their specific tropes and strictures give them continuity while their tendency to assimilate elements of contemporary culture gives them continuing relevance. Because "the superhero has a mission to preserve society, not to re-invent it" (77), s/he embodies the mythical values assigned to her. Batman, in *The Dark Knight Returns*, rebels against this ideal, chastising Superman for his allegiance to law and order above justice. *The Authority* is, of course, an explicit denial of the stricture against re-inventing society.

More importantly, the serial nature of the comic book creates a strange narrative state that amplifies the mythical effect of the superhero. For the bulk of comic book history, change in the superhero narrative was restricted to a limited timeframe—a storyline or often a single issue. The superhero's essential characteristics remained the same from issue to issue so that readers could follow the stories told at any one time. In "The Myth of Superman," Umberto Eco suggests that this unchanging character results also from the fact that the superhero cannot age and thus only the history relevant to the story at hand resides in the superhero's memory. The myth also defines those unchanging key parts of the hero's character. Any "one element of a character's myth can be used to generate a potentially unlimited number of texts, even texts which seem to 'tell the same story'" (Reynolds 48). With no memory and an unchanging set of traits, the superhero becomes very much like a member of a mythological pantheon. Just as the Greek god Zeus ruled with a fist full of lightning bolts and used disguises to hide his philandering from his jealous wife, so Superman embodies American idealism, hides his identity, and agonizes over Lois. The chronological order of events in these mythological structures do not matter—whether Perseus came before Heracles matters no more than whether Mxyzptlk appeared before Lex Luthor.

With the emergence of Marvel and the extension of story length, another concept arrived to help maintain the mythical state of the super-heroes: continuity. While careful attention to continuity may appear to erase the hazy history mentioned above, it actually supports the mythological structures of superhero comics. Reynolds writes: "Continuity, and above all metatextual structural continuity, is the strategy through which superhero texts most clearly operate as myths. Continuity provides the interaction with the audience which characterizes mythological discourse.... The continuity is the *langue* in which each particular story is an utterance" (45).

In short, continuity provides a method for maintaining the structural necessities mentioned above *and* allowing time to progress. Time both moves forward (in continuity and in adopting elements of contemporary culture) and stands still (in the hero's costume, attitudes, and symbolism). Continuity also provides guidelines within which new writers can tell stories about the hero. Writers will often reinterpret a superhero's origin story to "bring some new aspect of the character to light" (48). In doing so, the bullpen of writers working on a given superhero comic become like oral storytellers, shifting elements of their poems around to suit the audiences and the constraints of meter. In the balance between constant mythical elements and changing story lines allowed by continuity, comic books found a way to maintain their mythical characters for decades.

In the second half of *Superheroes*, Reynolds suggests that the revisionist forces shaping comics since the late 1980s disrupt this mythological function. Reynolds points to several factors that allow these new texts to alter the way superhero comics work. First, he highlights the significant emergence of the "graphic novel" as a change in the superhero comic market. The inclusion of the creators' names, the publication of collected editions (or *trade paperbacks*) on high-quality paper stock, and the price of these editions all point to an intentional literary thrust in the authorship of these comics. Second, Reynolds highlights the revisionist inquiry into the superhero genre. In *The Dark Knight Returns*, for example, "the political underpinning for superhero actions was examined [and unlike previous such explorations] ... this questioning has reached a point where there are no longer any (offered) solutions" (101). Works like *The Dark Knight Returns* and *Watchmen* disturb static signification, the mythological aspect of superhero comics; they question the unchanging nature of the serial superhero. So what happens to superhero comics when revisionist approaches disrupt the balance created by the mythological form?

Ellis' work after *The Authority* and *Planetary* holds one answer. Ellis' more contemporary work has begun occupying the space cleared by the revisionist comics of the late 1980s and 1990s. In particular, three of his works, *Transmetropolitan*, *Global Frequency*, and the Apparat comics singles push the boundaries of the superhero genre and suggest just how open comics can be.

At the same time, Ellis' approach to writing comics pushes his stories away from the mythological limitations on the superhero genre by means of science fiction. Where many superhero writers are constrained by the mythological requirements of the serial narrative, the writer who approaches comics as science fiction can move in different directions. Most obviously, the writer can leave the boundaries created by the mythological continuity Reynolds describes. In some ways, superhero comics become science fiction by default when their mythological elements are removed. Ellis makes the most of such expanded possibilities by side-stepping the continuity constraints in favor of original works. Such texts allow him to write "speculative fiction" that needs not rely on the genre's continuity requirements. For instance, Ellis crafted *The Authority* to explore the *idea* of superbeings and the Justice League of America. Yet the originality of his characters gives him the freedom to move them beyond normal continuity and constraints. He is able to tease out, following Miller's lead from *Dark Knight Returns*, the ramifications of the superhero team.[5]

In doing so, Ellis explores how writers and artists can make use of the ground cleared by the revisionist wave of the 1980s. Like the "soft" science-fiction writers of the 1960s, modern comic writers can use the now-flexible boundaries of the genre to expand its possibilities.

TRANSMETROPOLITAN

Two years before *Planetary* launched, Ellis began writing a comic that would ultimately last five years: *Transmetropolitan*. In many ways, the comic— sometimes abbreviated as *Transmet*—is the first of Ellis' new brand of superhero comics. *Transmet* has all the hallmarks of a superhero comic and yet simultaneously disrupts the traditions of the genre in several key ways.

Ellis has crafted a text that shares many key tropes of the traditional superhero comic. Working from Reynolds' list of superhero tropes (16), it becomes clear that Jerusalem is modeled in the superhero vein. Reynolds describes the superhero as someone "marked out from society" whose "devotion to justice overrides even his devotion to the law." The superhero's exceptional skills contrast strongly with the ordinary people around him, and "although ultimately above the law, superheroes can be capable of considerable patriotism and moral loyalty to the state, though not necessarily to the letter of its laws." Reynolds explains that Superman fits each of these tropes very well—obviously his superhuman abilities mark him as different, but his wholesome upbringing on a farm gives him a sense of justice to match his super strength. He also strongly values justice, even if he needs to dodge the letter of the law occasionally in order to be just (16).

Transmetropolitan's protagonist, Spider Jerusalem, shares many of these traits. His preferences and lifestyle set him apart from the hoi polloi populating The City—the series opens with Spider, drawn to look remarkably like Alan Moore, hiding out in his mountain compound. Like Superman, he's drawn distinctively: his costume is less flashy (a suit with distinctive two-colored eyeglasses) but he has tattoos. His "superpower" is his weekly column, which he regularly uses to promote justice. The comic articulates a world that has gone mad, making the normal man a superhero, his relatively ordinary ability to write becoming his superpower. Jerusalem regards defending freedom as his personal responsibility: "There's people like me there to squeeze the President into doing what's right" (*The New Scum* 94).

At the same time, *Transmet* violates several of Reynolds' key tropes—Jerusalem has no superpowers, no alter ego, and no special magic. In light of these changes, it becomes clear how remarkable *Transmet* is—Ellis used the conventions of the superhero genre to create and publish his comic about a gonzo journalist. While the comic was published by a mainstream press, its content might have relegated it to the independent shelf if not for these generic tropes. The fight for freedom of the press in a dystopic future is a far cry from the capes and briefs of traditional superheroes.

But the derivations from Reynolds' character schema are not what make *Transmet* interesting. Rather, it is the way the text violates other tropes of the superhero comic to advance a more developed, complex story than would otherwise be possible. Specifically, the five-year run of the comic involves—primarily—a single storyline. While this is not uncommon in recent comics (*100 Bullets* is a prime example of a similar arc), extended story lines that change the basic relationships of the characters are rare in mainstream serial comics. In his short piece about the end of *Transmetropolitan*, Cory Doctorow reflects on Ellis' ambitious five-year story arc: "Comics repel the casual reader with open-ended story arcs. That's how publishers lure you into buying a Spider-Man funnybook every month, so you shoulder-surf Peter Parker in one adventure after another. Not so with *Transmet*, which unfolds in three acts throughout 60 issues—each a complete tale and an inextricable part of the beginning, middle, and end of the meta-story" (Doctorow).

Because *Transmet* was both limited in scope and did not need to answer to a continuity established before the author began writing the comic, Ellis was able to push the boundaries of where the narrative could go.[6] While individual episodes did often offer closure to the reader, they also usually played to the metastory that did not give the reader such room.

Second, *Transmetropolitan* made the shift from the superhero serial's usual mythological melodrama to science fiction. As alluded above, Reynolds suggests that the sense of wonder often evoked by superhero comics is produced using science as a kind of modern magic. He writes: "Science is treated as a special form of magic, capable of both good and evil. Scientific concepts and terms are introduced freely into plots and used to create atmosphere and add background detail to artwork—but the science itself is at most only superficially plausible, often less so, and the prevailing mood is mystical rather than rational. Explicitly 'magic' powers are able to coexist quite comfortably with apparently scientific ones" (16).

While it can be solidly argued that a significant body of science fiction, often called "soft" sf, relies on its concepts as ethical backdrops rather than as "plausible" ideas, there exists a strong difference between these stories and superhero comics. Because superhero comics rely on science as a background to uphold the mythologies of their heroes, their science

Spider Jerusalem stands separate from the people around him but still plans to defend them, just as superheroes usually do. From page 6 of *Transmetropolitan: The New Scum* (New York: Vertigo, 2000).

works solely as a mystical force, separating the story from the reader's world and life-experience. Soft science fiction, on the other hand, explicitly uses the sf elements to highlight and connect with elements of the reader's world.

For example, Ursula LeGuin's novel *The Left Hand of Darkness* takes as its premise a planet where people are androgynous, their gender only emerging during a specific phase of the month, called *Kemmering*. LeGuin includes almost no science to suggest how such a thing might be possible, but rather explores the sociological ramifications of a genderless society by drawing on models and cues from contemporary culture. *X-Men*, by contrast, also explores questions of prejudice and racism, but it does so using dubious science to explain its characters and, at the same time, make them otherworldly. Science fiction presents seemingly different people in ways that highlight their similarity to ourselves; mythical structures do the opposite.

Transmetropolitan's move, then, is to embrace the broad tradition of science-fiction at the same time as it draws upon the mythological superhero. In doing so, Ellis provides a bridge between the two and piggybacks the legitimacy that science-fiction stories developed in the 1960s. Whereas the mythological component of comics essentially excluded them from being science fiction, Ellis' narratives open a space to consider the changing and evolving world of tomorrow—a world rejecting to the rigid narrative structure of traditional superhero comics.

THE FUTURE OF SUPERHERO COMICS

Warren Ellis is one of the most prolific comic writers working today (second only, perhaps, to Brian Michael Bendis). Ellis produces so many comics that any scholar (or fanboy) has trouble keeping up. In recent years, though, he has produced two comics that seem to build within the space he opened up with *The Authority* and *Transmetropolitan*. These two comics play with the superhero genre in the way science-fiction stories have played with mainstream culture—they suggest alternate paths for mainstream comics to take, places for the superhero genre to go. *Global Frequency* and the Apparat singles function like science-fiction thought experiments or, to use a comic book trope, alternate futures for superhero comics. If the revisionist 1980s and '90s (crowned by *The Authority* and *Planetary*) signaled an apex for the superhero comic as we know it, where can these comics go next?

GLOBAL FREQUENCY

Published in 2002 and 2003, this twelve issue series imagines a worldwide task force of 1001 people of varying expertise who work to counteract worldwide threats. The group's coordinator, Miranda Zero, organizes the activities of the Global Frequency by means of a central operator—a woman named Aleph—and mobile phones. The Global Frequency deals with a vast variety of threats, from invading alien thought memes to psychotic terrorists to malfunctioning secret government space weapons.[7]

Like a more traditional superhero comic, Ellis and his co-creators (each issue is drawn by a different artist) use emblems to signify the "team" aspect of the group, and Ellis recycles the trope of a central control dispatcher he used in both *StormWatch* and *The Authority* as well as the public nature and role of the group. He also adapts several elements from *Planetary*, including the virtually limitless resources of the shadowy agency and the short narrative arcs of one or two issues per story. *Global Frequency* also brings back a similar array of enemies and villains as that which emerged in *Planetary*.

In light of the shifting ground under the superhero narrative, *Global Frequency* might very well function as Ellis' answer to the superhero team comic. We might even suggest it as the bastard child of *Planetary* and *The Authority*, the former having returned from its hiatus and begun publication during *Global Frequency*'s run. If *Planetary* is, as Klock argues, the comic that cleans out the attic of the superhero genre, *Global Frequency* might be the new tenant. Beyond adapting elements of his previous team comics to the new text, Ellis makes some important changes that reverberate both within the genre and with the larger culture.

One of the more important changes occurring in the shift to the 1001 members of the Global Frequency is the integration of the digital mind-set into the superhero comic. Whereas most superhero teams have a central base of operations, the Global Frequency could best be described as rhizomatic. For example, in the recent Marvel comic *The Ultimates*, the super-team operates out of a government funded high-tech base in Manhattan harbor called the Triskellion. *The Authority*, similarly, works from a giant interdimensional "shiftship" that orbits the Earth. *Global Frequency*, on the other hand, does not have a base of operations. The Global Frequency operates rhizomatically, its members living in semi-secret until they are activated; GF functions much like a revolutionary group—only its leaders know very much about who the members are, and members only know one another when they work together on a job. The only regular locale revealed in the series is Aleph's command center, which functions more like a switchboard than a gathering place. *Global Frequency* explicitly engages with real-world technological networking as an essential part of its operations. Aside from the satellite cellphones each member of the GF carries, the series features spy satellites, internet connections, LAN systems, spy cameras, unmanned flying drones, GPS tracking, and more.

Global Frequency also shifts the criteria for choosing its heroes. The heroes in teams such as JLA and *The Authority* have stunning, outrageous superpowers that virtually assure their victory in any conflict they face (one side effect of these power bonanzas is to demand uber-powerful villains, as in each storyline of *The Authority*, whose first three story arcs pit them against an army of super-powered villains, an alien invasion force from a technologically superior alternate universe, and God). These superheroes represent straightforward causes and easy-to-solve problems. Their black and white approach to the world reinforces the mythological aspect of their texts, an approach parodied in *The Authority*. By contrast, the individual members of GF come from all walks of life. In the twelve issues, we see numerous military or intelligence operatives, but we also see a venture capitalist with his own spaceship, a *le parkour* runner—someone who treats "the city as an obstacle course…. Like Tarzan with buildings" ("The Run" 3)—and many others. The Global Frequency demands numerous talents and a wide variety of inputs.

Like the rhizomatic organism it is, the GF also adopts people as it needs them. Several times in the series, characters will declare themselves members of the GF, and deputize others by saying (or shouting) "you are on the Global Frequency!" (*GF7* 5). As such, the group embodies some of the key elements of digital culture, using emergent strategies to connect disparate members. The ordinariness of each individual member is trumped by their ability to work together efficiently. In essence, GF embodies Ellis' hope for the Internet as a source of communication and community. Where top-down hierarchies like *The Authority* fail to successfully navigate (or just outright reject) the challenging waters of world government, *Global Frequency* regularly makes use of non-superpowered people to save the world.

A final key distinction between Global Frequency and other super teams is its focus on realism in its stories. *Global Frequency* embraces the science-fictional model mentioned above—nearly every GF story plays out one or more of scientific developments that have emerged recently. As opposed to traditional superhero stories, in which science simply replaces magic as an explanation for the exceptional people in the stories, *Global Frequency* wrestles with real scientific dilemmas such as stem cell research (*GF* 9) and the decay of Cold War weaponry (*GF* 12). In doing so, the comic becomes science fiction, and thus pushes the superhero genre into new territory.

APPARAT COMICS

In late 2004, Warren Ellis published four comic "singles." As he explains in the notes at the end of each issue, he imagined the four comics, each a first issue for an imaginary comic series, to be the comic book equivalent of the musical single. He writes: "The Apparat Singles Group. An imaginary line of comics singles. Four imaginary first issues of imaginary series from an imaginary line of comics, even. This is what I think adventure comics would look like today if you blanked out the last sixty years of superhero comics. Yes, there would still be elements of great strangeness, because that's what the pulps traded on" (*Simon Spector* afterward).

Ellis describes the comics, published under their own imprint, as imaginary comics from an alternative history in which superhero comics did not overrun the rest of the pulps. Ellis imagines his four comics as future versions of pulp genres from the twenties: *Frank Ironwine* plays on the classic detective story; *quit city* asks how aviation heroes might have evolved; *Angel Stomp Future* seeks to mimic the mad, raucous, vicious science fiction of early pulps; *Simon Spector* comes closest to the traditional superhero genre, inheriting its tropes from urban pulp heroes like Doc Savage. As a group, Ellis imagines that the Apparat comics function like experimental trajectories, suggesting different ways the medium might evolve from its roots.

At the same time, these non-superhero comics converse with the superhero genre, drawing on it, informing it, and ultimately suggesting where it can go. The following brief survey avoids Ellis' explicit intent (to engage with four prominent pulp genres) in favor of elucidating the conversation these comics hold with the superhero genre. Ellis suggests that the Apparat Singles Group works like "response songs." The following sections touch briefly on the implications of these responses not to the pulp genres they draw from, but the superhero comics they stand against. If the Apparat Singles Group is "Elsewhere" fantasies at the level of genre, these analyses focus on the lessons the components teach about superhero comics.

FRANK IRONWINE

Frank Ironwine tells the story of a police detective and his new partner. Ironwine's methods are careful but intuitive—he works by understanding people rather than by focusing on clinical examination of the evidence. Ironwine's approach to crimes is "that minds and feelings [are] the way into crimes. That and maps" (*Frank Ironwine* afterword). Ellis explains this as a reaction to the current trend in crime fiction—the tendency to focus on the procedural, the CSI effect. Frank focuses on people and uses his understandings of social interaction to solve crimes.

It's no accident that Ironwine is the counterpoint to the colorless characters on CSI. Ellis complains that police procedurals have drained humanity from detective work, so he created a detective who works via his sense of the human. At the same time, Ironwine stands in opposition to the technological doohickery of the prototypical superhero detective, Batman. For instance, when Ironwine examines a crime scene, he uses no machines at all—he kneels on the floor, smells the air, examines the carpet, and draws conclusions. "It's not about blood chemistry and DNA and analyzing farts. It's about people. And history. Every damn time" (6). He also approaches interrogations differently. His scolding of his new partner explains just how different his approach is: "If that's what it takes. You hug them, you hold their hands, you touch their faces, you kiss them if that's what it takes. Anybody, *anybody* walking into an interrogation room is scared. I don't care what they say, how they handle themselves—they're scared of something.... In that room, you take that fear away. You bring them out of what they've done and you take it out of their hands" (14). Ironwine approaches interrogation as a humane act.

By contrast, Batman often uses methods the police would not be allowed to use. In *Dark Knight Returns*, for example, Batman brings a captive villain up to the top of a skyscraper and hangs him from a gargoyle to make him talk. Klock argues that the violence in *Dark Knight Returns* functions emblematically, reminding readers of all the violent acts that have occurred before. Ellis' diametrically opposed detective, in working by empathy, highlights the cruelty and viciousness of the vigilante model, and suggests an alternative to the model we've seen on comic covers for the last 80 years.

ANGEL STOMP FUTURE

The most blatantly science-fictional of the Apparat pieces, *Angel Stomp Future* follows an ultra-sexy "doctor" in a disgusting, trash-infested future as she explains how the future is horrible. Each panel bursts with throw-away ideas—robots having sex, a trash can for the disposal of unwanted children labeled "Retroactive Abortion Device," people with every cyborg contraption imaginable—as well as images of grit, dirt, and scum. Juan Jose Ryp's art overwhelms the reader with detail, and the black-and-white presentation makes some of the images nearly inscrutable. The overflow of information feels very much like what *Transmetropolitan* was moving toward. Spider Jerusalem's world was nearly as chaotic as this, and nearly as shocking.

At the same time, *Angel Stomp Future* steps further away from the super-hero model, expanding the premise started in *Transmet* and explicitly engaging with a science-fiction aesthetic, rather than a magical-mytholog-ical one. Ellis acknowledges as much in both his afterword to the comic and in the comic itself, in which Angel says: "This is science fiction. Come [*sic*] from the word scientifiction, coined by a publisher of electrical mag-azines called Hugo Gernsback.... The essentials never change. I mean, from where you are now imagine going back a hundred years. It's only the details and the consumer goods that change. The scope of your experi-ence changes, but the essentials remain the same" (7, 14).

Angel Stomp Future embraces all the elements of the science fiction genre, but it also serves a metaphorical purpose—it embodies the possi-bilities for the future of superhero comics. Angel's speech describes the process of science-fiction authorship: changing a few details to highlight the effect they have on culture. The comic also exacerbates the disinte-gration of the line between villain and protagonist, as Angel turns out to be malevolent toward her dystopian surroundings.

In fact, her attack on her culture—the launching of a deadly meme-virus—positions her as the antithesis of a superhero (or science-hero). She seeks to destroy the world rather than save it. This malevolence echoes the problems that arise in *The Authority* during Mark Millar's run. In par-ticular, the members of the super-team get so headstrong that they begin to neglect their duties in favor of debauchery and drugs. When they're forced out and replaced by corporate-sponsored copies, it becomes clear how the superhero can easily slip into the role of super villain.[8] Because Angel ends up being a super villain, the comic's title could use a pronoun and tense correction: Angel Stomps on the Future.[9]

QUIT CITY

In *quit city*, Emma Peirson resigns her commission with the Aeropi-ratika, a sort of heroic group of pilots, and returns to her hometown. She finds that everyone she knew has been following her career as a superstar pilot, and are both shocked and disappointed that she has quit. Her jour-ney back into regular life shapes the issue of the comic. All heroic events occur in the past, referred to only in dialogue. In his afterword to *quit city*, Ellis explains that his solution to the lost glamour of the pilot was to make the comic about someone who has lost her own glamour—hence, a character who quits the romantic life of the aviator.

quit city is the most 'conventional' of the Apparat comics, in that it most directly mirrors another body of work. Unlike the other three comics, *quit city* fits nicely into the rose-colored nostalgic/revisionist cannon most represented by Kurt Busiek's *Astro City* or Jeph Loeb's *A Superman for All Seasons*. In *Astro City*, the everyday and the superheroic are mixed, giving the reader another perspective on the events of the superhero world. The resulting stories reinforce the superhero mythos, shoring up the genre's boundaries as Cawelti suggested such nostalgia does. Cleverly, *quit city* uses the same nostalgic drive, drawing on the trope of the pilot hero, but shifts into an exploration of more mundane questions of day-to-day human existence (such as how to return to one's hometown). By avoiding the reaffirmation of its generic parent, *quit city* represents a metaphorical retort to the kinds of stories told in *Astro City*. Ellis here suggests that such comics can focus on superheroes as people without returning to the superhero mythos; he urges us to consider whether we need the *super* in *superhero*.

SIMON SPECTOR

Simon Spector embraces the pulp genre most closely associated with superheroes: adventurers. Like the science heroes such as Batman and Ironman, Spector operates from a position of wealth and (slight) madness. *Simon Spector* tells the tale of a wealthy detective who uses a special drug to greatly speed up his incredible powers of cognition. He uses this increased speed to hunt down and ultimately execute one of his old villains.

Ellis suggests, again in the afterword to the issue, that Spector draws on the old pulp heroes such as the Shadow or Doc Savage. These characters, Ellis reminds us, operated in a very different way from the super-powered Boy Scouts that were emerging in American comics: "These were the guys. The antecedents of the American superheroes, and sharing something of a tone with the British stuff too. These were the guys who didn't screw around. They were stinking rich, mad as arseholes and so bored or otherwise that they couldn't help but run around and get entangled with the bad guys. And did they turn the bad guys over to the cops? Did they hell. They shredded the bad guys with hails of bullets" (*Simon Spector* Afterword).

Ellis saw the pulp heroes as operating on their own authority, acting on their own sense of justice and with little regard for the law. As such, Spector represents the superhero as he would have evolved if the mythical, status-quo-protecting persona had not taken over comics books. As such, Spector represents the antithesis of Frank Ironwine, and the logical end of Batman. Ellis suggests that this trajectory—toward an almost mad hero with little regard for the law beyond his own sense of justice—is the ultimate result of the superhero genre. Indeed, Simon Spector would fit right in on the Authority's shiftship.

CONCLUSION

Much of Ellis' recent work seeks to push comics in new directions. While he has been contributing to several superhero comic lines (such as *Ironman* and the Marvel Ultimate universe), the remainder of his work opens new spaces for mainstream comics to go. His work on *The Authority* started with the superhero premise and brought out its dark ramifications. *Planetary*, simultaneously, began dismantling the history of superhero comics, engaging with (and rewriting) golden and silver age heroes to open spaces for other kinds of comics. Having cleared a path for comics to take (and created an audience for his own work), Ellis introduced three possible futures for superhero comics: *Transmetropolitan* smuggled a complex story with many non-traditional elements to a mainstream audience using tropes of the superhero genre; *Global Frequency* explored a different kind of solution to the superhero team comic in the networked democracy; finally, the Apparat comics posited four alternative futures that tease out, in classic science-fiction form, the ramifications of different elements of the genre.

At the same time, Bloom's "anxiety of influence" continues to haunt Ellis' work. Despite efforts from Ellis (and other writers, like Grant Morrison) to elude the superhero influence in mainstream comics, they are always already in conversation with the genre. Even Ellis' experiment in comics that suppose what comics would be like without superheroes can't help but engage in conversation with those superheroes. Thus, despite the trek through the revisionist cycle and the metacritical destruction of the conventions governing the genre, mainstream comics still find themselves haunted by superheroes.

Where superhero comics will go from here remains to be seen. The kinds of complex stories Ellis tells are becoming more common. Nontraditional comics such as Garth Ennis' *Preacher* and Brian Azarello's *100 Bullets* use some superhero tropes to create stories that are not about superheroes. Other comics, such as Brian Michael Bendis' *Powers* and Brian Vaughn's *Ex Machina* market themselves as superhero comics and then craft tales that elude easy classification within the genre. This is not to say that traditional models of superhero comics do not still thrive. Rather, that paths have opened in recent years for the genre to expand, for it to produce altered and expanded stories. We can only hope such paths continue to diverge in the years to come.

NOTES

1. Readers of *Powers* may object that the comic, in its later story arcs, returns powers to Walker and imbues Pilgrim with same. I suggest that the comic's early work establishes its characters in a different way than most superhero comics have previously, thus opening up a new way for readers to encounter the superhero figure.

2. Two other comics in recent years have made similar moves. *Top Ten*, which first appeared in 1999, imagined a city in which every resident was a superhero, as were police. *Gotham Central* (2003) focuses on the police in Gotham City. Of these two comics, the latter is much closer to the original concept of *Powers*, since the main characters must deal with the superheroes and supervillains around them.

3. Eco describes the conundrum of the mythological comic book superhero as being a character who must exist in entirety *and* function within standards of modern storytelling in which surprise and narrative twists play a prominent role. He suggests that Superman's specific problem is one of time—each time he accomplishes something, he gets one step closer to death and thus advances in a way that mythological characters cannot do. Eco writes: "The stories develop in a kind of oneiric climate—of which the reader is not aware at all—where what has happened before and what has happened after appear extremely hazy. The narrator picks up the strand of the event again and again, as if he had forgotten to say something and wanted to add details to what had already been said" (114).

4. Comics have often been described as "power fantasies" for young male readers. Matthew Pustz writes: "Many of the stories appealed to these children through very direct identification. Kids may have been attracted to Superman because of his colorful costume or his amazing feats of strength, but his unassuming secret identity as Clark Kent helped make the Jerry Siegel and Joe Shuster creation into, in the words of historian Jim Steranko, 'the graphic representation of the ultimate childhood dream-self'" (27).

At the same time, comic companies have a long history of courting active and rabid fanship among their readers. The most prominent stereotype is the "fanboy," someone who strives for coverage in both readership and ownership of his favorite titles. Fans who attained such coverage joined an insider's club and "saw themselves as superior to people who read other comic books or did not read comic books at all"(53). Thus *The Authority* embodies not only a physical power fantasy, but a mental one—the "good guys" are finally in charge.

5. Ellis fans will object that he has been writing comics for mainstream presses all along as well—for example, he recently finished a long story arc for the Marvel "Ultimates" universe that re-tells the Galactus storyline. I suggest that Ellis' work in already-established comics tends to be much less innovative than his original work. While he does regularly discuss the need for comic writers to push boundaries, he hasn't, to my knowledge, undertaken a major campaign to revise the shape of an established comic line, as Grant Morrison did in his run on *New X-Men*. Significantly, Morrison published his own "Manifesto" as part of the trade paperback for *New X-Men*. His essay calls for (and predicts) the kinds of changes I suggest occur in Ellis' work. I see the discovery of multiple instances of such innovation as helping to connect my local (and admittedly insular) argument to a more global picture of the superhero genre as it exists presently.

6. For the opposite side of this phenomenon, see Brian Michael Bendis' *Avengers: Disassembled*, in which he killed several members of the team and was savaged for it by the fan community. Klock also reminds us that Ellis made a similar move with another team comic—*StormWatch*—but *StormWatch*'s short run and smaller fan-base gave him some cover under which to do it.

7. Once again, we see a similarity between Ellis' work and that of Grant Morrison. In this case, Morrison's 13-issue series, *The Filth*, seems remarkably similar to *Global Frequency*. Morrison's series follows an extra-dimensional police force that handles the most extreme and horrible criminals or crimes. Far more surreal in its narrative style and method, one might suggest that *The Filth* goes even further in exploring the kinds of openings Ellis explores in *Global Frequency*. (The author thanks Terrence R. Wandtke for his excellent comments in revising this piece, particularly in bringing to mind the parallels between Morrison's work and Ellis.')

8. Mark Millar returns to this theme in volume 2 of *The Ultimates*, which features an Amer-

ican super-team being displaced by a world coalition that views the American activities as overstepping the bounds of responsible superheroism.

9. Regular Ellis readers will recognize the three word imperative form of the title from his popular "Edison Hate Future" feature on warrenellis.com.

WORKS CITED

Busiek, Kurt. *Astro City: Life in the Big City.* New York: DC/Wildstorm, 1999.

Cawelti, John. "Chinatown and Generic Transformation in Recent American Films." *Mystery, Violence, and Popular Culture.* Madison: U of Wisconsin Popular P, 2003.

Doctorow, Cory. "Exit Transmet: Graphic Novel of the Decade Fades to Black." *Wired.* 10 December 2002. 25 May 2006. *http://www.wired.com/wired/archive/10.12/play.html?pg=4.*

Eco, Umberto. "The Myth of Superman." *The Role of the Reader: Explorations in the Semiotics of Texts.* Bloomington: Indiana UP, 1979.

Ellis, Warren. *Angel Stomp Future.* Rantoul: Apparat Comics, December 2004.

_____. *The Authority: Relentless.* New York: DC/Wildstorm, 2000.

_____. *The Authority: Under New Management.* New York: DC/Wildstorm, 2000.

_____. *Frank Ironwine.* Rantoul: Apparat Comics, November 2004.

_____. *Global Frequency: Detonation Radio.* New York: DC/Wildstorm, 2004.

_____. *Global Frequency: Planet Ablaze.* New York: DC/Wildstorm, 2004.

_____. *quit city.* Rantoul: Apparat Comics, December 2004.

_____. *Simon Spector.* Rantoul: Apparat Comics, December 2004.

_____. *Transmetropolitan.* New York: DC/Vertigo, 1997–2002.

Klock, Geoff. *How to Read Superhero Comics and Why.* New York: Continuum, 2003.

LeGuin, Ursula. *The Left Hand of Darkness.* New York: Walker, 1969.

Miller, Frank. *The Dark Knight Returns.* New York: DC Comics, 1986.

Pustz, Matthew. *Comic Book Culture: Fanboys and True Believers.* Jackson: UP of Mississippi, 1999.

Reynolds, Richards. *Super Heroes: A Modern Mythology.* Jackson: UP of Mississippi, 1992.

PART III

SUPERHEROES IN
THE MULTI-MEDIA AGE

Wonder Woman as World War II Veteran, Camp Feminist Icon, and Male Sex Fantasy

MARC EDWARD DIPAOLO

Beautiful as Aphrodite Wise as Athena Strong as Hercules and Swifter than Mercury!

WHO IS WONDER WOMAN?

A warrior pacifist, a feminist sex symbol, a foreign-royal-turned-American-immigrant, and a devout pagan living in a secular age, Wonder Woman is a heroic figure who embodies a set of seemingly contradictory character traits. These traits, all of which have been a part of her persona since she made her debut in *All Star Comics* #8 in 1941, conspire to make her a highly complex and controversial figure. Seemingly torn between being an escapist action hero and an activist role model for young women around the world, Wonder Woman satisfies both roles when she is presented as having a charismatic, three-dimensional personality that comfortably contains these contradictions.

Unsurprisingly, different creative teams from different decades have pulled the character towards the political right (see comics written and drawn by Frank Miller and John Byrne during the 1990s) and towards the left (George Perez's stories from the 1980s); but the character has been at her most interesting, both dramatically and socially, during periods of great social unrest and military conflict—when she was a New Deal patriot during World War II, a symbol of ascendant feminism during the 1970s, a voice of the opposition during the Reagan years, and a meditation on power and responsibility during the current War on Terror. It is during these eras of global conflict that she speaks as a priestess praying for a time when soldiers will finally lay down their weapons and people from all cultures will finally live in peace.

I will argue that the stories which come closest to convincingly depicting Wonder Woman as a soldier of peace are the original, World War II era comic books and the episodes of the 1970s television series *Wonder Woman* featuring actress Lynda Carter's pitch-perfect portrayal of the heroine. Both the early comic books and the 1970s television adaptation cast the Amazon princess as more of a negotiator than a warrior, more of a women's advocate than a pin-up girl—but they also present her as a rich, complicated figure who has the potential to be all of the above. That having been stated, I agree with cultural critics such as Gloria Steinem and Matthew J. Smith, who have asserted that Wonder Woman should ideally promote peace over war, feminism over conservatism, and multiculturalism over American Imperialism because she acts as one of the few progressive alternatives to the male-centric sensibilities still dominating popular culture.

Unfortunately, Wonder Woman's status as an icon of feminism and an advocate of peace during wartime has often been undermined by those who are invested in domesticating the character and making her less threatening to sensitive male egos. In some instances, more politically reactionary writers of the comic books have directly challenged her feminism by charging her with hypocrisy and "exposing" her divided loyalties. In other cases, artists and merchandisers have sold Wonder Woman posters, action figures, and comics that represent her as a wet dream in a star-spangled thong and not a "real" woman with a life beyond the one conferred on her by a lecherous male gaze. And so, even though the character has made a career of fighting Nazis and nuclear-armed terrorists, her greatest enemies have consistently been those in the real world who would marginalize her significance in the history of both the feminist movement and "heroic fiction." After all, as one of the earliest popular icons of twentieth-century feminism, Wonder Woman deserves to be treated with respect by those who currently write adventures with the character, and should not be sanitized by clever marketing, turned into a one-dimensional fetish object, or appropriated by a writer with an axe to grind against everything she stands for.

CREATING AN ICON: THE WORLD WAR II ERA COMIC BOOKS

Wonder Woman, a princess of the Amazons also known as Diana of Themiscyra, was created in 1941 by psychologist William Moulton Marston, a student of the psychological effects of mass media on the individual spectator, an advocate of the reformation of criminals, and an early developer of the lie-detector test. According to biographer Les Daniels, Marston believed that the antisocial, violent tendencies in humanity were undesirable masculine traits that were best subdued by the socializing and loving influence of a powerful maternal figure. He felt that society in general would be a more peaceful place if "women's values" were cherished and if men willingly submitted themselves to female dominance. For Marston, the inducement for men to relinquish their power and reform the excesses of the patriarchy would be the sexual appeal of the dominant female.

Marston created the comic book character Wonder Woman to be both strong and sexy as a means of encouraging women to emulate her unapologetic assertiveness. He also hoped to convince men that strong women were more beautiful than passive ones and were worthy of love and respect instead of fear. Therefore, Marston designed Diana's adventures to advance his political agenda and psychological views, while hoping that her serialized exploits would offer an alternative to the grotesque comic books that flooded the market (such as *Dick Tracy*, a strip saturated with violence that he regarded with great personal reservations). As a devotee of Classical mythology, Marston found a precedent for his empowered female hero in the story of the Amazons: a race of proud women warriors from ancient Turkey who were subdued by Hercules and whose queen, Hippolyta, was ruined by her love of men. Marston crafted Wonder Woman to be the greatest member of this warrior race.[1]

According to Daniels, Marston was encouraged to use the Amazons as models for his super heroine by his creative collaborators and muses, trailblazing lawyer Elizabeth Holloway Marston and psychologist Olive Byrne (or Richard), the mothers of his children and the women with whom he had a polygamous relationship. Whether Wonder Woman's Amazon heritage was Marston's idea, or Holloway's or Byrne's, the Greco-Roman underpinnings of the comic book represented a significant departure from the precedent set by the *Superman* adventures, which, as a secularized retelling of the Moses and Jesus stories, was based in Judeo-Christian lore and tailored to more contemporary sensibilities.

To help make the Amazons more successful role models for women, Marston rewrote the end of the established narrative, explaining that they eventually escaped their Greek captors. The first *Wonder Woman* comic book, which Marston wrote under the pen name Charles Moulton and which was drawn by artist Harry (H.G.) Peter, reveals that Hippolyta prayed to the goddess Aphrodite for deliverance from Hercules and his men. Aphrodite granted the Amazons freedom from bondage, provided they left the "civilized" world and founded a colony exclusively for women on "Paradise Island." Freed of their chains, the women would also have to permanently wear the manacles Hercules had placed upon their wrists as a grim reminder of what happened when they once allowed themselves to be dominated by men. Having fulfilled their end of the bargain, the Amazons earned the gift of eternal life, as well as superior strength and access to highly advanced technology, including invisible planes and telepathic communicators. The goddess also rewarded Hippolyta with a fatherless daughter—Diana, the only offspring ever produced on Paradise Island.[2]

And so, the Amazons lived in peace and isolation for thousands of years … until the outbreak of World War II.

Naturally, World War II was *the* significant historical influence on the Golden Age of comic books and *Wonder Woman* was no exception. In 1942s *Wonder Woman* #1, Marston reveals that "The planet earth … is ruled by rival Gods—Ares, God of War, and Aphrodite, Goddess of Love and Beauty." One of Peter's panel illustrations dramatically depicts the male Ares and the female Aphrodite facing off against one another in the stars with the Earth positioned as a contested prize between them. Ares proclaims, "My men shall rule with the sword!" and Aphrodite challenges, "My women shall conquer men with love!" The image strikingly crystallizes Marston's view of the world as defined principally by gender conflict, as opposed to by class, religious, or cultural strife, all of which would be equally valid ways of understanding the history of civilization and of warfare.[3]

Later in that same comic book, the narrator reveals that Ares has orchestrated World War II to set the world aflame. To wrest control of Earth from Ares, Aphrodite commands that the Amazons end their long period of isolation. They would send the wisest and strongest Amazon to aid the Allies. This "Wonder Woman" would protect the American home front from Axis spies and terrorists, promote the importance of women's rights, and preach the promise of peace. Again, global conflict is defined as a clash of male and female ideals as opposed to a clash of empires or of cultures. The result, while potentially simplifying the root causes of World War II from a historical perspective, offers intriguing food for thought, especially given the Nazi regime's anti-feminist policies.[4]

Even as Aphrodite orders the Amazons to join the Allied side, the tranquility of Paradise Island is disrupted by the unexpected arrival of the first man in history to set foot on its shores. U.S. Army Intelligence Captain Steve Trevor crashes his plane onto the beach after losing an aerial engagement with the Germans. As Diana tends to his wounds, both patient and nurse find themselves falling in love with each other. Eager to separate her daughter from Trevor's corrupting influence, Hippolyta holds an Olympics-style contest to determine which Amazon would become Wonder Woman, Aphrodite's champion and Trevor's escort home. She forbids her daughter to participate in the contest, but Diana enters in secret, as a masked contestant, and proves herself to be legitimately the best athlete on an island of super powered women. Winning the right to the title Wonder Woman, Diana forsakes her immortality for love and for duty by leaving her home and her people.[5]

Heartbroken at losing her daughter, Hippolyta nevertheless gives Diana her blessing and sews her daughter an ambassadorial uniform made of the colors of American flag, a symbol of Diana's pledge to protect Democracy and to adopt America as her new homeland. Hippolyta also gives her a golden lasso that has the magical ability of forcing those caught in its links to tell the complete truth. Upon arrival in Washington, D.C., Diana assumes the identity of war office secretary Diana Prince and disguises herself in dowdy clothes and oversized glasses. From that vantage point, Diana monitors enemy activity. She also remains close to Trevor, the man she loves but is wary of becoming romantic with, partly because he is so enamored with his dream-visions of Wonder Woman that he cannot see the beauty lurking behind his secretary's plain façade.

This "origin" is perhaps one of the richest in comic book history, and the story of how the daughter of a queen became a super hero remains one of the best Wonder Woman stories, which is why it is so often retold—as it was in the Carter television series, 1987's *Wonder Woman Vol. 2* #1, and 2001's *Justice League* cartoon (which brought Diana into the 21st century by having her leave Paradise Island to fight off a Martian invasion). In each retelling, certain elements of the story are changed or given a different amount of dramatic weight, either through dialogue, visuals, or the structure of the plot; consequently, the central themes of the story change to match the times and a given creator's voice. Sadly, as compelling as the origin story is, it has not penetrated the public consciousness the way that Superman's origin story has—*everyone* knows about Kryptonite, the Kents, and Jimmy Olsen—but there is no guarantee that anyone reading this essay would have known Wonder Woman's story in advance. This is ironic since her origin was complete and complex from the beginning, while the back stories given to Superman and Batman evolved incrementally over the course of many years and through contributions from a variety of writers.

Americans basically know what Wonder Woman looks like, thanks largely to merchandizing and a fond (if vague) memory of the old television show; they have a general idea that she is a feminist, but they are unlikely to know the full political and thematic significance of her exploits, nor are they even likely to know that she was created during World War II as a patriotic feminist symbol akin to Rosie the Riveter. Indeed, Rosie the Riveter is an ideal parallel figure for Wonder Woman since, as merciful as the Amazon was to her enemies and as eager as she was to reason with them before resorting to violence, there was no question which side she was on during World War II: that of America. And she states repeatedly that she fights for America because America fights for women's rights around the world.[6]

Marston and Peter pitted their Amazon champion against Nazis who were clearly bloodthirsty, sexually deviant pawns of Ares. They were insane, had no moral center, and sported stereotyped names and features. They were also frequently portrayed as sexually repressed and would-be rapists, greeting the sight of Wonder Woman's exposed flesh with either too much moral outrage or too much lust, and failing the test of reacting to Diana's appearance in a well-adjusted manner.[7] Hitler himself appears in *Wonder Woman* #2, as a drooling maniac eager to shoot his own best men for insubordination even as he absorbs subconscious psychic commands from Ares to escalate his military campaign against the Allies.[8] This scene is emblematic of *Wonder Woman*'s consistent portrayal of the Nazis as "evil" pagans and Diana as a "good" pagan. Diana's paganism, a worship of Aphrodite, is shown to be maternal, environmentalist, and natural, while Hitler and the Nazis worship Ares in a manner that is industrial, martial, and anything but natural. Perhaps the most imaginative story that illustrates this is the adventure from February 1943's *Sensation Comics* # 14, in which a fir tree in the snow-covered border between the United States and Canada literally talks to Wonder Woman, betraying the nearby location of a secret Nazi base. As the story's narrator and central character, the fir tree is effusive in its praise of Diana's virtue and helps her rescue the mother of two small children from being raped and killed by Nazi soldiers.[9]

Not *exactly* figures of fun, Wonder Woman's enemies were still not granted depth of characterization, given any kind of respect as worthy opponents, or allowed a forum to express a cohesive political philosophy. The inevitable consequence is that she is pitted against straw man opponents, who are no match for her super powers, even if they attack her in tanks, submarines, or planes. (Nor are they any match for her ideologically because their philosophy is empty and inarticulate.) Indeed, they are only interesting as threats when they discover how to nullify her super powers. In a weakness that resembles Superman's vulnerability to Kryptonite, the earliest *Wonder Woman* adventures feature a heroine who loses her powers when she allows herself to be manacled by a man.[10] During these early adventures it is only when Diana is tied up that is she in any danger, and the real suspense comes when the audience works to figure out whether she will trick her way out or whether the local Holliday College For Women sorority sisters will come to her rescue.

Despite the uninteresting villains (which have plagued *Wonder Woman* adventures from the beginning) the early Marston-penned comics are compelling reads primarily in their political commentary and in their depiction of female friendship. The aforementioned Holliday College women appear frequently during Marston's tenure on the comic book, which lasted until his death in 1947, and their leader, the comically overweight Etta Candy, is a loyal friend to Diana (rather than a rival who is envious of the Amazon's perfect figure). Depictions of female friendship are as rare in popular culture as they are in serious literature, so the camaraderie demonstrated between Wonder Woman and the various women she encounters in her 1940s adventures, be they sorority sisters, nurses, teachers, or even misguided villainesses, may be found in precious few comic books, before or since, with the notable exceptions of Alan Davis' *Excalibur* and Gail Simone's *Birds of Prey*.

Although the sensibilities of an action-oriented comic strip are not conducive to showing Diana merely "hanging out" with other women characters and enjoying their company, the women in these early adventures are always there to help one another, rally together under a united political front, and even go to prison to protect one another. Their feelings of sisterhood are presented as strong enough to encourage women on the side of the Axis to reconsider their allegiances and join their sisters on the side of right and democracy. In these comic books, Wonder Woman advocates a new standard of sisterhood which challenges the jealous female competition that the dominant cultural climate of patriarchy fosters. She also expresses concern with the plight of the poor working woman during wartime. In these ways, Diana questions the American culture that she champions, showing that it is possible to be a patriot and still be a progressive. In typical New Deal fashion, her somewhat Marxist-feminist leanings are not traitorous, but help inspire improvements in the American standard of living and make the United States stronger as it continues its conflict with Nazi Germany.

For example, in *Sensation Comics* #7, Diana encounters a grieving mother whose son, Danny, died of undernourishment after she could no longer afford to buy milk for him.[11] Wonder Woman promises to send milk to Danny's equally undernourished sister every day, and to investigate the causes of the price-gouging. She confronts the head of the International Milk Company, Mr. DeGyppo, who resents her claims that the company is behaving immorally, since "Everything we do is absolutely legal!" (105). In retaliation, Diana attacks the milk company's public image by organizing a massive protest featuring banners that read: 'The International Milk Company is starving America's children!' (110). Thanks to the publicity provided by print journalists and newsreel grinders, her protest is a success and milk is made affordable once again.

In a story with similarly populist and feminist overtones, the following issue sees Diana confronting department store owner Gloria Bullfinch for underpaying her overworked female employees. While Bullfinch wines and dines in high society, her staff is suffering from exhaustion and cannot afford to pay for the medicine they need to keep trudging away at their grueling jobs. When one employee collapses and another steals medicine on her behalf, Bullfinch's lackeys see to it that the sick one is fired and the thief is imprisoned. Infuriated by this injustice, Wonder Woman hypnotizes Bullfinch into thinking that she is a working-class woman and orders Bullfinch to take a job in her own department store. Once she is sure that Bullfinch has learned her lesson, Wonder Woman lifts her spell and allows Bullfinch to reassume control of the store. Fortunately, Bullfinch's latent feelings of sisterhood are awakened and she learns to value the women in her employ, offering them more equitable pay and more reasonable work shifts.[12]

Like DeGyppo, Bullfinch was seduced into working against the best interests of her country by a foreign spy of the opposite sex. Consequently, the presence of that "alien" enemy elides the possible criticism that the comic book is anti–American and anti-capitalist. Still, Wonder Woman's insistence on combating homegrown economic evils—war profiteering, low wages, etc.—as well as enemy soldiers and saboteurs suggests that her patriotism, and her allegiance to democracy and capitalism, depends entirely on America delivering on its promises of *true* freedom and *true* equality for all. The implication is, should America ever stray from the path of righteousness, Wonder Woman will cease wearing the colors of the American flag. (In fact, in the 1978 comic book "Superman Vs. Wonder Woman: An Untold Epic of World War II," written by Gerry Conway and drawn by Jose Luis Garcia-Lopez, Superman fights to make sure that America develops nuclear technology before the Axis does. However, Diana fights both Superman and the Axis to make sure that *no one* develops nuclear technology, because she doesn't trust America, or any other nation, with such destructive power.)

The two Marston stories described above are emblematic of the early Wonder Woman adventures that have provided a vision of female friendship and solidarity and inspired generations of women—including luminaries such as the previously mentioned Gloria Steinem, Judy Collins, as well as hosts of others—to fight for the betterment of women's positions in society. Steinem, who honored her childhood hero by printing a "Wonder Woman for President" headline on the cover of the first issue of her *Ms.* magazine (December 1971), has written extensively about the appeal of the character, but has also acknowledged that the Amazon's relationship to men is as problematic as her relationship to women is admirable. As she explained in a 1995 essay on the heroine,

> Of course, it is also true that Marston's message wasn't as feminist as it might have been. Instead of portraying the goal of full humanity for women and men, which is what feminism has in mind, he often got stuck in the subject/object, winner/loser paradigm of "masculine" versus "feminine," and came up with female superiority instead.... No wonder I was inspired but confused by the isolationism of Paradise Island: Did women have to live separately in order to be happy and courageous? No wonder even boys who could accept equality might have felt less than good about themselves in some of these stories: were there *any* men who could escape the cultural instruction to be violent?
>
> Wonder Woman herself sometimes got trapped in this either/or choice, as she muses to herself: "Some girls love to have a man stronger than they are to make them do things. Do I like it? I don't know, it's sort of thrilling. But isn't it more fun to make a man obey?" [276–277].

Steinem is correct in identifying Wonder Woman's conflicted heart, especially concerning her relationship to Steve Trevor. It is interesting that Diana is so uneasy around Trevor, the man she presumably loved enough

In *Superman vs. Wonder Woman*, Superman takes President Franklin Delano Roosevelt's word that the United States will never use the atom bomb while he is president. However, Wonder Woman indicates to her mother that she believes a future president will. From page 31 of *Superman vs. Wonder Woman* (New York: DC Comics, 1978).

to sacrifice immortality for. After all, Trevor is hardly presented as a male-chauvinist. He is a capable soldier, spy, and tactician who expresses unwavering admiration for Diana's unearthly power when a lesser man might feel threatened by her. (During one adventure, when he fails to jump out of the way of an explosion, as she does, she asks, "Are you hurt, Steve? Why didn't you jump like I did?" To which he replies, "Jump like you? What am I, a kangaroo?") He gives credit where it is due, invariably telling his superiors that they have Wonder Woman to thank, not him, whenever she saves the day. In fact, Trevor appears to only have two flaws: he is a little too militaristic for Diana, and he consistently fails to react correctly to her clothing.

Diana's fashion sense is symbolically linked to her politics. Her half-nakedness is part and parcel of her political agenda, so those who are uneasy about her clothes are often uneasy about her broader message of female empowerment. When Diana confronts the world with her exposed flesh, she expects a well-adjusted reaction. The first time she encounters American clothing in *All Star Comics* #8, she is puzzled by how conserva-

tive the women's fashions are. "There's so much material in these dresses
... but they *are* cute!" she says, talking as if she had the sensibilities of Eve
before the Fall. Leaving the store after choosing to stay dressed in her
Wonder Woman costume, Diana encounters throngs of people on the
streets who "are amazed to see the scantily clad girl walking about so unconcerned." When old women react with jealousy ("The hussy! She has no
clothes on!" "The brazen thing!") and young men with lechery ("Ha! Sour
grapes, sister! Don't you wish you looked like that!"), Diana is mildly put
out that her flesh causes such a stir in either direction. While she does
blend in with mainstream American society by dressing conservatively as
Diana Prince, she finds the clothes as confining as if she were wearing a
corset or a nun's habit; so, when she transforms from Diana Prince to Wonder Woman for the first time, she shouts with triumph, "It feels grand to
be myself again!" as she discards her civilian attire.[13]

Even though Steve does not react with lust or fear to her half-nakedness, as those on the streets do, he does deify "Wonder Woman," and Diana
does not feel that his reaction to her is healthy. When she rescues him from
the Nazis, he exclaims, "Wonder Woman! My beautiful angel!" And she
replies, "What's an angel? I'd rather be a woman" (42). Deifying "Wonder
Woman" seems to be an understandable sin for the oft-rescued Steve to
commit, but it also seems to be too much for Diana. She wants him to see
her as a flesh-and-blood woman, and not as a romanticized ideal. Steve
also compounds this mistake by writing off his secretary—the more dressed
down Diana Prince—as a possible romantic interest. He does not see the
potential of an ordinary woman to be extraordinary, nor does he see that
there are many kinds of female beauty (not just the flashy Amazonian
kind).

Because Wonder Woman herself has such anxiety about male-female
romance, her relationship with Steve Trevor has always been a non-starter.
In fact, like the Lois Lane–Superman relationship, which tread water for
decades, writers faced the challenge of keeping the Wonder Woman–
Trevor relationship interesting. More often than not, the solution was to
write Trevor out of the comic book, or to kill him, only to resurrect him
from the dead later. However, when the saga of Diana of Paradise Island
briefly came to an end in 1986 with the publication of issue #329, that
"Final Issue" featured the marriage of Diana and Steve and their bodily
assumption into Mt. Olympus. Obviously, the "match made on Olympus"
ending seems too "pat" and too "domestic" an end for the Wonder Woman
saga. On the other hand, each time Steve or any of Diana's other love
interests disappear from *Wonder Woman* adventures, many fans lose hope
that Diana will ever be able to find love, or demonstrate to her readers
how a true (heterosexual-homosexual-polygamous) romantic relationship
of equals can be achieved.

It is significant that the Wonder Woman who appears in comic books today, the same one that was revamped and modernized during the 1980s in a story crafted by George Perez, left Paradise Island purely out of a selfless sense of duty, charged with preventing Ares from escalating the Cold War tensions between Russia and the United States into a nuclear conflict. She had no real romantic interest in Steve Trevor. As with the early Marston issues, Perez's adventures showed that Wonder Woman's most rewarding relationships were with female friends, especially mother-figures, including Classics Professor Julie Kapatelis, and Julia's daughter, Vanessa, who looked up to Diana as an older sister. Her asexuality assured, the new Wonder Woman has sometimes been criticized by readers for being frigid, and writers have addressed the issue by suggesting that she has unrequited romantic feelings for Superman, that she had brief flirtations with Aquaman, and feels unresolved sexual tension whenever she is with Batman (who is equally attracted to her, but is also equally afraid of the opposite sex, dooming the relationship even before it begins).[14] When writer-artist Phil Jiminez challenged this frustrating cycle by proposing a storyline in which Wonder Woman would finally lose her virginity to African-American character Trevor Barnes, the resultant fan outcry over the sexy, inter-racial relationship prevented the story from seeing print.[15] Diana's dalliance with Hindu god Rama was also cut abruptly short when protests from the religious community deemed the romance sacrilegious.[16]

The sexual content of the comic book has always been controversial, to the extent that the Holliday girls were written out of the series following the publication of *Seduction of the Innocent* (1954). (The book was a study of juvenile delinquency in which social critic and psychologist Dr. Frederic Wertham pointed to the lesbian overtones of Wonder Woman's relationship to the sorority sisters.) After the congressional hearings caused by Wertham's book, *Wonder Woman* became far more conservative in its sensibilities. Since the dominant cultural mood of the McCarthy-era 1950s suggested that it was not possible to be both a progressive and a patriot, Diana chose patriotism over feminism and socialism. She fell silent on political issues and became a fickle flirt. Before long, the Amazons disappeared from the narrative and after losing her super powers, Wonder Woman took to studying karate under Chinese mentor I Ching.[17] Thanks largely to an intervention by Steinem, who hated the new direction the comic book had taken, the Amazons and the "original" version of Wonder Woman returned to the comic book in 1973. Two years later, a television pilot inspired by the early Marston-written comic books appeared, *The New Original Wonder Woman* featuring Lynda Carter, and it soon evolved into a television series.

Lynda Carter: *The New Original Wonder Woman*

Given the timing of *Wonder Woman*, which ran from 1975 to 1979, the series served as a celebration of the then-recent strides made by the women's movement. It also acted as a tribute—or as a "thank you"—to the super heroine who, as a creation of the 1940s, helped lay the groundwork for feminism's contemporary successes. As the series' executive producer Douglas S. Cramer observed, "*Wonder Woman* came along at a time in the 1970s that was absolutely right ... [when] the women's movement was hitting its stride, where feminism and all that it conveyed ... was ... exploding across the country."[18]

In the recent DVD releases of the entire television series, the legacy of the show was examined, as was its portrayal of the character, both as a feminist icon and a sex symbol. Naturally, much attention was paid to the revealing costume that Carter wore in the title role. After all, as sexy as Wonder Woman was in the comic book, it was even sexier seeing a flesh-and-blood woman on television wearing such a revealing outfit—especially a woman as beautiful as Carter. In an admittedly self-promoting DVD special feature, the subjects interviewed agreed that, as sexy as Carter was and as revealing as the costume was, the television Wonder Woman was remarkably "sexy" and "not sexy" at the same time. In the special "Beauty, Brawn, and Bulletproof Bracelets," Carter herself remarked that the costume "felt like a second skin. I really didn't feel too self-conscious oddly. Maybe I should have but, you know, don't forget, this was the 'ban the bra' time, this was sexual freedom, this was bikinis and midriffs and that was the timing and I really wasn't thinking of being sexy either." Carter added that she was always determined to play Wonder Woman as an inspiration to women, and that is why few women saw her as a threat to their self-esteem.

Painter Alex Ross, whose depictions of Wonder Woman rank with Garcia-Lopez's and Perez's as among the most recognizable artistic renderings of the character, also felt that Carter's look in the costume was striking but not threatening to women. He said: "Here's this woman—a very gorgeous woman—running around half-naked, essentially wearing ... a swimming outfit and somehow she comes across as not being ultra sexual and, in fact, she is this symbol to young women—or women of any age—as not being defiled by that exposure. Essentially, the character was taken as what [she] ... was meant to be, as an object of energy in motion, not as of corrupted sexuality or something that was just ... for the boys" (Beauty, Brawn and Bulletproof Bracelets, DVD special feature).

The observation is quite true in many ways, but it is also important to point out here that Steinem felt that Carter's Wonder Woman was "a little blue of eye and large of breast" for her taste, so it is conceivable that Carter's stunning looks were off-putting to some women viewers. On the other hand, it is also possible that Carter's good looks had exactly the effect on the male viewers that Marston wanted his Wonder Woman to have—they were initially attracted to her by her beauty, and later learned to respect her for her intelligence, spirit, personality, and good deeds.

The early installments of the series were remarkably faithful to the spirit of the comic book, including all the major elements of the mythos and episodes directly adapted from Marston tales. The Nazis remained Wonder Woman's main foes, but they were presented in an even more broadly comic fashion on television. Their philosophy was just as empty as before, only now the series could operate with the knowledge that the Nazis were ultimately vanquished. In fact, the show had and an air of nostalgia about it, hearkening to the "simpler times" of World War II, when it was easier to be a liberal patriot than it was in the years following Vietnam and Watergate.

To many, Lynda Carter "is the living, physical embodiment" of Wonder Woman—a gorgeous actress who brings "a sense of grace and style and dignity" to the character. From a promotional photograph for the second season of *Wonder Woman* (Warner Bros, 1977). Copyright owned by Warner Bros. Photograph owned by author.

In general, Wonder Woman was as reluctant to use force in the series as she was in the comic, and virtually always contented herself with rendering her enemies unconscious or tying them up. Also, as with the comic book, she would reason with opponents before fighting them and, in the case of Fausta, the Nazi Wonder Woman, she convinced her enemy to defect to America, a land that treated its women better.

The Holliday girls are notably absent, but Etta Candy was included as another of Trevor's female staff members. Most significantly, most of the trappings of Greek mythology were removed from the series, and the secret of the Amazon's power was revealed to be superior technology fueled by the discovery of Feminum, a rare element unearthed in the mines of Paradise Island. The move made the show less mystical in its feel than the comic, but the fact that Wonder Woman now only had her mother to answer to, and not the gods as well, helped make the character more assertive (and more of a free agent).[19] Indeed, Carter's Wonder Woman goes to America to fight the Nazis and to be with Steve, but she is not spurred on by a command from Aphrodite. Therefore, Diana's dramatic choice is not to obey Aphrodite over her mother, but to defy her mother despite her own misgivings about breaking her mother's heart.

Nina Jaffe, author of several children's books featuring the heroine (including *Wonder Woman: The Journey Begins*), explains: "To be like her mother, she has to defy her mother. Queen Hippolyta led her own people in a battle for freedom. At a certain point, Wonder Woman realizes that she wants to take on the challenges that someone like her mother would and, in order to do that, she has to rebel. She has to disobey her mother."[20]

The television pilot movie emphasizes this domestic, generational element of the conflict above the feelings of love Diana has for Steve, and the shift in emphasis makes for a rewarding and fascinating mother-daughter conflict on screen.

While Hippolyta loves Diana, she grows concerned over the months following Diana's departure that her daughter has become too involved with Trevor, too warlike, and too prejudiced against the Nazis. These concerns are dispelled during the two-part adventure *The Feminum Mystique*, in which the Nazis discover Paradise Island and conquer it. The Nazi ringleader forces the Amazons to mine Feminum for Hitler, and plans to send the women back to Berlin "for study and possible breeding." While the Amazons are genuinely horrified that war has come to their home and haven, some viewers may suspect that Hippolyta allowed the Nazis to conquer the island just to see if they were are as bad as Wonder Woman reported they were. When Hippolyta is convinced that the Nazis are genuinely evil and beyond reasoning with, she decides that they have failed her test and orders Diana to lead a rebellion to liberate the Amazons.

While Hippolyta reveals in this episode that she suspects her daughter and Major Trevor have a sexual relationship, it is not clear that she is correct in this assumption. The first season episodes feature several sly remarks that, like the double entendres in *The Avengers* series, suggest that the lead characters are lovers without showing any romantic encounters during the actual episodes. Whether or not their relationship is a sexual one, both Diana and Steve are presented as equally respectable, heroic figures, and they work well together as a team when taking on villains like the Nazi counterfeiter code-named "Wotan" in "The Last of the Two Dollar Bills." Episodes such as this present a model friendship-romance that serves as the 1970s "television action series" equivalent of a Spencer Tracy and Katharine Hepburn romance of equals.

The sometimes arch, sexy dialogue between the leads is also part of the somewhat campy quality to the series. The show is never as campy as the Adam West *Batman* television series, mostly because Carter plays Wonder Woman with great seriousness and integrity and does not mock her own character. To that extent, the show fits perfectly Susan Sontag's definition of successful camp. According to Sontag, camp is "high spirited and unpretentious" (Sontag 278), is anti-elitist in its sentiments, and features garish costuming, a fascination with the androgyne, and a "relish for the exaggeration of sexual characteristics and mannerisms" (279). Carter's Wonder Woman is simultaneously quite masculine in her feats of strength and in her Amazonian prowess, just as her grand beauty and buxom figure make her "flamboyantly female" as well. Also, as far as Sontag is concerned, the best "camp" is played as serious, while "camping," done deliberately, is less successful. At times, the series features guest actors in the role of villains, such as the Nazis in the premiere television movie, who are "camping" in a manner that is wince-inducing, while Carter's performance is more successful because it is serious.

The series as a whole also grew less light-hearted during its second season, as its setting was brought into (what was then) the present. It was revealed that, following the defeat of the Nazis, Wonder Woman returned to Paradise Island for several decades to live in peace with the Amazons. When word eventually reaches her of the existence of an underground, international terrorist ring armed with nuclear weapons, her fear of nuclear war prompts her to return to America to lead the fight against terrorism. Since the series moves from taking place during a conflict of the past to a conflict of the present, the tone becomes notably more somber. When Diana returns to the U.S., she is a veteran at overcoming culture shock and acclimates more easily the second time assuming an American identity. However, she is understandably shocked by the inflation that has raised rents markedly since the 1940s and is disappointed that women haven't come further in achieving equality with men since the end of the war.

WONDER WOMAN AS FEMINIST, FEMINAZI, NEO-CONSERVATIVE, AND SEX SYMBOL

It is somehow appropriate, perhaps symbolic, that the Carter series was cancelled in 1979. Its final episodes marked the end of the liberal 1970s and the beginning of twelve years of the Ronald Reagan and George H. W. Bush administrations, and the feminist backlash that accompanied them. During this time period, Wonder Woman's perception among the general public suffered. Even during the presidency of Bill Clinton, and the all-too-brief resurgence of feminist sentiments during the 1990s, the character was oddly absent from the public scene. This was especially strange, given the arrival of derivative characters on television such as *Xena: Warrior Princess* and *Buffy the Vampire Slayer*. In fact, Wonder Woman was a source of embarrassment to Lucy Lawless, the actress who played Xena. Lawless continually refused to even consider playing Wonder

Woman in a revival series or movie, even though she was already playing an anti-hero variation of the character.

The sales of the *Wonder Woman* comic book, which have often not been good, were particularly low over the past several decades and, as in the I Ching period, several of the writers and artists attached to the series have tried to make the character more accessible to the largely male, conservative comic-book-buying audience by emphasizing her sexuality or downplaying her feminism. Some of her appeal was rediscovered thanks to her inclusion in the *Justice League* cartoon, and many episodes of that series, especially those written by Dwayne McDuffie, have made her a compelling, three-dimensional character. However, this new version of Diana is quite martial and humorless—far more so than Carter's and Marston's visions of the character ever were, making her more like the borderline-fascist Batman or the belligerent Hawkgirl than she really should be.

Since the *Justice League* cartoon reminded comic book fans that the character had great potential, Wonder Woman has had a renewed presence in the DC Comics line of comic books, and has played especially prominent roles in *Justice League of America* comics and in epic graphic novels and miniseries such as *The OMAC Project* and *New Frontier*. However, the Wonder Woman who has appeared in these stories represents a significantly different brand of feminism than the one from the television series. Unlike earlier incarnations of the character, who would never consider killing, the new Wonder Woman is presented as too pragmatic and too ruthless to spare the life of an opponent she sees as both deadly dangerous and irredeemable. On the one hand, her position is presented as far more reasonable than Superman's and Batman's, who have argued the position (that used to be taken by Wonder Woman herself) that it is always wrong to kill an enemy, even if that enemy is Adolf Hitler or the Joker. On the other hand, in both storylines, Wonder Woman is presented as being *too* violent and *too* ruthless to be truly heroic, and her honor and purity is somewhat stained by the blood on her hands.

In *New Frontier* (2004), in a segment set in Indo-China shortly before the Vietnam War, Wonder Woman liberates a group of women who have been raped and imprisoned by guards and enables the former victims to avenge themselves by machine-gunning their oppressors to death. A shocked Superman protests her role in the execution of the rapists rather than join her and the vindicated women in a drink from a celebratory goblet of mead, and she demands that he leave. In *The OMAC Project* (2005), telepathic villain Maxwell Lord robs Superman of his free will and orders the Man of Steel to kill Batman and Lois Lane. When Wonder Woman determines that the only way to free Superman from Lord's influence is to kill Lord, she does so without compunction or guilt. Footage of her snapping Lord's neck with her bare hands makes national news, causing Wonder Woman to be publicly disgraced, accused of betraying her pacifist convictions and put on trial for murder. Although she is eventually cleared of all charges, she still surrenders her costume to skulk off into exile for a year. In both *New Frontier* and *The OMAC Project*, Wonder Woman has had to suffer great public shame, penance, and physical beatings before either Superman or Batman would deign to forgive her.

These storylines are not the only recent ones in which Wonder Woman has been criticized by her fellow heroes for being too much of an ideologue, too militaristic, and too underdressed. In *Wonder Woman: Spirit of Truth* (2001), Superman tells Wonder Woman that she is too much of an aristocrat and too arrogant for people to relate to, let alone listen to. He advises her to humble herself, live like a common woman, and dress more conservatively when visiting Muslim countries so as not to frighten the natives. In *JLA: Golden Perfect* (2003), even Wonder Woman's lasso of truth rebukes her for being too much of an ideologue. When Wonder Woman grows too overzealous in her potentially misguided protection of a young, Messianic boy, the lasso disintegrates and the world is almost destroyed in a mystical tidal wave of moral relativism that sweeps reality. Only when Wonder Woman supplicates herself before the Fates is the lasso repaired and is "truth" restored. In addition to the humiliations Diana has suffered in these stories, she has been effectively fired and replaced on no less than three occasions since her life story was begun anew in 1987. First she was replaced by the Amazon Artemis, then by Hippolyta herself, and, most recently, by Donna Troy. Diana has been killed and resurrected, made a goddess and then kicked out of Olympus; and her fellow Amazons have seen their Paradise Island invaded, destroyed, and shunted off into another dimension an absurd number of times.

Admittedly, many of these stories, on their own, have their share of high drama. Some, especially *New Frontier* and *Kingdom Come*, are wonderfully written and include some classic moments with the character. However, *collectively* these stories seem to rebuke Wonder Woman harshly even as they work to restore her to a position of prominence in the comic book world. The modern-day Wonder Woman is strong and admirable, but she is also frightening and reckless in a way that she arguably would not be if more women writers and artists were assigned to craft her adventures. It would not be unreasonable to suggest that, as interesting as the latest version of Wonder Woman is—she is now an unpredictable agent of chaos in the DC universe—she is the epitome of the "Feminazi" that Rush Limbaugh made famous in the 1990s when he compared abortion rights activists to perpetrators of the Holocaust. These days, Wonder Woman is a ruthless, sexless, pagan woman with blood on her hands (who has more in common with her archenemies the Nazis than she would ever be willing to admit). The male writers who have penned her stories of late love to imply that Wonder Woman would be a lot nicer if she'd just have sex with Batman, put some more clothes on when she goes out in public, and shut up with the annoying politics already.

Even as the darker Wonder Woman has gained prominence in the comic book world, writers such as Phil Jiminez have worked hard to write and draw stories with the character that are truer to the legacy of a more liberal, kind-hearted Wonder Woman from both the early Marston comics and the Carter TV show. According to Jiminez, he draws Wonder Woman to look as much like Carter as possible because she "is the living, physical embodiment of this character." She brings to Wonder Woman "a sense of grace and style and dignity [and regality] which you don't often see in most female characters ... in comics today," who are usually presented "as sex vixens or ... kittenish or just as men in women's clothes."[21]

As an openly gay creator, Jiminez's more politically liberal sentiments have informed the way he writes the character. Sadly, Jiminez's highly political stories were lightning rods for controversy. For example, in *Wonder Woman Vol. 2* #170, Jiminez wrote a story in which Wonder Woman was interviewed on a talk show modeled after "The View" and openly discussed her political and religious philosophies. This is one of the monologues Jiminez, and co-scripter Joe Kelly, wrote for her:

> Women and their children must no longer fear abuse. *Anywhere* in the world. They must be given information that will help them remain economically self-sufficient, and in control of their bodies and reproductive lives. [My] Foundation's mission statement promotes the liberation of men, women, and children from the terrible problems that stem from antiquated religious philosophies and patriarchal fear—by educating them about alternatives. All human beings deserve to live on this planet without threat of violation, physical or spiritual, simply because of the body they were born in, the gender they were born to, or the region in which they live.

Dialogue such as this provoked an angry letter from a pro-life Christian reader, Chris Jackson, from Greenville, N.C., whose letter was published a few months later, in issue #173. Jackson felt that Wonder Woman's dialogue amounted to an attack on "freedom of religion." He identified her dialogue as Marxist, anti–Christian, and pro-choice propaganda. He wrote, "you've lost a longtime reader. Let me fill you in on a little secret: Most of us don't buy comic books to have our personal beliefs ridiculed or stoked by some funnybook writer." Editor Eddie Berganza replied to the letter by saying, "Wow. Sorry that Diana's message of tolerance exposed your intolerance.... [i]f you feel that 'valuing each other simply because we exist' is a wrong message, then Diana would ask you to look more closely at the teachings of your beliefs."

While Berganza may have had the last word here, Jackson's sentiments may have won the larger battle. It is notable that each time writers such as Jiminez, Trina Robbins, or Greg Rucka tackle Wonder Woman's liberal political beliefs—say, by having her fight domestic violence or write a controversial non-fiction book analyzing contemporary culture—fans react negatively and respond by not buying the comic. DC Comics, then, responds in kind by minimizing the political content or placing a greater emphasis on (admittedly) cool fight scenes with mythological opponents such as Circe or Medusa. Oftentimes fans claim they are reacting to bad writing more than bad politics, or they argue that controversial politics have no place in comic books which are marketed towards children. Whatever the reason, the consequence has been that the more traditional-yet-still-more-progressive Wonder Woman has been replaced by a more militant Wonder Woman who, despite being a murderess, is more palatable to the tastes of an audience who would rather see her kind of feminism unleashed on America's enemies than the more pacifistic feminism represented by Marston's Wonder Woman.

As Lillian Robinson, author of *Wonder Women: Feminism and*

Although Wonder Woman is supposed to be sexy, artists such as Mike Deodato, Jr., have sometimes risked alienating the character's female fans by rendering Diana with the provocative lines of "bad girl art." From page 4 of *Legends of the DC Universe*, Issue 4 (New York: DC Comics, 1998).

Super Heroes, observed, Wonder Woman *is* still relevant. She can still be a hero and a role model, even to the young women of today: "Anyone who realizes that she has the power within her to make changes, not just for herself, but for women, can be Wonder Woman. You have to take what she does and extend it into the terms of your real world. If you want to fly through the glass ceiling, if you want to bring about an end to domestic violence, if you want to bring pay equity for working women, she's there to be that kind of icon."[22]

Whether Wonder Woman will succeed in inspiring young women today will partly depend on who gets to tell stories with the character, and on how her image is "marketed" to the young. If her comic books continue to be drawn by the likes of Adam Hughes, Terry Dodson, and Mike Deodato, Jr., who are masters at rendering Diana as luscious eye-candy for horny men of all ages, then women will likely be too disgusted by the display to embrace the character as anything more than a degrading, *Sin City*–style pretense at feminism.[23] If she is used only as an image to merchandise—as one of many "outfits" to slip on a Barbie doll—then her feminist message truly will be smothered by corporate administrators. And if she continues to be an Amazon in the Classical sense, a relentless, bloodthirsty foe of dictators, then her appeal will not outlive the martial sensibilities of the Bush-Cheney White House years. However, it is equally possible that Robinson is right, and the world is waiting for Wonder Woman to return and to be a positive role model for women across the world once again.

It is not yet clear what kind of Wonder Woman will appear in the upcoming feature film. Previously slated to be written by *Buffy the Vampire Slayer* creator Joss Whedon, his camp, post-modern sensibilities may have worked for Wonder Woman, and made up for the fact that, once again, a male had been hired to write her exploits instead of a woman (as his commissioned script trumped an earlier submission by feminist historian and screenwriter Laeta Kalogridis). In the meantime it is possible that a woman writer and a woman artist will be hired to write the comic book regularly.[24] If so, perhaps female creators will have better luck in presenting a progressive Wonder Woman to the public whose appeal hearkens back to the Carter television series that dazzled men and women of all political stripes and sexual orientations.[25]

NOTES

1. According to historian Sue Blundell, author of *Women in Ancient Greece* (1999), the mythical Amazons referenced by Homer shunned marriage and family while embracing traditionally masculine pursuits such as hunting and warfare. As Blundell argues, ancient Athenian women could have interpreted the legend of the Amazons as containing "heartwarming messages about the empowerment of women," but, more likely, "the majority of women subscribed to the prevailing view" that the Amazons were barbaric figures and "rejected the warrior woman's example" (61–62).

2. Well, maybe not the only offspring. Some stories—in comics and in the 1970s television series—have featured Donna Troy, who is sometimes presented as Diana's sister ... but not always. The explanation for Donna's presence has changed repeatedly and is, frankly, confusing beyond belief. In any event, the character more often appears outside of *Wonder Woman* comic books (as a major figure in the pages of *The New Teen Titans,* for example) than she does in the *Wonder Woman* title proper, so I like to disregard her presence whenever I can.

3. This comic book was reprinted in *DC Archive Editions: Wonder Woman Archives Vol. 1,* New York: DC Comics, 1998.

4. As historian Jill Stephenson wrote in "The Wary Response of Women," "It is generally safe to say that in the Nazi view, women were to be 'wives, mothers, and homemakers'; they were to play no part in public life, in the legislature, the executive, the judiciary, or the armed forces. Hitler himself frequently expressed opposition to women's participation in politics, claiming that it sullied and demeaned the female nature, as he saw it. It was partly Hitler's personal attachment to the image of women as 'mothers of the nation' which delayed and then vitiated the introduction of labor conscription for women during the Second World War, although in his *Gotterdammerung* mentality early in 1945 he was prepared to see women enlisted as soldiers and sent to the front" (168–169).

5. That having been stated, as a possible consequence of the comic never going out of print (and of her story cycle constantly being "rebooted," retelling her adventures from the beginning), Wonder Woman has not, to my knowledge, ever really had to face the consequence of giving up her immortality. To this day, she remains eternally young. Even in stories set in the future, such as the non-canonical miniseries *Kingdom Come,* she still appears to be in her prime. Menopause never seems to be an issue for her either, as she gives birth to Superman's child after they are married in the novel version of the story.

6. While American culture was hardly free of sexism, it was, in contrast with Nazi Germany, a much more feminist-friendly culture during the World War II era, lending credence to Marston's thesis that a feminist's natural allegiance would be to the Allied Forces and not the Axis. As Susan M. Hartmann, author of *American Women in the 1940s: The Home Front and Beyond,* explained, "The [wartime] need for female labor lent a new legitimacy to the women worker.... While the women who replaced men in aircraft factories, ordnance plants and shipyards were most numerous and visible, the labor shortage also opened doors for women musicians, airplane pilots, scientists, athletes, and college professors." And, for the first time, discussions of pay equity were taken seriously. (20–23).

7. Marston's suggestion that the Nazi thirst for warfare was fueled by sexual repression carries some weight when one considers biographical evidence which points to Hitler's own bloodlust being fueled by his sexual inadequacies. Historians such as Ken Anderson, in his 1995 essay "Hitler and Occult Sex," have argued that Hitler's horror of Jews, and thirst for conquest, were outgrowths of his own sexual repression, and fear of women (159–160). Also, the connection between Hitler and Ares evokes Hitler's real-world fascination with the Occult and paganism, and the fact that, between 1940 and 1945 paganism was "publicly commended by the Nazis and publicly practiced. Nazi-sponsored pagan 'cults' revived the pre-Christian shrine to Wotan [German God of War] at the Heiliger Berg near Heidelberg.... The old stone gods of the Germanic race had been taken out of storage, dusted down and revitalized" (Prittie 74).

8. This story is featured in the reprint hardcover called *DC Archive Editions: Wonder Woman Archives Vol. 2,* New York: DC Comics, 2000.

9. Ibid.

10. The content of Marston's early *Wonder Woman* adventures, as drawn by Harry (H.G.) Peter, has given many commentators pause, largely because of the bondage imagery that can be seen throughout, which has sometimes been viewed as an indication of Marston's sexual kinkiness, while other times explained as a convention of the super hero narrative, since villains almost always tie up the heroes they capture. See Smith, Robbins, and Steinem. Also, during the 1990s, "bad girl" comics such as *Lady Death* took their lead from the tradition of bondage imagery Marston set the precedent for, producing kinky representations of tied-up women that few feminists would take kindly to.

11. Reprinted in *DC Archive Editions: Wonder Woman Archives Vol. 1,* New York: DC Comics, 1998.

12. Ibid.

13. See *DC Archive Editions: Wonder Woman Archives Vol. 1*, New York: DC Comics, 1998.

14. That having been stated, there is something very romantic, and very comical, about two sexist, sexually repressed warriors doing an awkward mating dance. Although they traditionally operate in different comic book universes and have been kept separate for decades, recent years have seen Batman and Wonder Woman together and acting like a dysfunctional couple in the *Justice League* and *Justice League Unlimited* cartoons (as well as in issues of the *JLA* comic book by Joe Kelly). Wonder Woman and Batman have also been adversaries in physical conflicts with an erotic undercurrent, as in the graphic novels *Trinity*, *Wonder Woman: The Hiketeia*, and *JLA: A League of One*.

15. See rumor postings on *The Comic Bloc Forums*, especially on http://www.comicbloc.com/forums/archive/index.php/t-11159.html.

16. See Wikipedia entry on *Rama (comics)* at http://en.wikipedia.org/wiki/Rama_(comics). The Rama romance was central to comic books scripted by the underrated Eric Luke.

17. This era of the comic book inspired the Cathy Lee Crosby *Wonder Woman* television movie, which preceded the production of the more faithful, Lynda Carter television series; it is not widely regarded as a "legitimate" Wonder Woman film by fans of the character.

18. See "Beauty, Brawn, and Bulletproof Bracelets: A Wonder Woman Retrospective."

19. To that extent, this version of the character is more her own woman than the comic book heroine seen since the series, who not only has to answer to female gods, but feels great reservation whenever she is asked to pay homage to the male chauvinist likes of Zeus in comic book stories written by Eric Luke, George Perez, John Byrne, and Greg Rucka.

20. See "Wonder Woman: The Ultimate Feminist Icon."

21. See "Revolutionizing a Classic: From Comic Book to Television—the Evolution of Wonder Woman from Page to Screen."

22. See "Wonder Woman: The Ultimate Feminist Icon."

23. In her article "Superwomen? The Bad-Ass Babes of Sin City—Or Are They?" Dana Leventhal criticizes the portrayal of women in the film adaptation of Frank Miller's Sin City. As she observes, "On the one hand, the women can be seen as warrior-goddesses, magnificent and luminous; on the other, they are morally dubious prostitutes and strippers, victims and servants of debased male gratification.... In the end, the women are simultaneously exalted and loathed as the objects of male fantasy."

24. To make "fannish" suggestions, Gail Simone, Linda Medley, Wendy Pini, and Trina Robbins are accomplished women writers who would be well-suited for the *Wonder Woman* comic book.

25. In "Female Bonding" (*Bitch Magazine*, Issue 33, Fall 2006), KL Pereira expresses similar sentiments about the choice of Joss Whedon as the architect of Diana's big screen debut. Like me, Pereira hopes that Wonder Woman can be revitalized as a feminist icon and rescued from bland comic books and crass merchandizing. Although the overall arc of my argument parallels hers, she focuses more on the empowering motif of lesbianism and erotic bondage imagery. Also, Pereira finds Perez's comic books and Carter's Wonder Woman far less compelling than I do.

WORKS CITED

Anderson, Ken. "Hitler and Occult Sex." *Hitler and the Occult*. New York: Prometheus Books, 1995. 159–166.

"Beauty, Brawn, and Bulletproof Bracelets: A Wonder Woman Retrospective." *Wonder Woman: The Complete First Season*. Warner Home Video, 2004.

Blundell, Sue. "Women in Myth: Amazons." *Women in Ancient Greece*. Cambridge: Harvard University Press, 1995. 58–62.

Collins, Judy. "Foreword." *DC Archive Editions: Wonder Woman Archives, Vol. 1*. New York: DC Comics, 1998. 5–7.

Conway, Gerry. "Superman vs. Wonder Woman: An Untold Epic of World War II." *All New Collector's Edition*. New York: DC Comics, 1978.

Cooke, Darwyn. *DC: The New Frontier, Vol. 1*. New York: DC Comics, 2004.

_____. *DC: The New Frontier, Vol. 2.* New York: DC Comics, 2005.
Daniels, Les. *Wonder Woman: The Complete History.* San Francisco: Chronicle Books, 2000.
Dini, Paul. *Wonder Woman: Spirit of Truth.* New York: DC Comics, 2001.
Hartmann, Susan M. *American Women in the 1940s: The Home Front and Beyond.* Boston: Twayne/G.K. Hall, 1982.
Jiminez, Phil. "Amazons Attack!" *Wonder Woman* 2 (173). New York: DC Comics, 2001.
_____. "She's a Wonder." *Wonder Woman* 2 (173). New York: DC Comics, 2001.
Justice League (a.k.a. *Justice League Unlimited*). Warner Bros. Animation. 2001–2006.
Leventhal, Dana. "Superwomen? The Bad-Ass Babes of Sin City—Or Are They?" *Bright Lights Film Journal.* August 2005. 25 October 2006. http://www.brightlightsfilm.com/49/sincity.htm.
Marston, William Moulton. *DC Archive Editions: Wonder Woman Archives, Vol. 1.* New York: DC Comics, 1998.
_____. *DC Archive Editions: Wonder Woman Archives Vol. 2.* New York: DC Comics, 2000.
_____. *DC Archive Editions: Wonder Woman Archives Vol. 3.* New York: DC Comics, 2002.
Messner-Loebs, William. "Moments." *Legends of the DC Universe* 4. New York: DC Comics, 1998.
Moeller, Christopher. *JLA: A League of One.* New York: DC Comics, 2000.
Pereira, KL. "Female Bonding." *Bitch: Feminist Response to Pop Culture* 33 (Fall 2006). 34–39.
Perez, George. *Wonder Woman, Vol. 1: Gods and Mortals.* New York: DC Comics, 2004.
_____. *Wonder Woman, Vol. 2: Challenge of the Gods.* New York: DC Comics, 2004.
_____. *Wonder Woman, Vol. 3: Beauty and the Beasts.* New York: DC Comics, 2005.
_____. *Wonder Woman, Vol. 4: Destiny Calling.* New York: DC Comics, 2006.
Prittie, Terrence. *Germans Against Hitler.* Boston: Little, Brown, 1964.
"Revolutionizing a Classic: From Comic Book to Television—the Evolution of Wonder Woman from Page to Screen." *Wonder Woman: The Complete Second Season.* Warner Home Video, 2005.
Robbins, Trina. *The Great Women Super Heroes.* Massachusetts: Kitchen Sink Press, 1996.
_____. *Wonder Woman: The Once and Future Story.* New York: DC Comics, 1998.
Rucka, Greg. *The OMAC Project.* New York: DC Comics, 2005.
_____. *Wonder Woman: The Hiketeia.* New York: DC Comics, 2002.
Simone, Gail. *Birds of Prey: Sensei & Student.* New York: DC Comics, 2004.
Sontag, Susan. "Notes on 'Camp.'" *Against Interpretation and Other Essays.* New York: Picador, 1990. 275–292.
Smith, Matthew J. "The Tyranny of the Melting Pot Metaphor: Wonder Woman as Americanized Immigrant." *Comics and Ideology. Popular Culture/Everyday Life Series, Vol. 2.* Eds., Matthew P. McAllister, Edward H. Sewell, Jr., and Ian Gordon. New York: Peter Lang, 2001. 114–128.
Steinem, Gloria. "Introduction." *Wonder Woman: Featuring Over Five Decades of Great Covers.* New York: Abbeville Press, 1995. 5–19.
Stephenson, Jill. "The Wary Response of Women." *The Nazi Revolution.* 3rd edition. Ed., Allan Mitchell. USA & Canada: D.C. Heath, 1990. 167–175.
Wagner, Matt. *Trinity: Superman, Batman, Wonder Woman.* New York: DC Comics, 2004.
Waid, Mark. *Kingdom Come.* New York: DC Comics, 1997.
Wonder Woman: The Complete First Season. Warner Home Video, 2004.
Wonder Woman: The Complete Second Season. Warner Home Video, 2005.
Wonder Woman: The Complete Third Season. Warner Home Video, 2005.
"Wonder Woman: The Ultimate Feminist Icon." *Wonder Woman: The Complete Third Season.* Warner Home Video, 2005.

WORK CONSULTED

Goossen, Rachel Waltner. *Women Against the Good War: Conscientious Objection and Gender on the American Home Front, 1941–1947.* Chapel Hill: The University of North Carolina Press, 1997.

Smallville *as a Rhetorical Means of Moral Value Education*

ROBERT M. MCMANUS
AND GRACE R. WAITMAN

If a couple of Superman fans such as ourselves can serve as representatives for the collective consciousness of Americans, we can safely say that one only needs to hear the name "Superman" to ignite the flame of childhood memories. One of the authors of this chapter, Rob, acted out his own imaginary Superman scenarios as a child, refusing to wear any clothing save his Fruit-of-the-Looms underwear and T-shirt with a large "S" scribbled across the chest in crayon. He battled imaginary villains and took refuge in his fortress of solitude composed of sofa cushions and his grandmother's crocheted afghans. It is doubtful that he would be wearing clothing today if it were not for his mother's last ditch attempt to clothe him in a pair of Superman-inspired pajamas, complete with a cape, and his sister convincing him that Superman wore a red and blue costume on color T.V.

By contrast, Grace first encountered Superman in the 1978 film *Superman* when Christopher Reeve swooped in to save Margo Kidder. She watched the movie with her father, who embarked on a study of Superman as part of his academic research. She was captivated by the Man of Steel's ability to fly; a talent she vowed to acquire by the time she grew up, despite her parents' uncertainty about the idea. By the time she was in college and viewed *Lois and Clark: The New Adventures of Superman,* her love affair with the Superman mythos and all its attendant glory had flared full-scale. (She had inherited her father's fascination, and then some.) Her college roommate thereafter commented on her predilection for all things Superman, and *Smallville* proved to be no exception. It would seem the Man of Steel has made his mark on everything from popular culture to the ivory tower; we will examine this intersection throughout this chapter.

One of the newest incarnations of the Superman story is found on the television series *Smallville.* The Warner Bros. series' retells the life of Superman, a.k.a. Clark Kent (played by actor Tom Welling), as a teen growing up in Smallville, Kansas, discovering his powers and ridding Smallville and Metropolis of its kryptonite-infused villains in a fresh take on the life of this superhero. It takes advantage of Superman's apocryphal lost years and creates a history for Clark Kent's entourage, including Jonathan and Martha Kent (John Schneider and Annette O'Toole), Lana Lang (Kristin Kreuk), Chloe Sullivan (Allison Mack), Lois Lane (Erica Durance), and, of course, Superman's arch nemesis Lex Luthor (Michael Rosenbaum). The introduction of Lex Luthor and his friendship with Clark Kent in the teen and young adult years of Superman's life is a significant revision and a particularly interesting retelling of the Superman myth. The show has consistently received high ratings since its debut in 2001 and throughout its subsequent six seasons, especially in the hard to reach demographic of males age 18–34. It garners between six to eight million viewers weekly (Aurthur B9). The show's essential makeup is a synthesis of superhero, family drama, and teen drama genres that have been popular on the WB, now CW, network.[1]

There have been numerous historical and critical studies focusing upon the Man of Steel (e.g., Eco; Yeffeth). Such a ubiquitous story is certainly worthy of scholarly study, specifically in regards to the potential persuasive appeal this story might have on such a large audience. Additionally, as the study of rhetoric has expanded within the last three decades to include popular culture texts such as television shows, these studies have used gender-based approaches to examine the implications televised texts have upon audiences' perceptions of femininity and masculinity (e.g., Dow; Robinson). As Superman's profile has expanded in academic studies, the rise of feminist criticism has also increased accordingly. Throughout this chapter, we will be blending these approaches to examine the way *Smallville* teaches its viewers to be "good" men and women and encourages its viewers to adopt a very particular value system.

We believe that the Superman story in general, and specifically the television show *Smallville,* has the potential to influence audiences and help shape their values; or more specifically, we believe *Smallville* helps shape its audiences' view of morality, cultural identity, and gender roles. Umberto Eco acknowledges the reader's role to construct meaning in his germinal work *The Role of the Reader,* specifically in regards to the Superman myth. This line of thought is also very much in keeping with modern rhetorical scholarship, pioneered by such rhetoricians as Kenneth Burke and Barry Brummett. Burke and Brummett suggest that audiences may look to popular culture texts such as television shows as "equipment for living" and apply the concepts they are presented to other areas in their lives (Burke 253–262; Brummett 97–99).

Henry Giroux makes a similar assertion to the powerful influence of popular culture texts, specifically youth-centered entertainment such as *Smallville.* He states that such forms "inspire at least as much cultural authority and legitimacy for teaching specific roles, values, and ideals [as] more traditional sites of learning such as public schools, religious institutions, and the family" (Giroux 24–25). The same could be said of *Smallville* and the instruction it provides in the proper way to be a man or a woman. *Smallville*'s creator, Alfred Gough, summarizes our thoughts best when he says, "[T]here is something about Superman that permeates the American psyche. Perhaps it is because he symbolizes the best of what we want to be" (Hinson 10). Assuming Gough is correct in his assessment, a text this powerful deserves our critical attention.

As we proceed through this chapter, we will draw on the mythological implications of the Christ story, the concept of the American dream, and feminist theory to examine the ways *Smallville* addresses its audience and potentially helps to shape its views. The first section specially looks at the way *Smallville* draws upon the Christ story to create a world of moral absolutes, and in so doing persuades audiences to draw clear divisions between right and wrong, good and evil. The second section draws upon the work of Walter Fisher to examine the way *Smallville* encourages its viewers to embrace a particular version of the American Dream. Finally, the third section will utilize Judith Butler's scholarship to examine the implications *Smallville* may have on its audience's concept of gender roles.

SMALLVILLE'S MORAL UNIVERSE

One of the distinguishing characteristics of *Smallville* is its clear boundaries of right and wrong—good and evil—despite the apparent complexity of its characters and their situations. This is particularly true given the ubiquitous nature of the Superman story and its audience's knowledge of the ultimate outcome of its characters; Clark Kent *will* become Superman and Lex Luthor *will* become his archenemy. *Smallville* embraces this view rather than reinterpreting Clark Kent as a flawed or "tragic" hero, as has been done with the most recent incarnations of other superheroes such as Batman. The producers of *Smallville* have developed an extensive narrative structure based upon the Superman myth, and in so doing have created a particular moral universe in which they invite their audience to take part. Annalee R. Ward, in her book *The Morality of Disney*, eloquently explains the rhetorical implications of such a creation: "When a narrative that moralizes builds on myth, the result is axiological advocacy; the story, although it may entertain by virtue of its being a narrative, promotes certain values over others (Ward 13).

It is well understood, even by the layperson, that Superman draws upon the Christ story. In both the Superman and the Christ stories, a child—an only son—is sent by his father to save the world from evil. Both children are endowed with supernatural powers. Both are tempted to use their power for personal gain. Both overcome their temptation. Both die.

Both are resurrected. Both seek to save the world from ultimate evil. Thus, the linking of Superman to the sacred, spiritual, and transcendent is a well-established homology.

Indeed, this link to the sacred or the spiritual is seen throughout the *Smallville* series. For example, in the pilot episode, Clark Kent is captured by Smallville High School's football team and placed upon a post in a cornfield, symbolizing a "crucifixion" of the good by the evil—Clark Kent as Jesus Christ, as it were. Kent as symbol of savior is figuratively and literally seen throughout the series, whether it be found in the Remy Zero's theme played at the beginning of each episode, appropriately titled "Save Me," or in the many episodes in which the plot entails Clark Kent saving his friends and family from certain doom, and in even some instances, raising the dead: as in "Reckoning," where Clark implores his god-like father to turn back time

Superman depicted as a Christ-figure; Clark "crucified" in a Smallville cornfield. From the cover of the DVD box set *Smallville: The Complete First Season* (Warner Bros., 2003).

to raise Lana Lang from the dead, or in "Fever" in which Clark Kent uses the space ship that transported him to earth from his home planet Krypton to resurrect his mother.[2]

But more particular to *Smallville* is that the moral universe it creates has distinct boundaries between good and evil, not unlike the Christ-Lucifer dichotomy of the Gospels.[3] These boundaries are metonymically created through the show's primary protagonist and antagonist, Clark Kent and Lex Luthor. Clark Kent represents "truth, justice," and, "other stuff," as he says ("Drone"); whereas Lex Luthor represents, lies, selfishness, and ultimate evil.[4]

One particular episode where this is clearly seen is "Hourglass" in which an elderly woman who has the gift of seeing the future glimpses into the lives of Clark Kent and Lex Luthor. She sees Clark Kent surrounded by the graves of his friends and family but she then later explains to him that she has seen several visions of his future in which Superman/Clark Kent has rid people of pain and despair, despite his personal suffering. She says, "I think that's your destiny, Clark. To help people; to save them from fear and darkness." She then shows Clark a vision of him saving women and children from burning buildings and car crashes. Contrarily, when reading Lex Luthor's future, the old woman sees Lex standing in the Oval Office dressed in white, then in a field of flowers which crumble to dust at his touch and turn into the charred remains of thousands of bodies as blood rains from the sky. The old woman then dies after seeing the horrors of Lex's future. In creating such a clear-cut division between good and evil, audience members are encouraged to side with the good and decry the evil found in these character's forms. But unlike the "real" world in which these divisions are not so easily deciphered, *Smallville*'s universe calls for a clear division between ultimate good and ultimate evil, not unlike the Christ story.

Another way the producers of *Smallville* create this division between good and evil is through the use of light and shadow throughout the series. Michael Osborn's work on archetypal metaphors is a well-established theoretical approach in rhetorical-critical studies. Osborn's observation that light and dark metaphors "express intense value judgments and thus may be expected to elicit significant value responses from an audience" has particular relevance to the way *Smallville* creates a world with clear moral boundaries between good and evil (Osborn 118). Although originally applied to verbal texts such as speeches, Osborn's approach has recently been applied to visual formats such as those found in television and film (Ward 48–50). This use of light and dark to create moral distinctions is mirrored in *Smallville*. Clark Kent is often seen bathed in the light of the bright Kansas sun, and even, in one episode, is mistaken as an angel by one of his young admirers because of the light surrounding his face. Kent's loft in his family's barn looks out to the sun, the sunset, and the stars hovering over the Kansas prairie; later, in his fortress of solitude, Kent is positioned in the bright light of the Arctic snow and ice. Lex Luthor, on the other hand, is routinely set in the dungeon-like shadows of his family's castle that has been moved from Scotland and rebuilt in Smallville, Kansas. The lighting in his palatial office is painfully dim and the only natural light to make its way into the office must pass through opaque stained glass windows.

Even the costuming on *Smallville* encourages these distinct divisions. Clark is most always clothed in primary colors of red and blue, unless he is under the effect of red Kryptonite, which negatively affects his desire to do good, in which case he wears black, such as in the episodes "Red" and "Exodus." Whereas Clark is usually dressed in bright primary colors such as his trademark red jacket and blue shirt, an obvious prototype to his future red cape and blue tights, Lex is usually clad in black with only a hint of muted colors such as a mottled blues or grays.[5] When forced outdoors, Lex is usually seen wearing sunglasses to block the light, whereas Clark only wears sunglasses when he has been negatively affected by red

Kryptonite that causes him to "go to the dark side" of his personality. The series encourages us to see otherwise complex characters such as Clark and Lex in terms of the simplistic binaries of good and evil through the environments in which we find them, through cinemagraphic elements such as lighting and costuming, and most often through allusions to their future. This separates us from the reality of the situation itself. For example, Lex actually develops a very good excuse for obsessively and secretly seeking Kryptonian technology; within the course of the series Lex is possessed by an evil Kryptonian and wants to protect himself and his world from a similar fate.[6] On the other hand, Clark often questions his actions and whether he should interfere with other people's lives and destinies— a question that is worth asking and yet is never answered in the series. Once again, however, the visual use of light and dark metaphors helps to establish a very clear moral universe, which the audience is encouraged to embrace and apply to their own experiences.

The clear dichotomy of good and evil presented in *Smallville*, metonymically represented by the show's primary protagonist and antagonist, helps to persuade its viewers that a "good" man has a clear moral distinction between right and wrong, good and evil (and will position himself on the right side of this clearly defined boundary if he or she wants to be a good person). The potential disturbing consequence of this moral universe is that it implies that there is "one right way" to be. If audiences consciously or subconsciously apply this piece of equipment for living their lives, they are encouraged to see clear divisions between good and evil in their own world. Such thinking leads to a potentially dangerous form of moral absolutism that discounts individual choice or cultural relativity that is so important to human understanding in an increasingly pluralistic world. It encourages the viewer to arbitrarily create divisions between us and them, the sheep and the goats, the axis of evil and the allies of good. Viewing the world as complicated, containing subtleties of moral distinctions, is discouraged. Or, as Lex Luthor says, "It's a complicated world, Clark. Only the naive view it in black and white" ("Aqua").

In addition, Lex Luthor and Clark Kent use many of the same tactics to overcome the obstacles that are presented to them. Most notably, both Luthor and Kent will resort to extreme violence if pressed. Admittedly, Kent's aims are usually to protect others when using violence, whereas Luthor's are suspicious and assumedly to protect his own interests; nevertheless, both characters willingly use violence to achieve their goals. Both characters willingly lie or obfuscate the truth when questioned as to their intents or methods of obtaining their goals; whether it be Clark Kent protecting his identity as Superman, or Lex Luthor protecting his own quest to discover the source of Clark Kent's strength (or further his own power and fortune), the methods used are remarkably similar. *Smallville* does not provide the viewer with a transcendent defining source of good or evil;

rather the show is remarkably humanistic in its seemingly purposeful lack of religious or transcendent authority. We know what is "good and evil" because the characters intuitively know the difference.

Ironically, the extreme moral absolutism in the world of *Smallville* may lead to extreme moral relativity in the "real" world. The message to viewers is clear: the ends justify the means if your intent is right and you are on the side of "good"—however "good" may be defined for you as an individual. Thus, *Smallville* creates a moral universe with clear boundaries between good and evil and encourages its audience to do the same, but does not provide any transcendent voice to authenticate one's definition of good and evil; thus, it may call the viewer to define his or her own choices as "good" and use whatever means necessary to achieve their ends (with potentially negative consequences).

SMALLVILLE'S DEFINITION
OF THE AMERICAN DREAM

The moral universe established in *Smallville* also has implications for the viewer's embracing of a particular view of America and the American Dream. In his article "Reaffirmation and the Subversion of the American Dream," Walter Fisher provides another potentially heuristic tool to understand the implications that *Smallville* may have on its viewers. Fisher posits that the "American Dream" is actually two "dreams" or "myths" that are simultaneously held while competing with one another. One is the moralistic myth of universal egalitarian brotherhood; the other is the materialistic myth of individual success (161). Fisher explains:

> The materialistic myth is grounded on the puritan work ethic and relates to the values of effort, persistence, "playing the game," initiative, self-reliance, achievement, and successes. It undergirds competition as a way of determining personal worth, the free enterprise system, and the notion of freedom, defined as freedom from controls, regulations, or constraints that hinder the individual's striving for ascendancy in the socio-economic hierarchy of society…. The moralistic myth is well expressed in the basic tenets of the Declaration of Independence: that "all men are created equal," men "are endowed by their Creator with certain inalienable rights…." These tenets naturally involve the values of tolerance, charity, and true regard for the dignity and worth of each and every individual [161–162].

These competing views of the American dream are embodied in the characters Lex Luthor and Clark Kent, with Lex embodying the materialistic and Clark embodying the moralistic. For example, a continuing scene throughout the *Smallville* series is that of Lex's father, Lionel (John Glover), "mentoring" Lex to help him achieve wealth and power. Indeed, Lionel is an exemplar of the materialistic myth portion of the American dream in that his mother and father were poor American immigrants but he rose to be a titan of industry. Lex follows in his father's footsteps, attempting to overthrow his father's company, LuthorCorp, and desiring to obtain more wealth and power. Clark, on the other hand, is raised by Jonathan and Martha, who mentor him to care for his fellow human beings. For example, in *Smallville*'s second season, Clark finds a message from his biological father. The message tells Clark to rule his new planet and conquer the weak race that inhabits it ("Exodus"). Jonathan Kent encourages Clark to use his powers for the benefit, and not the destruction of, all humankind. The differences between Clark and Lex are traditional and are ascribed to a rural-urban dichotomy. Lex comes from the big, bad city of Metropolis, and Clark lives in the creamed corn capital of the world, Smallville. Lex is positioned as the urban invader ravaging the land and livelihoods of poor rural farmers. When Clark is under the influence of red Kryptonite, which negatively affects his personality, not only does he abandon Smallville for Metropolis, but he abandons his moralistic American dream for a materialistic one ("Red"; "Exodus"). His adopted father, Jonathan Kent, must remind him of the "true" American dream and reaffirm the moralistic myth ("Exile"). By creating such a sharply divided moralistic universe and positioning the chief protagonist as the keeper of the moralistic myth and the chief antagonist as the keeper of the materialistic myth, the creators of *Smallville* encourage their audience to champion one dream in favor of the other.

The creators of *Smallville* continue to mirror Fisher's observations of the dualistic nature of the American dream by following these myths to their extremes. Fisher observes that each of these myths have their own potential for destruction: "In naked form the [materialistic] myth is compassionless and self-centered; it encourages manipulation that leads to exploitation.... [The moralistic myth appeals] to our better nature; however, that appeal is predicated on the arousal of guilt for what we are in respect to what we should be. Put another way, in order for one to be moved by moralistic appeals, one must condemn himself in some way or other" (162).

It is noteworthy that Lionel Luthor actually had his immigrant parents killed to collect the insurance money to start his business and obtain his version of the American dream. Likewise, Lex will stop at nothing, including lying to Clark about his friendship and interest in him, exploiting victims of Kryptonite poisoning for his own financial and Machiavellian purposes, and killing those who threaten to come between him and his quest for personal wealth and power. Lex is the materialization of the materialistic myth.

Clark, conversely, must sacrifice himself—both literally and figuratively—for the good of humankind. He does not allow himself to share his secret powers or alien identity with others because of the burden it will cause them. He offers himself as a sacrifice to save his friends, family, and ultimately all of human kind from certain destruction. For example, Clark's self-sacrificing instincts even extend to the point that he can never reveal his secret powers and alien status to Lana. When he does tell her, this step results in very grave consequences when Lana loses her life. Jor-El, Clark's biological father, agrees to turn back time and allow Clark the opportunity to save Lana, but the result is that Clark's adopted father, Jonathan Kent, dies in the process ("Reckoning"). Such dire results implicitly remind him—daily, through the shroud of his enduring grief—that with his great powers comes great responsibility, including his self-sacrificing attempts to protect Lana and his other friends and family, almost from himself, as it were. He repeatedly condemns himself psychologically as well as physically to save the universal brotherhood. That is, after all, what makes him Superman. Clark Kent is the materialization of America's moralistic myth.

Walter Fisher notes, "In dichotomizing into materialistic and moralistic myths, there is danger that one may assume that there is virtue in one and only vice in the other. But this is an inaccurate view. Both are based on traditional American values" (163). *Smallville* presents both versions of the American Dream, but calls its audience to choose one myth over the other—the moralistic—in their quest to become more "like" Superman.

SMALLVILLE'S INTERPRETATION
OF PROPER GENDER ROLES

Thus far, we have presented elements of *Smallville* that apply to its audience in general; however, the rhetorical implications of *Smallville* have further implications for specifically male and female audiences. If, indeed, Clark Kent, a.k.a. Superman, serves as a role model for moral and mythical behavior, it is logical that he would also serve as a role model for how to be a "man" and how men should be perceived.

Women in *Smallville* obtain their identity from the men in their lives. In *Smallville*, three adolescent female characters hover as satellites around the burning star of Clark Kent. Lana Lang, Chloe Sullivan, and Lois Lane are three of Clark's closest friends, and the most significant triumvirate of women in his life, save for his mother, Martha Kent. The series exalts a certain kind of manhood and by extension, a specific version of masculinity—one which corresponds to the system of morality embodied and enacted by the Man of Steel.

Along the same lines, the series also prefers a particular conception of femininity. After all, any female who enjoys the elevated status of being friends with Clark Kent—and thereby, Superman—must also engage in actions which correspond with his same sense of morality. The overall trajectory of character development for Clark Kent—and also, those characters who remain close to him—must uphold the strict sense of morality embodied and enacted by a superhero whose very existence signifies "truth, justice, and other stuff." If Superman becomes exalted for his allegiance to this narrowly defined code of conduct, any individual with whom he maintains a significant friendship will be viewed in a similarly positive light. But with great acclaim comes great responsibility—or, at least, adherence to a strictly delineated moral code. Therefore, *Smallville* cultivates constructions of gender identity which remain limited by the type of man that Superman must inevitably become.

Specifically, Clark cannot remain good friends with any person who could negatively influence the moral integrity of the future Superman. In the case of these three females, this standard proves particularly significant, because any one of the three girls represents a potential love interest and match for Clark. Indeed, two of the three girls—Lana and Lois—serve as his official love interests from the legendary narratives of the Superman mythos, albeit from two different periods in his life. For Clark to sustain any continuous interest in any female, that woman must somehow prove "worthy" of attracting the attention of such an alpha male as Superman/ Clark. If the woman acted in a morally "corrupted" manner, she could not only prove a negative influence on Clark himself, but she could also imperil the integrity associated with Superman's judgment; after all, he cannot hold in high esteem any woman whose own level of morality does not approach his own.

According to this logic, the constructed gender identity of each of these three females remains inextricable from her relationship to Clark within the sphere of *Smallville.* Judith Butler alludes to the interdependent quality of the traditional patriarchally based understanding of gender roles when she explains that "the process of meaning-constitution requires that women reflect that masculine power and everywhere reassure that power of the reality of its illusory autonomy. This task is confounded, to say the least, when the demand that women reflect the autonomous power of masculine subject/signifier becomes essential to the construction of that autonomy and, thus, becomes the basis of a radical dependency" (Butler 57–58).

Butler's theory of the patriarchal sphere suggests that the projection of male autonomy and power actually proves illusory, because it remains dependent on women to sustain a certain role which reflects this display of masculine power. In other words, male figures can only project an autonomy which remains misleading. To sustain such an autonomy, cultural representations must promote a mode of understanding which requires women to reassure the integrity of this illusion; thus, this mode of depiction—though it clearly privileges the male figure and accords him a greater independence and power—remains reliant on the female to sustain the illusion of the autonomy of this power.[7]

This power structure retains a dialectic quality, as Clark Kent's spotlight would be seriously altered without his interactions with Lana, Chloe, and Lois. Similarly, if his relationship with them changes for any reason, their independence equally becomes influenced. For example, near the conclusion of the second season, Clark temporarily sustains a romantic relationship with Chloe instead of the more platonic friendship they have shared until that point. However, in this relationship, he remains trapped between her affections and the connection he still feels with Lana. When he and Chloe break up, her jealousy over his interest in Lana causes her to forge an alliance with Lionel Luthor, in which she agrees to investigate Clark. Chloe herself possesses significant prowess as an investigative reporter. But instead of being able to use her talents as a means to extinguish her emotional investment in Clark (perhaps by turning her attention to writing stories instead of festering over his rejection), her frustration over his preference for Lana causes her to expend her investigative talents in an unproductive manner. She aligns herself with the negatively viewed Luthors, and for several episodes after Clark discovers her transgression, he refuses to trust her. By entering into Lionel Luthor's employ, she behaves in a manner that contradicts Clark's moral system. This development causes him to view her in a negative manner, to the extent that he treats her with almost the same level of disdain that he usually reserves for Lionel Luthor himself. Only after she concedes that her behavior was a mistake and makes concessions to Clark (and acts against Lionel) is she able to re-enter Clark's good graces.

At the beginning of the sixth season, Chloe and Clark also seem on the verge of a romantic connection, until her relationship with Jimmy Olsen eclipses this possibility. Her significance as a character necessarily relies on the nature of her relationship to Clark. Chloe's identity remains contingent on Clark's judgment of her behavior, and her motivation seems to stem only from her feelings for Clark, instead of factors which would allow her to maintain a more independent identity, such as that of an assertive reporter. Through occurrences like this one, the program reminds its viewers that the female characters' significance typically stands in relation to their association with Clark; therefore, they can never truly sustain any type of behavior which would not correspond with his and the Kents' black-and-white conceptions of morality and acceptable behavior.

Indeed, if the female characters continuously acted in ways that did not meet with the Kents' approval, they would all be construed as "bad" girls, or as a potentially negative influence on Clark. Lana, Chloe, and Lois must engage in actions which meet with male approval, usually that of Clark or Jonathan Kent, in order to be considered positively within the sphere of the series. They can only cultivate identities that remain dependent on a patriarchal-like consensus about acceptable standards of female agency. Butler further asserts that a gender is the "repeated stylization of the body, a set of repeated acts within a highly rigid regulatory frame that congeal over time" (Butler 43). In essence, the repeated actions of Lana,

Chloe, and Lois remain constrained by the "highly rigid regulatory frame" of the moral system embodied by Clark, as the future Superman, because each of these three characters sustains a close, if sometimes strained, relationship to Clark. Thus, they must construct identities that inevitably earn his approval. Granted, they are supporting characters in a larger series that revolves around the iconic Superman. But this type of presentation nevertheless constructs an identity of femininity that places implicit limitations on the agency they can exert. Their interests must always remain secondary to the greater concerns of Superman. After all, if the Man of Steel has the larger community's interests in mind, how could the considerations of an individual female possibly be viewed as important?

Ultimately, the series will culminate in Clark donning the famous blue tights and red cape. Clark himself remains equally hampered by this same "highly rigid regulatory frame," as even the adolescent Clark cannot *sustain* any behavior that could compromise the strict moral codes upheld by his future self. In all of the adolescent characters on *Smallville*, the series must inherently confer approval on behavior that would adhere to the rather stringent standards of morality embodied by Superman, and also discourage those actions that could jeopardize Clark's future moral integrity. Just as Clark's developmental path charts a particular course as an "appropriate" one by which to arrive at manhood, the female characters who spend the most time with him must equally engage in actions that construct them as a particular type of woman. The actions they take determine the type of woman who can be viewed in a positive light within the realm of *Smallville*.

Therefore, if Lana, Chloe, and Lois can only act with a greater amount of agency when it doesn't threaten the limelight of Clark, the significance of their roles will always invariably be subsumed by his brightness. And if these three female characters can only engage in actions that remain heavily influenced by the looming Kryptonian presence of Clark, such a presentation could instantiate barriers to the potential autonomy allocated to them. Their implicit subservience could also suggest to female viewers of *Smallville* that a woman can only consider herself influential if she defines herself in relation to a male. Their interaction with Clark—and their dependence on his moral "approval"—could also reinforce the limitations of conventional gender roles that exist within a patriarchally oriented sphere.

Arguably, all three females act with a certain modicum of agency. As the series has progressed across its six season run, all three of the adolescent female characters have grown more independent and assertive—partially because they have gradually become full-fledged adults but also because their lives have undergone complicated twists. All of the female characters engage in active roles to a certain extent. Within this circle, Lana Lang remains the most passive; although, admittedly, even she has her moments. Chloe Sullivan acts extremely independently—except in her relationship with Clark. In the earlier years of the series, her intense romantic interest in Clark often impaired the amount of independence she could exert. After she gains knowledge about Clark's powers and secret origins, however, she cultivates a closer friendship with him. Somewhat ironically, this development allows her to fulfill her wish to be more intimate with him—as friends if nothing more, although their friendship has repeatedly crossed the barrier into a romantic liaison several times during the series. Of the three, though, Lois Lane constantly acts with the most assertion and authority. Her independence stems in part from her late entrance into the series; her character was already eighteen years old and the viewers did not witness her coming-of-age experiences in the same way as Lana and Chloe. However, Lois can likely sustain her autonomy because she has the most distant relationship from Clark. Lois and Clark interact quite frequently—during Clark's adventures, through the various friends they have in common, and also because Lois maintains a close relationship to the Kent family, especially because she works for Martha Kent. Overall, their relationship is marked by an overt dislike of each other, and the two rarely fail to engage in verbal sparring whenever they come into contact.

During the sixth season, Lana appears to develop more agency, as she leaves Clark Kent to be with Lex Luthor. In her relationship with Lex, she exerts a much greater amount of agency. However, her agency remains contingent on Lana acting in ways which correspond much more closely with the behavior of the Luthors; that is, she challenges people's authority and threatens her elders. These actions represent a definite departure from her behavior as Clark's girlfriend as well as her more stereotypical representation of a wholesome "small town Kansas girl earlier in the series." By contrast, her relationship with Lex has fostered in her patterns of behavior which remain construed as decidedly evil. Thus, Lana still can only act within the boundaries imposed on her by a traditional understanding of gender roles.

Ironically, Lana exerts the greatest agency as a result of supernatural means. When she becomes possessed by a spirit ("Spell"), or falls ill because of a poisonous flower ("Nicodemus"), or when she becomes infected with a vampire-like serum ("Thirst"), Lana's motivation always stems from some external source. Her behavior—as it falls outside the moral codes embodied by Superman—becomes identified as deviant and outside the parameters of sanity. In this vein, her "transgressions" become stabilized when Clark again "saves" her at the conclusion of each of these episodes. She must return to the passive role afforded her by the traditional gender roles, which *Smallville* seems to instantiate.

Chloe is very active, independent and resourceful, except where her interest in Clark lies, at least during the earlier years of the series. Chloe served as the "woman" in her family from the time she was five, when her mother left. After Clark becomes the "man" of the Kent family, these two friends fill similarly mature positions—replete with greater responsibilities—and their identities change as a result. For example, in the later years of the series, Chloe is no longer preoccupied with her own interest in Clark, especially after she learns the true nature of Clark's powers. Rather, Chloe's affection for him has deepened by her increased knowledge, and the fact that he does act as a savior. The *Smallville: The Visual Guide* relates that after Chloe's disclosure to Clark that she knows about his secret, she becomes his "close confidante" and the "brains behind his brawn" (Byrne 65). In their escapades together, he frequently requests her help before he has conferred with anyone else, and her capacity to act as both his confidante and a viable source of accurate information ensures his reliance on her. In the wake of the complete dissolution of his relationship with Lana, Chloe serves as an implicit "stand-in" for Clark's (absent) romantic interest. However, she can still express continuous awe about the breadth and depth of his powers, and Chloe alone can serve as a more objective appreciator of Clark's powers. The other people who have knowledge of his secret all have different kinds of ties with Clark. His mother will obviously think highly of him, heat vision and super speed notwithstanding. Equally, Lionel Luthor will always have some diabolical ulterior motive where Clark's abilities are concerned, despite his allegedly philanthropic interest in Martha Kent and her state senatorship. Chloe exists as the only permanent character who can reflect the audience's surprise and delight at Clark's capacity to rescue those in danger as he evolves into the future Superman.

Already eighteen when she arrives in *Smallville*, Lois acts on a more sophisticated and adult level than had been previously exhibited by Lana and Chloe during the first three seasons. Unlike Lana and Chloe, she bears the advantage of having completed her early and middle adolescence off-screen. In addition, the almost militaristic upbringing she has received from her father, General Sam Lane, has imbued her with a take-charge attitude, and a dynamism which marks her as an extremely assertive and confident female character. Her identity still remains determined by her relationship to Clark, as she often accompanies him on an adventure and occasionally, serves as the object which he must save.

Nevertheless, on a certain level, her eventual destiny of becoming involved with Superman allows the adolescent Lois to maintain a modicum of distance from the Clark Kent in *Smallville*, the nascent Superman. Ultimately, she will become Clark's match (or, at least, Superman's, depending on which version of the mythos one might consider). However, *Smallville* focuses on Clark's development into Superman, and the program has repeatedly confirmed that it will sustain a "no tights, no flight" policy—or, that Clark will not fly until he dons the actual blue and red costume of the Man of Steel. Therefore, Lois and Clark cannot conceivably enter into any kind of serious romantic relationship during the period of Clark Kent's life on which *Smallville* focuses.

At one point in the series, Lois and Clark investigate Chloe's disappearance together. Near the end of the episode, Clark is about to be obliterated by a hit man who can transform his extremities into weapons—specifically, solid steel blades. Lois immediately "saves" Clark by aiming an electric ray at the hit man, which stuns him. Clark then assists her by turning his heat vision onto the hit man so that the villain dissolves into molten liquid. After the exchange, Lois remarks, "I don't know how you ever survived without me," to which Clark retorts, "How did you get here, anyway?" Lois then responds, "What do you mean, how did *I* get here? How did *you* get here?" ("Gone"). Beneath their acerbic banter, Lois continuously challenges Clark to rise to her level, to push past the boundaries of his own self-doubt and recriminations to take an action-oriented perspective in response to his problems, both physical and psychological.

Lois's sassy, take-charge attitude thus forces Clark to rise to her level by inciting him to take a step forward from the more meandering quality of his relationship with Lana, which the audience realizes must be tragically doomed in their knowledge of how Clark's life will eventually unfold. The challenging nature of Lois implicitly signifies that Clark himself requires a strong woman to provoke him into action. This conception of Lois signifies that Superman needs a strong female counterpart. Lois's assertive style provokes Clark into responding on her level. She doesn't allow him to remain trapped in a passive state, paralyzed by emotion, but instead reminds him—and none too gently—that he has within himself the capacity to change, at least partially, the negative circumstances of his condition. Her direct teasing and sarcastic comments might seem like a mildly antagonistic overlay, but, practically speaking, she has goaded Clark out of his bad humor and shown him the potential that he does still control and the power which he can still exert. Perhaps Lois herself represents the idea that all superheroes need a female counterpart who acts more assertively. After all, in *Smallville*, Lois has displayed a romantic predilection for superheroes: her romantic encounters include Aquaman and the Green Arrow. Traditionally, however, Lois dismisses the idea of a romantic relationship with "just" Clark, and instead, she prefers the "ideal" man of Superman. As a result, her preference ensures that even Lois, as a strong and outgoing female character, remains (somewhat) entrapped in a traditional and rather subservient position.

The female characters in *Smallville* can exhibit agency and autonomy, but they do so either within a limited framework, or if they do take actions outside acceptable boundaries, they usually return to actions that fall within the parameters of "acceptable" conduct by the conclusion of a particular episode (or series of linked episodes). Although the females might possess limited autonomy, the structure of *Smallville* reinforces the "process of meaning-constitution" outlined by Butler because the female characters still construct a gender identity through their relationship to a male character.

Ultimately, all of the characters must construct identities which correspond with their respective futures within the larger Superman mythos. The audience has always already had foreknowledge about the outcome of the series; therefore, Lex Luthor can never fully be redeemed, just as Clark and Lana can never enjoy a successful romantic future. Finally, anyone who remains close to Clark must generally adhere to a traditional, Kent-based understanding of morality. Thus, while the cultural sphere of *Smallville* offers temporary possibilities of independence for the female characters in the Superman mythos, the space itself remains situated as predominantly patriarchal, and suggests that females can possess autonomy only within parameters defined by more conventional gender roles.

CONCLUSION

This chapter has examined *Smallville* and has viewed it as a rhetorical text that has the potential to influence its audience's values, specifically in regards to its sense of morality, cultural identity, and gender roles. *Smallville* creates a moral world for its viewers free of moral ambiguity and calls its viewers to do the same, but offers no transcendent authority on which to base its conceptions of good and evil. The means used by the forces of good and evil within *Smallville* are remarkably similar, potentially calling the viewer to embrace a moral relativism and action using any means necessary in order to achieve "good" ends. *Smallville* also beckons its viewers to embrace one particular version of the American dream; that is a moralistic myth of universal brotherhood that calls the viewer to guilt and sacrifice of one's self in order to help society fulfill this dream. Finally, *Smallville* presents a world with specifically prescribed gender roles that privileges patriarchy and limits the agency of women to act without a male reason or counterpart. This view of the world has potential negative implications specifically for female audiences; if they apply this particular piece of "equipment for living" to their own lives, the belief that women are capable of acting autonomously is subverted.

However, when all is said and done, we still like *Smallville*. Although Rob no longer runs around the house with an "S" scribbled on his T-Shirt, he will most probably still wear the latest in Superman red-and-blue silkscreen fashion; Grace will most probably still secretly wish for the ability to fly; and both will most probably continue to be avid fans of the series. Our criticism of *Smallville* has afforded us the ability to delve deeper into our passion for "all things Superman." Superman, and now *Smallville*, is part of the collective consciousness of America, and we have attempted to expose what lives at an unconscious level within the series. Our deeper look into *Smallville* has led us to question some of the implications of the messages the show presents to its viewers. As Richard M. Weaver notes, "Ideas have consequences." We have simply examined a few of the ideas presented in the *Smallville* series and have suggested the potential negative consequences of those ideas. It is in the spirit of better understanding the power the Superman mythos has upon audiences that we have explored this issue. Indeed, it is in the very spirit of Superman and all that Superman stands for that we present this chapter. That is, in the spirit of truth, we question the moral absolutes and the particular version of the American dream presented in *Smallville*; in the desire for justice, we want women to have a voice without the necessity of male influence or agency; and we will continue for fight for ... some other stuff.

NOTES

1. The three theoretical approaches we use later in this paper—mythological structure, competing American dreams, and feminism—loosely correspond with these genres.

2. The Superman myth has often capitalized upon its parallels with the Christ story, such as in *Superman* (1978), the first of the Superman Trilogy, in which Jor-El, Superman's Kryptonian biological father, refers to sending his only son to save the world; this is but one of many obvious references to the Christ story in this film and throughout Superman mythology in general.

3. Indeed, if there is a tragic hero in *Smallville*, it is Lex Luthor as a version of Milton's Satan.

4. The choice to change Superman's slogan from fighting for "Truth, Justice, and the American Way" to "Truth, Justice, and other stuff" has proven controversial for the producers of the Superman franchise. The creators did this to make Superman more applicable in a global context and more palatable to larger audiences. The most recent incarnation in *Superman Returns* (2006) also uses a variation on the latter of these phrases as the Superman slogan. Nevertheless, Superman's red and blue costuming and his position in the American conscious still encourage the viewer to see him as representing distinctly American values and interests. For more information on this discussion, see Christopher Campbell's "Truth, Justice, and the Worldwide Box Office" (www.cinematical.com).

5. It is worthy of mention that as the creators of *Smallville* establish a clear moral universe between good and evil, they do so by using the colors of the American flag, red and blue, and Clark Kent himself supplies the third color, white. Thus, the *Smallville* viewer may read that a "good" person is a "good *white* person." Likewise, viewers might also read: A good person is a "good American," whatever the way "good" is defined in the world of *Smallville*. We will discuss this later implication in more detail in the next section of this paper.

6. Terrence R. Wandtke, this volume's editor, made this observation.

7. Grace's colleague, Aimee Frederickson, was essential in helping to implement the gender theories of Judith Butler in this essay.

WORKS CITED

"Aqua." *Smallville*. Warner Bros. DVD, 2006.

Aurthur, Kate. "Young Male Viewers Boost 'Smallville.'" *New York Times* 20 May 2006, late ed: B9.

Brummett, Barry. *Rhetorical Dimensions of Popular Culture*. Tuscaloosa: University of Alabama Press, 1991.

Burke, Kenneth. *The Philosophy of Literary Form: Studies in Symbolic Action.* Berkeley: University of California Press, 1973.

Butler, Judith. *Gender Trouble: Feminism and the Subversion of Identity.* New York: Routledge, 1999.

Byrne, Craig. *Smallville: The Visual Guide.* New York: Dorling Kindersley, 2006.

Dow, Bonnie J. *Prime-Time Feminism: Television, Media Culture, and the Women's Movement Since 1970.* Philadelphia: University of Pennsylvania Press, 1996.

"Drone." *Smallville.* Warner Bros. DVD, 2003.

Eco, Umberto. "The Myth of Superman." Trans., Natalie Chilton. *Diacritics* 2 (Spring, 1972): 14–22.

_____. *The Role of the Reader: Explorations in the Semiotics of Texts.* Bloomington: Indiana University Press, 1979.

"Exile." *Smallville.* Warner Bros. DVD, 2004.

"Exodus." *Smallville.* Warner Bros. DVD, 2004.

"Fever." *Smallville.* Warner Bros. DVD, 2004.

Fisher, Walter R. "Reaffirmation and Subversion of the American Dream." *Quarterly Journal of Speech* 59 (1973): 160–7.

Giroux, Henry A. "Animating Youth: The Disneyfication of Children's Culture." *Socialist Review* 24 (1994): 23–35.

"Gone." *Smallville.* Warner Bros. DVD, 2005.

Hinson, Hal. "*Smallville*: Getting to the Heart of a Hero." *New York Times* 27 January 2002: C10.

"Hourglass." *Smallville.* Warner Bros. DVD, 2003.

"Nicodemus." *Smallville.* Warner Bros. DVD, 2003.

Osborn, Michael. "Archetypal Metaphor in Rhetoric: The Light-Dark Family." *Quarterly Journal of Speech* 53 (1967): 115–126.

"Pilot." *Smallville.* Warner Bros. DVD, 2003.

"Reckoning." *Smallville.* Warner Bros. DVD, 2006.

"Red." *Smallville.* Warner Bros. DVD, 2004.

Robinson, Lillian S. *Wonder Women: Feminisms and Superheroes.* New York: Routledge, 2004.

"Spell." *Smallville.* Warner Bros. DVD, 2005.

"Splinter." *Smallville.* Warner Bros. DVD, 2006.

Superman. Dir. Richard Donner. Warner Bros., 1978.

"Thirst." *Smallville.* Warner Bros. DVD, 2006.

"Unsafe." *Smallville.* Warner Bros. DVD, 2005.

Ward, Annalee R. *Mouse Morality: The Rhetoric of Disney Animated Film.* Austin: University of Texas Press, 2002.

"Wither." *Smallville.* Warner Bros. DVD, 2006.

Yeffeth, Glenn. *The Man From Krypton: A Closer Look at Superman.* Dallas: BenBella Books, 2005.

"Le Western Noir":
The Punisher *as Revisionist Superhero Western*

LORRIE PALMER

The man in black with vengeance in his heart has come roaring onto our movie screens in many guises, across eras and vastly different pop culture landscapes. Whether he is a cowboy, a Jedi knight, or a comic book character, he answers some urge in us to see both darkness and light in our heroes. With two film adaptations (and a sequel in the works), the Punisher, in his evolution, and with his genre roots buried deep in our collective cinematic myths, is worth a closer look. As a character, The Punisher first appeared in Marvel Comics' *The Amazing Spider-Man* #129 in 1974. Starting out as a foil for Spider-Man, he gradually evolved into a post–Vietnam anti-hero in the vein of cinematic vigilantes like the ones in *Dirty Harry* (1971) and *Death Wish* (1974). He had no superpowers or hi-tech gadgets, just his specialized Marine Corps training and his own implacable determination to right society's wrongs by eliminating the villains who perpetrated them.

The director of the 2004 film version of *The Punisher*, Jonathan Hensleigh, is mindful of a plotline "straight out of Othello" (Hutchins) which partially aligns the film's protagonist, Frank Castle, with Iago because he shrewdly plays on the jealousies of his enemy, instigating the action of the story. Both the comic and film versions revise Shakespeare's villainous prototype as an anti-hero, leaving his dark impulses intact. The film's producer talks about the character as one who has to pick up the mantle of justice when regular law enforcement fails: "It has to do with this whole system in which he has been a willing soldier not giving him the justice that he feels is deserved when killers walk free" (*Comics2Film*). Therefore, the filmmakers looked at not just action films but "crime sagas and westerns made between 1960 and 1978" (*Cinema Review*), an indication of the intricate ancestry that can be claimed by *The Punisher*. Hensleigh was inspired by the dark action films of the 60s and 70s made by directors such as Sergio Leone, Clint Eastwood, and Sam Peckinpah. Likewise, comic book writer Garth Ennis, born in Belfast and raised on John Wayne westerns, further expands the character's genre influences in his graphic nov-

els through violent shoot-outs enacted by an increasingly tortured, solitary hero. This author's work (along with that of the other Punisher comic
book writers and artists) shapes a character arc in the Punisher that mirrors the iconography and evolution of the Western's complex protagonist.

The Western has been said to descend from multiple sources, including Victorian melodrama, an idea that lends itself to the built-in hybridity of the genre. Melodrama, in these early incarnations, was known for
"its aspect of excitation, its display of violent action" and the fact that its
"emphasis on excitation tied melodrama to urban modernity" (Singer 149).
Kenneth MacKinnon describes recent "male-oriented family melodramas"
(87) such as *The Godfather* and their portrayals of the "varieties of male
power within patriarchy, right down to what is clearly male powerlessness"
(97). These are concepts well-suited to genres that depict males in conflict
with each other, as they effectively cross generic boundaries. Films in the
noir tradition, such as *The Big Heat* and *Desperate Hours*, as well as quintessential Westerns such as John Ford's *Stagecoach*, *The Searchers*, and *The Man
Who Shot Liberty Valance*, are keen examples of melodramatic masculinity
functioning within those thematic structures so inimical to the Western.

In *The Big Heat*, Dave Bannion, although initially allied with the forces
of law and order (much like Frank Castle), becomes increasingly similar
to the villains he pursues after they murder his family. Seeking vengeance,
he breaks with traditional police procedure and steps into the dark, urban
world they inhabit as well as into their moral ambiguity. Likewise, when
the mild-mannered patriarch Dan Hilliard and his family are threatened
by the violent psychopath Glenn Griffith in *The Desperate Hours*, he must
find his own dark nature within that dangerous proximity. In his retaliation, he circumvents the police (who gather impotently outside), learns
to use uncharacteristic psychological cruelty to inflict pain, and ultimately
sends a man to his death without flinching.

In *Stagecoach*, *The Man Who Shot Liberty Valance*, and *The Searchers*, the
western frontier frames similar struggles in which men enact pursuit,
revenge, individualistic expressions of rough justice, and battles for family. The Ringo Kid in *Stagecoach* seeks the murderers of his father and
brother. In *Liberty Valance*, Tom Doniphan (again, John Wayne) must personally dispatch the villain when the politicians, the press, and the frontier authorities only talk about a better world.

In *The Searchers*, Ethan Edwards obsessively tracks down the Comanche
tribe that wiped out nearly his whole family. Ethan Edwards is a bleaker,
revisionist version of the straightforward pursuit of justice sought by Ringo.
Like Frank Castle, he loses part of his own better nature and flirts with
true madness on his bloody trek through enemy territory. This is especially
true in the Garth Ennis graphic novel *The Punisher: Born*, as Frank Castle
deliberately endures three tours of duty in Vietnam because he begins to
crave the violent quest, the brutality of the killing fields, and the unleash-

Thomas Jane stars as the Punisher in the most recent film version of the comic book anti-hero. From a promotional photograph for *The Punisher* (Lions Gate Films, 2004). Motion picture copyright owned by Lions Gate.

ing of his internal demons. He also believes that the connection he has to his family is his only hope of being rehumanized. The codes of the Old West, self-sufficiency and personal action, thread through all these narratives and continue on, within parallel themes, in film version of *The Punisher*. In each case, traditional forces of authority are inadequate, leaving the protagonist to enter into direct confrontation with the hostile foes arrayed against him (and a society unable to do so on its own). He must negotiate the shifting dynamics of male power and often adapt the villain's dark modus as his own in order to defeat him and gain vengeance and justice. This formula links melodrama, film noir and the Western to each other and Frank Castle's story to them all.

In *Super Heroes: A Modern Mythology*, Richard Reynolds describes the origins of comic book characters in a way that often parallels those of the Western protagonist. For instance, he writes that "[t]he hero is marked out from society" and that his "devotion to justice overrides even his devotion to the law" (16). Furthermore, the superhero, like the Western hero, suffers through personal issues involving family, vengeance, and guilt— especially as personified by characters like Batman, Spider-Man, Daredevil, and the Punisher. Reynolds also notes that a superhero's world "is one of mirror images and opposites" (68), a critical similarity to the movie cowboy (and his relationship with the villain) as I discuss him here. Through my close reading of *The Punisher* and my simultaneous, parallel examination of the characters and storylines of several influential Westerns, I will show how key aspects of the modern superhero are pre-figured in the Western film genre as well as how other generic elements from melodrama and film noir, through their own links to the Western, also color this increasingly nuanced figure.

For instance, a direct comparison in the motivation and character of both Ethan Edwards and Batman gives us an insight into the connection between the superhero and the Western hero. Reynolds could be describing both men when he says that "madness is a part of Batman's special identity, and that the protagonist's obsessive character links him with his enemies in a more personal way" (67). Thus is Ethan is paired with Scar, and Batman with his own antagonistic doubles such as the Joker.

Exploring film genre, Thomas Schatz writes that "the Western represents a basic story, which is never completely 'told' but is reexamined and reworked in a variety of ways" (37). Philip French speaks to the universality of this genre: "There is no theme you cannot imagine in terms of the Western, no situation which cannot be transposed to the West" (23). Throughout the history of the narrative arts, theater, literature, and myth, an oppositional structure has been the overriding method of storytelling. "The Western's essential conflict ... is expressed in a variety of oppositions" (Schatz 45). The most predominant of these was defined when Jim Kitses adapted "Lévi-Strauss's structural analysis of myth" into a "central antithesis between wilderness and civilization, from which all other conflicts derive" (Buscombe 292). Thus, the Western, with its eternal syntax of good versus evil, and especially with the moral ambiguities of later incarnations, provides a framework by which so many unexpected narratives may be examined.

The oppositions that are visible in the Western traveled forward through successive genre developments. The gangster genre of the '30s, along with the "hard-boiled detective film" of the '40s (Schatz 111) and the resulting evolution of '50s film noir all build on the basic mythology of the Western as one in which "a strong hero" (Wright 138) is "divided between two value systems" (Altman 220). In most cases, "he tends to generate conflict through his very existence. He is a man of action and of few words, with an unspoken code of honor that commits him to the vulnerable ... community and at the same time motivates him to remain distinctly apart from it" (Schatz 51). Our ingrained cultural notions of the Western hero as a man apart are echoed when the Punisher is described in a graphic novel as a man "above all laws, all codes, but his own" (Goodwin). His counterpoint is the villain, who can be both functional and symbolic, and who does "harm to the hero and to the society ... with impunity as far as the legal institutions of society are concerned" (Wright 65). These characters balance the narrative even when "the hero becomes very much like the men he is chasing" (Wright 156) by moving outside traditional authority and breaking the law himself. "Genre films regularly depend on

... dualistic structures" and "intertextual references" (Altman 24–25); it is through these that archetypal characters like the lone, laconic hero who slips over the line and the villain who frequently reflects that hero's darker self are threaded through our literature, our myths, and our movies. Therefore, we can follow a structural and thematic connection from Shakespeare to nineteenth-century melodrama to Westerns to film noir to present-day action films (and graphic novels along the way), right up to and including *The Punisher.*

When George N. Fenin and William K. Everson use the phrase "Le Western noir" in their book, *The Western,* they are talking about Anthony Mann, a director "brought up on hard-bitten city thrillers" (278) who also directed several films that are considered key examples of noir-ish Westerns of the 1950s. Thomas Schatz describes how "[John] Wayne's stoic machismo and [James] Stewart's 'aw shucks' naiveté are effectively inverted to reveal genuinely psychotic, antisocial figures" (40). The result is our understanding that genre can be as unfixed as any character wandering across a movie screen. Revisions in classic generic characterizations are what keep the form alive. And in whatever genre he comes, a film hero has a relationship with the natural world and with community in some form, and must confront the oppositions contained in these relationships. The Punisher moves within two worlds: one is the natural world, the family and its rituals, civilization. The other is the wilderness, the city, savagery. Genres such as the Western, film noir, and the melodrama contain the same oppositions, whether they are expressed through the use of a literal wilderness, an urban setting, or within domestic family space. In addition, there are often elements depicting varying expressions of ritual, along with masochism, sadism, and fetishism, within the narrative to bring deeper meaning to the relationship between the villain and the hero: to link them along an ambiguous moral spectrum and to situate them within multiple thematic oppositions. Through the use of iconographic imagery, Westerns and film noir can merge with graphic novels into a single film grammar that establishes a fluid hybridity between them.

When *The Punisher* opens, it is with the flourish of a spaghetti Western. The graphics, stark white letters on a black background, are soon riddled with bullet holes as the sound of a lone trumpet dominates the score. The writer and director, Jonathan Hensleigh, thus sets up his film with cues about its origins and its influences. The surname of the protagonist, Frank Castle, is itself a dualistic element that connotes both civilized community and militaristic fortification. In order that his ultimate identity as the Punisher, a man with "antisocial status" (Schatz 49), makes more of an impact, the film first shows us his life as a happy family man who has a successful career with the FBI. He has just finished his last undercover job, a sting operation to halt the sale of an illegal arms cache in Tampa, Florida. During the mission, Bobby Saint, son of local businessman Howard Saint (played by John Travolta) is killed. It is made clear that Bobby is presented with full knowledge of the illegality of his actions. His death, however, is accidental and Castle expresses anger afterwards at the unnecessary tragedy. He is then feted by his fellow officers in a retirement send-off before his departure for home.

Thomas Schatz describes the use of a critical doorway in *The Searchers* as a "visual motif" (76) indicating a character's relationship with civilization. Both this film and *Shane* frame their protagonists with the symbolic access points, like doors and windows, of a family space. In *The Searchers*, Ethan Edwards is filmed approaching an open door from the outside (in the film's most iconographic image) and walking away from it in the opening and closing scenes. In the latter, the mysterious gunfighter, Shane, stands outside the window of the Starrett homestead as he converses with Marian, a wife and mother who, despite their mutual attraction, he can never have, in a life he can never be a part of. These scenes highlight "the hero's basic inability to pass through that doorway and enjoy civilized existence" (Schatz 76).

Frank Castle's relationship to the domestic sphere is a revision of this theme. He is initially framed, lit by bright overhead rays beaming down, in the open doorway of his family home and, unlike the characters in the previous examples, he can enter through it comfortably. In both his working environment and his home, he is shown in these opening sequences to be a part of the world of family, institutions, and community. "He is upright, clean-living, sharp-shooting, a White Anglo-Saxon Protestant who respects the law, the flag, women and children" (French 48). He has loving relationships with his wife and young son and is looking forward to a long-awaited reunion with his extended family in Puerto Rico.

The dialectic relationship between civilization and savagery is explored in *The Punisher* through three family groups within the society depicted in the film. The Saints "represent unbridled market self-interest" (Wright 140) and yet are, on the surface, respectable. They are highly visible and wealthy; the Saint building, with its towering, cathedral-like roof, marks the city skyline as a distinctive symbol of power. Howard, his dark-haired wife, Livia, his two sons, his business associates, and his employees are shown nearly always dressed in black, which is also the color of his car. Like the Western villain, then, "he dresses in black, rides a dark horse and is doomed to die" (French 48). Thomas Schatz further describes a noir version of the Western villain, the gangster, who "must ultimately lie dead in the streets" (90), and who shows "irrational brutality ... enterprising business mentality" (87), and a "perverse devotion to his family" (88).

This last point is evident in the dark undercurrents of the Saint family, as it is revealed that Howard jealously covets his wife, despite their genuine affection. At the first sign of something amiss, he investigates behind her back rather than simply asking her for the truth, a fatal flaw that will be exploited by Castle. This family is about status. A pair of Harry Winston diamond earrings carries a nearly Hitchcockian object power. Castle delivers his first message to Saint on the golf course of his private country club. Howard Saint's remaining son, Johnny, who was one of the assassins of the Castle family, is shown coming out of a door with a sign above it that proclaims it to be "The Best Nude Bar" in the city. Along with his deceased brother, Bobby, he is clearly not a member of the upstanding working class that Frank Castle's family is shown to be. Family life at the Saint mansion is conducted through layers of security, with bodyguards and paid lackeys at each successive perimeter that surrounds them, proving, in addition, that "the bad guys are much richer than the good guys" (Wright 139–140). They are seldom shown outdoors, especially in daylight.

The Castle family is more casual and more ordinary: picnicking, swimming, walking on the beach in the idyllic setting of Aguadilla Bay in Puerto Rico. They also have a military tradition, with both Frank and his father having served. Frank's service, his power, has remained invisible to mainstream society through his involvement with Special Operations and a Counter Terrorism Unit. He and his blonde wife, Maria, are dressed in white clothes during a romantic beach scene in which they discuss how lucky they are to have each other, to have their family. The next morning, they talk about having another child as they watch their son, William, sleep. This family is about simple pleasures. During the family reunion, which takes place on the beach in front of his parents' modest island home, kids enjoy vanilla ice cream cones, couples dance in slow motion, Frank sits quietly, tilting his head back and breathing deep, the picture of contentment, while Maria and his son explore the wildlife near the surf.

The final family structure in the film is made up of the "social outcasts" (Schatz 50) that adopt Frank after his family's death, despite his deliberate attempt to remain apart. Just as "[t]here are three mediating figures in *Liberty Valance*," there are three characters who inhabit the isolated, run-down tenement apartment building "on the periphery of the community" (Schatz 50) that become his urban family. This dwelling is like "the Western fort manned by misfits" (French 20) and Joan, Mr. Bumpo, and Spacker Dave, like the microcosm of characters thrown together in *Stagecoach*, form a group that "represents a range of social issues" (Schatz 50) and, further, are all depicted as belonging to the working class. Joan is a waitress (like Hallie in *Liberty Valance*) who is trying to overcome an addiction to alcohol and abusive boyfriends. When we first see her, she is bent over a sewing machine working on the apron for her uniform and there is a jar of saved pennies in front of her. She is a "bruised and intelligent woman" that later speaks earnestly to Frank about a "commitment to reality" (French 143) when she points out that, in his quest for violent vengeance, he is no different than his enemies.

The heavyset Mr. Bumpo is an example of soft masculinity, with his penchant for preparing (and definitely eating) desserts while singing along to "La Donna è mobile" from Puccini's *Rigoletto*—food and opera as escape mechanisms. Dave, on the other hand, displays the badge of alienated youth, with multiple facial piercings on his eyebrow, his nose, his lower lip, and his tongue. He is estranged from the traditional support systems of parents and school. In his first scene, he is playing a computer game, scolding a figure on the screen for being a coward as well as a grave disappointment to his mother and father, hinting at personal experience. He is also the most benign example of masochism to be found in *The Punisher.*

This family is about sanctuary and, despite their outsider status, provides a human element to the nearly machine-like Frank Castle. They are comic relief, music, food, and loyalty in his cold world, whether he wants them or not. Furthermore, as in *Stagecoach,* they prove that "those who display the most nobility are the social outcasts" (Fenin 238). When Castle is in trouble, it is this new family unit that comes to his rescue, a revision of both the 'classic' and 'vengeance' hero in Westerns who "can take care of himself ... and needs no one" (Wright 138).

Thus, these three family groups embody "[t]he Western's essential conflict between civilization and savagery" (Schatz 48) with the Saint family on the savage side and the two families of Frank Castle on the civilized side. The urban setting of Tampa is the wilderness, the "contested space where forces of social order and anarchy" (Schatz 83) collide, and it contrasts with the natural world specifically associated with Frank Castle and his family structures. In the first scene with his son, he talks to him in the lush, green back yard of the family home. Later, there is the seaside family reunion. Finally, when he first drives up to the ugly tenement building where he will be living, the master shot reveals it to be located in a bleak, underdeveloped neighborhood next to a sad and scraggly empty lot. However, in the next shot, Joan is shown digging in the dirt, planting flowers, surrounded by a verdant patch of green next to the brick edifice of their home, as she turns to watch his car pull in. The city, as wilderness, is emphasized by long shots of the skyline dominated by towering vertical structures that bring to mind John Ford's favorite shooting location in Arizona's Monument Valley, "where awesome stone formations reach up to the gods but the desolate soil around them" (Schatz 47) is not arable enough to support the community that lives there. This isolated building is like the hardscrabble little settlement that tries to coax a living from the edge of the wilderness.

These oppositions are further demonstrated through the concept of high culture versus low culture. The strains of a Puccini opera accompany the most elaborate fight scene in *The Punisher* when Frank is nearly pummeled to death by a 6'11", 310-pound character known as "the Russian," a villain hired by Saint to kill him in a scene first enacted in Garth Ennis's

"Glutton for Punishment" chapter of *Welcome Back, Frank*. Good guys in both *Tombstone* (1993) and *The Man Who Shot Liberty Valance* recite the same ideas in the 'St. Crispin's Day' speech from Shakespeare's *Henry V*, with all these scenes serving to associate the forces for good with high culture. In a contrasting example, Howard Saint calls in a professional hitman, Harry Heck, from Memphis (played by country singer and actor Mark Collie) who shows up at Joan's diner with an ominous guitar case in hand. He opens it, looking directly at Castle, who is seated nearby and whose hand goes for his gun just in case the black-clad stranger does not pull out a musical instrument. Surprisingly he does and begins to sing a mournful and threatening country song which speaks of a time when Frank's time won't be his own anymore. This hired gun sports black nail polish and a tattooed teardrop by his right eye, affectations which place him squarely in the bad guy camp, and before he leaves the diner he tells Frank that he will sing the song at his funeral.

In *The Punisher*, it is through the elements of ritual, along with masochism, sadism, and fetishism, that further connections to the Western (and its generic offspring) are discernible. Ritual is depicted most notably in scenes of family meals and food that are inextricably linked with notions of family and community. The Castle family, even in so brief a period as they are onscreen, is shown sitting down to two large, communal dinners. There are toasts offered to family, the long tables are loaded with plates of food, and when assassins arrive on the scene, there is a shot of bullets shattering a large bowl of salad as the outdoor barbecue pit explodes. There are two later scenes that transfer the dining ritual to Frank's new situation. In the first, he is eating alone at a window table in the diner where Joan works and the only other patrons are Dave and Bumpo, who are eating at the counter. In the second, to show his gradual (if temporary) integration into the small group, he is interrupted in his solitary consumption of canned sardines by the invitation to have some real food with his neighbors. They sit down at a small dinette set to a regular meal of meat, vegetables and iced tea, all of which are served in retro kitchenware (frosted glasses and serving bowls in blue, yellow, and, most tellingly, tangerine and avocado) that harkens back to an old-fashioned era of nuclear families. Joan and Frank are like the parents of the two younger participants, as they all sit down at the dinner table and say what they are thankful for after such a satisfying supper.

Raising a new church in *My Darling Clementine*, the opening meal from *The Searchers*, and the predominance of the kitchen (and some extremely large plates of food) in *The Man Who Shot Liberty Valance* all speak to the presence and importance of ritual human behavior in Westerns. In contrast, the Saints are never shown eating together. After Bobby is killed, Howard, Livia, Johnny, and the family capo, Quentin Glass, sit around a glass table and toast their missing member, but there is no food in sight.

They do not partake in traditional family rituals and the setting of this one table scene takes place in their nightclub, called Saints & Sinners (an appropriate expression of genre dialectics), where they are surrounded by bodyguards and strangers. It is primarily the fringes of their home that appear onscreen: the balcony, the patio, the foyer, never a kitchen area, and, aside from Bobby's burial, their only forms of ritual are done individually, not as a family. Howard goes to the office at precisely the same time every day and Livia spends every Thursday night working out at the gym, getting her nails done, and going to the movies. Each one of them performs these routines like clockwork, providing Castle with the tools he needs to destroy them. Such negative connotations of ritual, therefore, emphasize the stark difference between the Saints and the more civilized family in the tenement.

There has always been "a strong undercurrent of masochism" (French 16), along with sadism and fetishism, in Westerns, as well as film noir and melodrama. For example, in the Western films directed by Anthony Mann, the "heroes are frequently wounded in painful ways which go far beyond the obvious purpose of providing a revenge motive" and beatings are often administered "at the hands of sadistic enemies" (French 118), which is clearly the case in John Ford's film when Liberty Valance repeatedly hits, kicks, and humiliates James Stewart's Ransom Stoddard. The horse head scene in *The Godfather* is a perfect blend of gangster sadism and Western semantics within a melodramatic family saga. In *The Punisher*, Howard Saint kicks at the prostrate lackey who led his son, Bobby, into the trouble that got him killed, then shoots a leg out from under another employee before killing him with two additional bullets. Livia Saint passes the decree that, not just Frank Castle, but his entire family, is to be killed to avenge Bobby's death. Later, after Castle has planted some incriminating evidence, Howard draws out the murder of his best friend and closest associate, Quentin, by slapping him, cutting his arm, and stabbing him several times as the man begs to know why. Furthermore, he invokes the name of Jim Bowie, who died at the Alamo, as he copies that frontiersman's ritual of kicking aside the furniture before a fight. Later, as lightning crashes, he is equally cruel to his wife for her perceived affair with Quentin (who, unbeknownst to her husband, was gay) before he throws her off a bridge to land in front of an oncoming train (a twist on the old melodramas where a righteous woman is on the railroad tracks). For his part, Quentin tortures young Dave by pulling out all the studs and small hoops that adorn his face in an effort to get him, or Bumpo, to tell them Castle's location. In their determined silence, with Joan hiding an unconscious Frank in a freight elevator beneath their feet, the makeshift family proves as heroic as any western hero.

Frank, through the bullet scars and the superhuman beatings he endures throughout, is a figure with both literal and "symbolic wounds"

(French 118) that position him "between subject positions of mastery and being mastered, sadism and masochism—and thus between traditional masculinity and femininity" (MacKinnon 86). This dualism leads logically from the division of "nineteenth-century stage melodrama into 'melodrama of action' and 'melodrama of passion'" (MacKinnon 94) to a film such as *The Punisher* in which both of these elements play out. Likewise, in the graphic novel, *Welcome Back, Frank,* writer Garth Ennis has a drunken doctor (shades of Doc Boone in *Stagecoach*) work on Castle after a brutal shoot-out. The doctor itemizes the weaponry and the wounds: "Six magnum loads.... Massive tissue damage, punctured lung, three broken ribs, fractured sternum, more blood out of you than in" (Ennis). The specificity of pain here points to Frank's doubled status as both a vulnerable, broken body and a nearly invincible warrior—a living embodiment of action and passion.

The body of Thomas Jane, in the character of the Punisher, is fetishized in this film adaptation, along with his weapons and his car. He is frequently filmed in fragments, with his biceps, his thighs, his lean waist, shown in various poses as he wraps himself around the engine of his car while rebuilding it or as he straps on various weaponry. He is shown to wear guns, virtually clothing himself in them in the way that female characters are often filmed putting on suggestive attire. The camera tracks slowly over his collection of military ordnance: grenades, arrows, shells, a hi-tech bow, and multiple guns. He is equated with all this hardware, even with machines, as close-ups of his arms and hands combine with both engine and weapon components to fill the frame. Likewise, in the comic book *The Punisher: War Zone,* Frank Castle's body is emphasized, depicted as overtly male, even homoerotic, sitting on his unmade bed clad only in underwear. His biceps are flexed, his calf muscles bulging, and his chest, back, and arms are covered in hair. The warrior's body, then, is a fetish symbol just like his weapons, especially every possible permutation of the gun. As a visual medium, the Punisher graphic novels are able to foreground the image of the gun through the exaggerated perspective found, for instance, in the artwork of Tim Bradstreet and Steve Dillon. Castle's guns are often drawn as they thrust toward the reader, enlarged and at a downward angle, emphasizing the Punisher's dominant stature. They are prominent in both the text and the art, clearly designated as fetish items.

The naturalness of Castle's earlier associations and his penultimate involvement with weapons and battle as "an archangel without wings, a superman whose main interest on this earth is to redress wrongs," (Fenin 30) comes down to a key opposition. "Because the Westerner exists on the periphery of both the community and the wilderness, he never loses touch with either world" (Schatz 51). The way Ethan understands Indian burial rituals in *The Searchers,* and the way that Bannion's capacity for violence comes to rival that of Vince Stone's in *The Big Heat,* is paralleled here with a symbolic ability possessed and utilized by Frank Castle. When he arrives at Saints & Sinners for his final showdown with Howard Saint, he spends several minutes in the woods nearby, a natural, outdoor space, fitting himself with guns, explosive devices, and a bow and arrow. Like the Indians in Westerns, he is skilled at this most stealthy of attacks. And like many examples of the Western genre, we hear the *phssst* of the arrow before we see it strike its first target, a guard outside the club. As he falls downward, out of the frame, we see Castle in the far distance firing his weapon from an elevated position, as Native Americans were often depicted doing from the bluffs and mountains of the Old West.

Interestingly, the second shot of Castle shooting his bow and arrow (featured earlier in this chapter) is done using the kind of iconographic pose one would associate with Robin Hood, not an inappropriate comparison because he later leaves behind money he has stolen from Saint's business for his three low-income neighbors. Iconography plays a large part in our relationship with genre films, especially as it regards the Western hero with "his horse, his gun" (Buscombe 286) and the tense shoot-out on Main Street. The composition of the shots in *The Punisher* depicting two showcase shoot-outs copies those used in virtually every example of the scene ever filmed. Castle, wearing a long black duster, pulls back the edge of his coat over his holster; "he wears a gun on his thigh" (Buscombe 203) and his hand is shown in close-up, hovering over it, ready to draw. The two men facing him do the same and there is a series of head shots and eyeline matches as they assess each other. When Castle gets the draw and fires two guns at once, spent shell casings are ejected past his head in a flurry of firing and his enemies are lifted off their feet in slow motion photography that is "as stylized, graceful and artfully choreographed as a ballet" (French 116), an effect that has been part of cinematic screen violence since Arthur Penn's *Bonnie and Clyde* and Sam Peckinpah's *The Wild Bunch.* Gangsters and cowboys tend to die well on film.

It is through iconographic symbols that further thematic connections can be made within the combined Western-superhero canon. For example, the set design in *The Punisher* forms a link to another, more mainstream superhero. In one of the nightclub scenes, there is a live band playing and behind them is a replica of the rotating double rings that are used in the trial scenes on Krypton in *Superman* and *Superman II.* These rings are the site of judgment, of justice, in *Superman* and, in their echo here at Saints and Sinners, ultimately evoke a similar image. Meaning-through-symbolism abounds in Westerns through icons such as the white hat (the good guy), the horse (the Old World), and the train (the New World, intruding).

In *The Punisher*, Frank Castle wears a t-shirt that his son gave him on the day he died. It is black with a white skull face on the front, which comes to symbolize the part of him that died with his family as well as his own eventual status as a bringer of death to those he hunts. Young William told him that it would "ward off evil spirits" and it becomes his dark identity when he goes into battle. In Ennis's *The Punisher: Born*, the white skull illustrates this duality by speaking to Frank Castle as an external voice, Death itself and at the same time, represents his own internal darkness. The film adaptations of other comic book heroes also use distinctive symbols such as the illuminated Bat signal in *Batman* and the flaming avian outline left behind in *The Crow* (both are, likewise, vengeance narratives). These later superhero films illustrate a shift from idealistic heroes with simple, more ideological goals ("Truth, justice, and the American way" in *Superman*) to personal, darker-themed, revisionist revenge tales. This transition mirrors the one that occurred in the Western film genre, as embodied in the character arcs found from *Stagecoach* to *The Searchers* and on through the nihilism of the Western's later cycle found in *The Wild Bunch* and *High Plains Drifter*.

This dark evolution of the Western genre is described by Thomas Schatz when he writes that legendary Western director John Ford "deconstructs and critiques" (77) the myths of the frontier, myths that he himself helped create in early Westerns like *Stagecoach*. Gung-ho Manifest Destiny and jingoistic ideologies gave way to cynicism and a fragmentation of Western heroes as they began to fight against even their own mythic identities. The cowboys themselves grew darker, more violent, and more divided within themselves in just the same way that comic book vigilantes, like the Punisher, would. Thus, the public personas and the secret identities of superheroes are the modern enactment of this evolving cultural representation.

In the same way that so many of these film genres are connected, so too are questions of fetishism and iconography to style, and they all find their culmination in visual aesthetics. "Really, it is not violence at all which is the 'point' of the Western movie, but a certain image of a man, a style, which expresses itself most clearly in violence" and "to work out how a man might look when he shoots" (Warshow 203). There is an element of this idea playing out when Travis Bickle practices pointing his gun at a mirror in *Taxi Driver*, itself a hybrid of influences which include film noir and Westerns, most notably *The Searchers*. In Amy Taubin's comprehensive exploration of *Taxi Driver*, she describes screenwriter Paul Schrader's and director Martin Scorsese's conscious, deliberate use of John Ford's Western as "the ur-text" for their film (19). When Travis points his gun at the mirror, examining how he looks in that pose, he is linked to the John Wayne character: "Ethan, the lone wolf, becomes Travis, the psychopath, trying to work out on his own what it means to be a man" (Taubin 20). The legacy of the Western gunslinger is fragmented within Travis, "who has problems with boundaries and with splitting" (Taubin 22) in his identification so that his own reflection is part pure image and part meaning, to him and to us. In other words, through the genre conventions of the Western and our own expectations as honed by those conventions, the image of a man with a gun is imbued with cultural, historical meaning. He, as a character, is made mobile across multiple genres and, in the case of the graphic novel, multiple media as well. Artist Steve Dillon, in *Welcome Back, Frank,* draws the Punisher in such a way that we see the Western hero, deliberately and clearly. In a Chapter 1 panel, he stands alone in the frame, wearing a long duster coat, with a holster strapped to each thigh, and a gun in his hand. All at once, we are looking at a revisionist cowboy.

Finally, *The Punisher* evinces a lineage to film noir through several elements, most notably through the use of deep space, glass imagery, wet surfaces, and oblique lines. In the aforementioned Robin Hood–inspired shot which takes place in the nightclub, there is deep horizontal and vertical space behind Frank Castle as he pulls back his bow; when we see Howard Saint enter the club, he is filmed through a wire railing that is rendered as oblique lines cut-

The typical well-muscled and well-armed comic book representation of the Punisher stylizes the character as a cowboy for a new age. From *The Punisher: Welcome Back, Frank* (New York: Marvel Comics, 2000).

ting across our field of vision. The walls and ceiling of his upstairs lounge area are composed entirely of a grid-like design of lines that also appears oblique from our perspective. "Obliquity adheres to the choreography of the city [and these] oblique lines tend to splinter a screen, making it restless and unstable" (Schrader 219). The 1988 film *Die Hard* provides a visual model for this, as it effectively transplants the technique so prevalent in '50s film noir into a modern action hybrid. *Die Hard,* itself evoking a clas-

sic Western by situating its isolated hero within a confined space where he
is forced to shoot it out against a superior force, depicts a world of oblique
lines in the walls, elevator shafts, ductwork, a zig-zagging conference table,
and stairwells that fill the frame throughout. Likewise, in *The Punisher*: outside the building, where Castle and Saint have their final confrontation,
each man stands at the narrow end of key oblique lines in the pavement,
which is wet. In fact, in nearly every scene shot in the city, the streets are
wet (though we never see rain) as they glisten with reflections. The theme
of glass furthers this noir tendency to emphasize water and reflective surfaces. Frank smashes through a glass display case to get his deceased
father's guns, the glass that he has been drinking copious amounts of Wild
Turkey out of drops from his hands to the floor (and falls toward the camera), the Saint building is a glass skyscraper, and Quentin's last name is
"Glass." By the time the explosions and gunplay of the final battle are over,
all of these ingredients have come into play as the villain lies dead in the
street; an urban frontier justice has been served and decades of film language have spoken.

The oppositional structure of civilization versus wilderness has been
rendered through a hybrid blend of genres, such as melodrama, film noir,
and the Western, bringing them all into alignment with this recent example of action cinema. Furthermore, distinct visual iconography and psychological undercurrents emerge from all these genres through the use
of symbols and in various depictions of sadism, masochism, and fetishism,
expressed through the mise en scène and plot of *The Punisher* as it explores
divergent forms of family and ritual. These characterizations of men who
suffer familial loss and issues of guilt, who seek vengeance when traditional forces of authority prove unable to attain justice, who ultimately
live apart from the society they protect—also enacted within the narratives
of Superman, Spider-Man, Batman, and The Crow—show that the modern comic book hero is the descendent of the Western hero. Frank Castle
fits the mold of a man who negotiates both society and the anarchic wilderness surrounding it. That he experiences both the intimacy of family
and the violence of solitary vigilantism is a revision of the Western arche-
type who can only observe hearth and home from the outside. The former trait, in fact, allies him with comic book characters like Clark Kent
and Peter Parker who are part of strong familial structures (despite Frank
Castle's later departure from society). With the film's modern weaponry
and contemporary urban setting, it further revises those found in Westerns; however, the basic narrative impetus, a search for justice, remains
the same. In both cases, it is the individual, not the institutions of society,
that must act to see this justice done.

Finally, the last scene in *The Punisher* provides visual and thematic cues
to the film's evocative generic lineage. Castle stands alone, armed, with
his car at his side on Tampa Bay's Sunshine Skyway. In voice-over, he gives

notice to evildoers everywhere that they will come to know him well, not as Frank Castle who died with his family, but as the Punisher. As the screen begins to fade to black, we realize that there is a brilliant sunset behind him. Calling up all our genre experience with classic Westerns, we imagine that we can hear the beat of a horse's hooves pounding in the distance and, if we squint our eyes, the diagonal steel cables of the bridge, soaring into peaks above him, almost look like mountains.

WORKS CITED

Altman, Rick. *Film/Genre*. London: British Film Institute, 1999.

The Big Heat. Dir. Fritz Lang. Columbia Pictures, 1953.

Bonnie and Clyde. Dir. Arthur Penn. Warner Bros., 1967.

Buscombe, Edward. "The Western." *The Oxford History of World Cinema*. Ed., Geoffrey Nowell-Smith. New York: Oxford University Press, 1996.

The Crow. Dir. Alex Proyas. Miramax Films, 1994.

Desperate Hours. Dir. William Wyler. Paramount Pictures, 1955.

Die Hard. Dir. John McTiernan. 20th Century–Fox, 1988.

Dixon, Chuck. *Punisher: War Zone*. New York: Marvel Comics, 2002.

Ennis, Garth. *The Punisher: Welcome Back, Frank*. New York: Marvel Comics, 2000.

Fenin, George N., and William K. Everson. *The Western, From Silents to the Seventies*. New York: Grossman, 1962.

French, Phillip. *Westerns*. New York: The Viking Press, 1973.

The Godfather. Dir. Francis Ford Coppola. Paramount Pictures, 1972.

Goodwin, Archie. "Marvel Super Action featuring The Punisher, #1." *The Essential Punisher, Vol. 1*. New York: Marvel Comics, 2004.

High Plains Drifter. Dir. Clint Eastwood. Universal Pictures, 1973.

Hutchins, John. "Jonathan Hensleigh, Writer/Director of *The Punisher* Interview." *Under Ground Online*. 6 December 2004. http://ugo.com/channels/filmtv/features/thepunisher/jonathanhensleigh.asp.

MacKinnon, Kenneth. *Love, Tears, and the Male Spectator*. New Jersey: Associated University Presses, 2002.

The Man Who Shot Liberty Valance. Dir. John Ford. Paramount Pictures, 1962.

My Darling Clementine. Dir. John Ford. 20th Century–Fox, 1946.

"Production Notes: The Punisher." *Cinema Review* 2004. 6 December 2004. http://www.cinemareview.com/production.asp?prodid=2488.

The Punisher. Dir. Jonathan Hensleigh. Lions Gate Films, 2004.

"Punisher Movie Update." *Comics2Film*. 17 October 2003. 6 December 2004. http://www.comics2film.com/FanFrame.php?f_id=3984.

Reynolds, Richard. *Super Heroes: A Modern Mythology*. Jackson: University Press of Mississippi, 1992.

Schatz, Thomas. *Hollywood Genres: Formulas, Filmmaking, and the Studio System*. New York: McGraw-Hill, 1981.

Schrader, Paul. "Notes on Film Noir." *Film Genre Reader II*. Ed. Barry Keith Grant. Austin: University of Texas Press, 1995.

The Searchers. Dir. John Ford. Warner Bros., 1956.

Shane. Dir. George Stevens. Paramount Pictures, 1953.

Singer, Ben. *Melodrama and Modernity: Early Sensational Cinema and its Contexts*. New York: Columbia University Press, 2001.

Stagecoach. Dir. John Ford. United Artists, 1939.

Superman II. Dir. Richard Lester. Warner Bros., 1980.

Superman: The Movie. Dir. Richard Donner. Warner Bros., 1978.

Taubin, Amy. *"Taxi Driver."* *BFI Film Classics*. London: British Film Institute Publishing, 2000.

Taxi Driver. Dir. Martin Scorsese. Columbia Pictures, 1976.

Warshow, Robert. "Movie Chronicle: The Westerner." *Partisan Review* 21 (1954): 190–203.
The Wild Bunch. Dir. Sam Peckinpah. Warner Bros., 1969.
Wright, Will. *Sixguns & Society: A Structural Study of the Western.* Berkeley: University of California Press, 1975.

The Nietzschean Influence
in The Incredibles
and the Sidekick Revolt

AUDREY ANTON

In every superhero story, one important element is always assumed and rarely analyzed: superheroes are super. Superman has super strength beyond that of any earthly man. Whether we're talking about the early versions of Superman that could leap over tall buildings with a single bound, or more recent depictions of Superman in flight, he is shown to have abilities that no man could develop regardless of the number of self-disciplined trips to the gym. Equally "amazing" is Spider-Man's ability to spin webbing from his wrists. This is not to mention the abnormal powers of the members of the Fantastic Four; it's not any person who can become invisible, stretch beyond human capacities, control fire, or demonstrate god-like strength. In a newer superhero team called the Incredibles, Mr. Incredible has superhuman strength while his wife, Elastigirl, has super-stretching abilities; their son, Dash, can run faster than any man alive and Violet, their daughter, can become invisible *and* create impenetrable force fields around various objects. Given these examples, it is easy to make the mistake of claiming that what is super about superheroes is their superhuman powers. But as Buddy (the kid known to himself as *Incrediboy*) tells us, "not every superhero has powers you know. You *can* be super without them." Brief reflection reminds us that much-loved superheroes such as Batman have no particular non-human abilities. Rather than throwing Batman (and other non-powered superheroes) out of the lot, thus destroying the childhood role-models of most of my friends, perhaps it is best to reconsider what puts the "super" in superheroes.

Then, what does it mean to be super? Can it be the fancy costume? Since the birth of the superhero genre, the superhero has donned some distinguishing style. While many exploit loud primary colors (and I am talking to you, Superman), Batman shows us that this is not required. Masks are helpful for concealing identities, but then again some superheroes, such as Superman, do not bother with them. Perhaps the cue is the cape. But this too seems to be going out of style. In *The Incredibles*, Edna Mode tells us that capes are not only unfashionable in the current superhero-scene, but they are also dangerous. She illustrates this point by listing the supers she knows to have died as a result of some tragic caped caper gone wrong. In her view, the cape could even interfere with a superhero's ability to do what he does. It would seem that although the outfits our superheroes wear are at times glamorous, they are not required for being super. If flair and loud colors were it, then we might have to accept Dennis Rodman and Marilyn Manson as superheroes. For obvious reasons, this won't do. Besides, our superheroes seem to be moving away from the costume racket. We see less and less of the disguise in movies such as the *X-Men* and television shows such as *Smallville* and *Heroes*. While snazzy attire is a common visual signifier of the superhero, it would be a grave mistake to conclude that the clothes make the man.

We know that superheroes are extraordinary and we are fascinated by what they do with their talents. But do we stop to consider what it means to be super? There are surely natural elements involved, such as abilities with which one is endowed. But we have already established that there are cases where powers were not involved. Batman is simply amazing at fighting crime and has developed such talents as acrobatics and rappelling. While he is superior in these areas, his abilities are not entirely unnatural for humans to have. Batman is just better at these things than other people, and he uses his talents overtly and unapologetically to regulate justice. Given this example, we can conclude that it is not super powers per se that make one super, but rather being super entails being superior. In this sense, the state of being super seems to include a relative element: the relation to that which is not super. And this dichotomy has been around in philosophy before our superheroes were conceived.

Perhaps we should go back to the ideas of that philosopher that have so inspired the creators of modern-day superheroes. Friedrich Nietzsche attempts to articulate a philosophy where humanity is divided in this sense just mentioned, and those who are super achieve such status naturally and independently of those who are not. Those superior people Nietzsche called noblemen. The noblemen are indeed human; yet they are fortunate in that they have many abilities and talents that, while human, are not common to every man. In addition to being talented and strong, these individuals have a further advantage: their will to power.

For Nietzsche, every living thing exhibits some will to power, or the life force that compels an organism to control and exploit resources. The nobles just exhibit a whole lot more than the rest of us. And there is the rub: the nobles have more potential than others and, comparatively, are better. The others, those Nietzsche refers to as commoners or slaves, can't help but resent the nobles for their fortune and strength. While the nobles are strong, Nietzsche admits that such an individual is vulnerable to inferior people. In fact, he postulates that such vulnerability resulted in the mediocrity we find in society today. For Nietzsche, the only way to force humanity to become an equal plane for all is to drag the nobles down rather than elevating the commoners. If mediocrity requires taking the "super" out of humanity, then mediocrity is an undesirable thing indeed.

Nietzsche's concern for humanity and his warnings against the detrimental power of resentment are not only popular topics of discussions between philosophers and literary theorists; his views have influenced popular culture for decades. In addition to the "will to power" mentioned above, pop culture frequently uses famous elements of Nietzsche's philosophy, such as his famous declaration "God is dead," and the opinion that whatever doesn't kill us makes us stronger. While Nietzsche's philosophy has stealthily infiltrated popular culture, its surreptitious infusion is often hard to detect and frequently only partially exemplified in its modified forms. In the previously mentioned superhero film, *The Incredibles*, one may find many correlations between the events of the film and Nietzsche's message, including his hypothesis of a slave revolt. And this recognition is vitally important, considering that this popular film is one of the ways in which superheroism has been first experienced by contemporary youth.

The film is primarily a story of two particular superheroes: Mr. Incredible and Elastigirl (though we learn of many of their colleagues throughout the film). Viewers are first introduced to these two characters as single people who marry each other early in the story. The movie introduces superheroes as helpful, talented people who are revered and loved by all. Their contributions to society are initially appreciated and they receive much publicity for their exemplary works. They make the world a better place for everyone in it. But such a happy story is certain not to last.

The commoners in the film benefit from the contributions the supers make to society since the supers can do all sorts of things that many people cannot. With time, the commoners begin resenting the supers as constant reminders of their own personal shortcomings. Commoners lobby to outlaw superhero activity. They don't want superheroes flaunting their extraordinary abilities around for everyone to see. Nietzsche might have seen this coming. Though this film does seem to exemplify Nietzsche's predictions and concerns, it does not provide an optimistic ending that Nietzsche could appreciate. A major theme in *The Incredibles* is that, when everyone is super, no one is. When such a society is realized, the death of the superhero and the birth of mediocrity are sure to ensue.

NIETZSCHE'S VIEW OF
HUMANITY AND BEING SUPER

In order to demonstrate that *The Incredibles* exhibits countless examples of Nietzsche's warnings against the infectious reign of mediocrity, it is necessary to first provide a synopsis of Nietzsche's view of humanity at its best and its worst. Nietzsche's views on this subject can be found in his famous and popular philosophical works, *The Genealogy of Morals, Beyond Good and Evil,* and his novel *Thus Spake Zarathustra.* Throughout these and others of Nietzsche's works, his belief that humanity is naturally unequal is evident. According to Nietzsche, some people are naturally strong and gifted with the talents and driven to lead and control. These people, otherwise known as the noblemen or masters, exhibit what he calls the will to power, which is the inner life force to dominate and exploit. The remainder of the human population that lacks a great amount of this quality is comprised of the slaves or commoners.

In a healthy and natural society, the noblemen rule the slaves while defining the purpose, value, and meaning of everyone's life. For Nietzsche, aside from what human beings create, there is no value. However, human beings could contribute value by declaring certain things to have positive, neutral, and negative worths. When one does this, such declaration manifests in language. The talented noblemen are naturally apt for such a post: "the right of the masters to confer names extends so far that one should allow oneself to grasp the origin of language itself as the expression of the power of the rulers" (Nietzsche, *On the Genealogy of Morals* 13). As a philologist, Nietzsche carefully considered the origins of various words. He suspected that the ancient roots of many of our terms (especially evaluative terms) came from noblemen of the past. The nobles would describe characteristics that resembled themselves to be good while other traits that did not resemble their strengths were considered bad. What was good according to noblemen involved strength, aptitude, and independence, because these types of traits not only belonged to the noblemen, but also distinguished them from the commoners.

For Nietzsche, the fact that the noblemen were good is not merely a linguistic one. Their superiority was evident, not merely apparent. However, Nietzsche did believe that we can gain understanding of natural goodness if we notice the traces of historical nobility in the roots of words: "It is of no small interest to note that, in those words and roots which designate 'good,' the main nuance, according to which the noble felt themselves to be men of higher rank, often still shows through"(Nietzsche, *On the Genealogy of Morals* 15). It is an objective fact that the noblemen had the traits that they called "good," and for this reason Nietzsche concerns himself with recalling their meaning.

While the noblemen were inarguably strong and talented, this is not to say that there is no role for relativity in instilling value and creating language. Negative terms essentially described a noticeable lack in a given trait exemplified by the positive terminology. Therefore, while weakness is a lack of strength, it is only "bad" because it fails to reach the high standard of nobility. In addition, one is weak in comparison to the strength of another. So the appropriate use of such terms is determined by relative conditions. In the case of the commoners, it is likely that Nietzsche would say that the strongest commoner was still weak compared to the weakest noblemen. The gap between noblemen and slaves was significant.

According to Nietzsche, society runs most smoothly when each individual is able to be what he or she is by nature. When the noblemen lead and create, and the slaves drone along, society functions at its best and, presumably, all people ought to be happy since they are doing and being whatever it is that they are capable of. The noblemen employ their will to power and thereby exploit the commoners. This exploitation does not entail destroying the commoners, but rather accepting their sacrifice as conducive to various projects.[1] Nietzsche likens this relationship to "sun-seeking climbing plants of Java ... *sipo matador*—which clasp an oak-tree with their tendrils so long and so often that at last, high above it but supported by it, they can unfold their crowns in the open light, and display their happiness" (Nietzsche, *Beyond Good and Evil* 258). The noblemen encircle, organize, and embrace the commoners and in return the commoners serve as a stable foundation from which the nobles may transcend themselves further still. While the image may appear parasitic, it is no different from the relationship found in corporate capitalist America. Where would the owners of Wal-Mart, McDonald's, and Microsoft be without their respective oak trees? Perhaps they would be crawling around the ground with the rest of us. Indeed, if they were, I'd have not had dinner before writing this paper, had nothing to wear, and had to have written this paper by hand.[2]

A wise libertarian once told me that the difference between a socialist and a capitalist is that a socialist looks at a rich man and exclaims, "No one should have so much" while a capitalist looks at the same man and insists, "Everyone should have so much!" (He was actually paraphrasing Phelps Adams.) While I appreciate his example, it is not clear that it is possible for everyone to have so much. We can't all be Bill Gates or Donald Trump. In fact, it may be logistically impossible. In order for Bill Gates to be Bill Gates, he needs people to work for him. He has so much that he could not possibly keep track and maintain it on his own.[3] If he were to try, he would not eat or sleep and would surely lose track of something. Now, if everyone who worked for Gates had as much as he does (and if they did, *why* are they still working for him?), then they too would need people to work for them, maintaining their capital. But wait! My libertarian friend's comment suggests that *everyone* should have so much. So their people should have people managing their stuff, and their people's people.... One can tell where this is going: absolutely nowhere (because it can't happen).

People don't want to admit that much of society is modeled off Nietzsche's account of the master and slave moralities. It is clear that some of society is. For Nietzsche, it is not a bad thing that Bill Gates[4] is able to "exploit" others to make billions. It is only bad when people delude themselves into thinking everyone can have what he has, or that no one should. It's a good thing for some of us to thrive. It is not possible for all of us to thrive in the same way. These facts together are realistically better overall for everyone than if no one thrived, period.

Nietzsche finds it unfortunate that there come times when somehow mediocrity is created and the rift between the two types of humans is clouded and confused. Slaves begin to think that they are noble, and noblemen find themselves ashamed of their gifts and begin denying them. Recent examples of the first instance are ubiquitous in society today. We have all seen those episodes of *American Idol* where the contestant is so obviously untalented that it is almost painful to watch. Upon receiving fair criticism, these contestants often lash out in rage. Instead of considering the possibility that they are not the next Kelly Clarkson, these folks insist that the judges simply don't know what they are talking about and cannot recognize true greatness when they see it! We all know what life is like when average people insist that they are amazing. But what is life like when the truly great are ashamed of their abilities? What happens when the exemplary among us feel the need to hide behind a mask and a cape just to be who they *are*? This is the perversity of modern day society for Nietzsche.

NIETZSCHE'S HYPOTHESIS OF THE SLAVE REVOLT

Nietzsche postulates that there was a time when all the slaves were slaves, and all the masters were masters. Everyone knew and accepted his role in society. But Nietzsche explains why this would not continue forever, for one thing is certain about the weak people, some day or other "*they* too want to be the strong" (Nietzsche, *On the Genealogy of Morals* 33). One day, some particular slaves realized the extreme discrepancy between the quality of their lives and that of the masters, and began to resent them.[5]

Resentment is a fundamental emotion that spurs any slave revolt. It is the impetus of revaluation and redefinition: "The slave revolt in morals begins when *ressentiment* itself becomes creative and ordains values: the *ressentiment* of creatures to whom the real reaction, that of the deed, is denied and who find compensation in an imaginary revenge" (Nietzsche, *On the Genealogy of Morals* 22[6]).

Resentment is an emotion that is characteristic of those who are weak. It is not something that strong people feel. The "deeds" that are the "true reaction" are how noblemen deal with issues of inequality. In other words, if a nobleman notices someone else has something he wants, rather than resenting that person, he is instead inspired to make himself worthy and capable of acquiring such goods on his own for himself. The slave does not react this way. He does not rise to the challenge of earning what he admires. Instead, it is out of resentment that he is "creative." But even this creation is dubious.

Noblemen do not even need to be inspired by what anyone else has to feel the need to achieve. If they did, their progress would depend on something outside of them. But their success is independent of anything else. They achieve because it is what they do. They need no other reason:

> This *necessary* orientation outwards rather than inwards to the self—belongs characteristically to *ressentiment.* In order to exist at all, slave morality from the outset always needs an opposing, outer world; in physiological terms, it needs external stimuli in order to act—its action is fundamentally reaction. The opposite is the case with the aristocratic mode of evaluation: this acts and grows spontaneously, it only seeks out its antithesis in order to affirm itself more thankfully and more joyfully [Nietzsche, *On the Genealogy of Morals* 22].

Typically, the nobleman aims to achieve simply so that he may grow and become even better than he is. But even if he is confronted with opposition, he uses such adversity for his cause of improvement. The nobleman believes in the cliché often mentioned as a mass culture popularization of Nietzsche's ideas: "Whatever doesn't kill me makes me stronger!"[7] He does not need a challenge to improve, but if he finds one, it too will contribute to his growth. As a result, the weakest nobleman grows both from his internal drive and competition with others, while the strongest nobleman also grows and improves continuously. Even being the best is not good enough; so long as one is not perfect, there is room for improvement.

Slaves have an entirely different mentality. Nietzsche postulates that the slaves wished to be like the nobles and enjoy the pleasures and benefits that the noblemen had. They saw that the noblemen's privileged position entitled them to all creation. However, they believed that they would never achieve such strengths and status on their own. Alone, and as individuals, they were too weak. Nietzsche believed that the slaves decided to start with the idea of value. Noblemen were those who decided what was good and were indifferent to what was bad. The slaves wanted to redefine good and bad in their favor. To do this, they needed to employ the influence of something stronger—or at least something apparently stronger. Thus began the invention of religion, and the Judeo-Christian monotheistic God. According to Nietzsche, the slaves invented a God, or a nobler master, who then redefined what was "good." In this redefinition, all that was considered "good" became strikingly similar to all that was previously viewed as slavish. An example of this could be when biblical texts espouse the doctrine "Blessed are the meek, the poor, and the lowly." According to Nietzsche, the success of the slaves prevents the rest of us from recognizing the change: "*The slave revolt in morality* begins: that revolt which has a two-thousand-year history behind it and which has today dropped out of sight only because it—has succeeded...." (Nietzsche, *On the Genealogy of Morals* 20[8]).

The slaves had to resort to referring to the authority of one higher because they knew that they didn't genuinely stand a chance against the nobles. The idea of a God who created all, including the noblemen, trumped all authority that they had. If they were strong and special, it was because God made them that way, and they ought to give thanks and be grateful to Him. In addition, they must use their gifts in the manner which He has designated them. The noblemen must use their good qualities and attributes to tend after the poor unfortunate slaves who need their help to enjoy a pleasant life. This kind of psychological warfare convinced the noblemen that they were mistaken about their nature: "The judgment 'good' does *not* derive from those to whom 'goodness' is shown! Rather 'the good' themselves—that is, the noble, the powerful, the superior, and high-minded—were the ones who felt themselves and their actions to be good" (Nietzsche, *On the Genealogy of Morals* 12).

Though the noblemen determined what was "good" before there was such a notion, the notion of goodness that we have today is far removed from its origin. This is because the "creative" powers of the men of resentment do not match, let alone transcend, the spontaneous and original creativity of noblemen. It is characteristic of a slave to recycle the terminology of the masters so that what is "good" is what they already *are*. Rather than change their situation, the slaves justified it:

> There is no doubt that they are miserable ... but they tell me that their misery is an election and a distinction conferred by God—one beats the dogs one loves the most.... Now they give me to understand that they are not only better than the powerful, the masters of the earth, whose spittle they are obliged to lick (*not* from fear, absolutely not! but because God commands respect for all authority)—that they are not only better, but also "have it better,' or will "have it better" one day (Nietzsche, *On the Genealogy of Morals* 31–32).

Instead of becoming good, it seemed more logical to the men of resentment to make "goodness" become them. Rather than elevate their status, it made more sense to drag down that of others. It is not that all men became equal; it is that all men *believed* that all men were equal. And this is the most damaging of all. Once we all believe we should be equal, what incentive is there to improve?

> The man of *ressentiment* is neither upright nor naïve in his dealings with others, nor is he honest and open with himself. His soul *squints*; his mind loves bolt-holes, secret paths, back doors, he regards all hidden things as *his* world, *his* security, *his* refreshment; he has a perfect understanding of how to keep silent, how not to forget, how to wait, how to make himself provisionally small and submissive. A race of such men of *ressentiment* is bound in the end to become *cleverer* than any noble race (Nietzsche, *On the Genealogy of Morals* 24).

This new race will surely be cleverer. It will be more cynical, more pessimistic, and more critical. Being clever is not necessarily being noble. Intelligence and devotion to truth may be attributes of one who is noble.

But cleverness is the abuse of reason. Nonetheless, it is a tough act to follow.

After this revolt, the noblemen no longer focused on maximizing their potential. Everyone helped everyone else, but no one helped anyone become great. Pride and ambition were outlawed. Mediocrity was born, and everyone was more or less the same. It would seem that this is the goal the common people in *The Incredibles* had in mind all along.

FROM NIETZSCHE TO THE INCREDIBLES:
OUR RESENTMENT AND MOTIVATION
FOR SUPERHERO REVISION

It has been a long time since Nietzsche first cautioned his readers to be aware of the weakness that lurks inside of every man. While he was hopeful that humans could face the responsibility to be their own gods, he was fearful that we might choose weakness over strength. The business of superheroes (whether in comics, television shows, or movies) seems to have captured an overarching theme in revision over time; a theme of utility. Jeph Loeb,[9] accomplished comic book writer and television producer, and Tom Morris,[10] distinguished philosopher and ethicist, discuss this aspect of revision in their article contributions to the recent book *Superheroes and Philosophy: Truth, Justice, and the Socratic Way*. Loeb and Morris write, "Many writers, artists, and other people who are in the superhero business have taken up this interesting task because we believe that the stories of these characters embody our deepest hopes and fears, as well as our highest aspirations" (Morris and Morris 11).

Superhero entertainment serves a purpose rather different from other forms of entertainment. Superheroes provide us with role models. As children, we are not only entertained by watching Batman and Superman, we want to *be* them. We dress up as superheroes for Halloween. Some of us (including my brother and me) paraded around in such costumes for as many months after Halloween as our parents would tolerate. Even within the meta-comic realm we see it. Within the storylines of comics and films, ordinary people find themselves inspired to rise to a given challenge and be super in just about every age of the superhero. Since the 1940s, we have seen examples of people inspired by a superhero to join his cause, such as Batman's Robin and Captain America's Bucky. In the 1980s we find that most of the heroes in *Watchmen* were ordinary people who, after the first hero took action, were inspired to join the cause. Likewise, Batman's new "Robin" in *The Dark Knight Returns* is a normal girl until the media devotes attention to the return of the vigilante crime fighter and she is suddenly compelled to join his cause.

Why does this happen in the superhero business more often than other forms of entertainment? Superheroes fix the types of problems (more or less) that we all fear. Superhero entertainment modifies, and sometimes glorifies, actual social situations and events and allows us to consider how we might hope a given person would act in these scenarios, as well as how we fear such a person might disappoint us. Without even recognizing it, we read and watch both individuals with careful anticipation and judge them with certainty, neglecting to admit to ourselves that both individuals *are* imaginary, fantastical versions of us.

As Jeph Loeb and Tom Morris suggest, superhero propaganda serves the purpose of addressing our hopes and fears in less-than-obvious ways. At times, this results in the inadvertent forgetfulness of the origins of those hopes and fears. As Nietzsche postulated, resentment stems from a desire to be good without the will to power; in other words, we want to be good without the hassle of *being* good. If superheroes are mechanisms for our impartial evaluation of our own goodness and we have revised their roles and appearance over time, perhaps we have revised our hopes and fears as well. Recent characterization in the superhero business suggests that we want to be as good as the heroes, without actually *being as good*. One particular example is Superman. The original Superman of George Reeves's day gallantly rescued helpless people while proudly proclaiming that he does it for "truth, justice, and the American way!" The later Superman of *The Dark Knight Returns* is a sell-out. He works for the government and complies with certain untruthful and unjust operations. Is this apparent shift indicative of more than a simple reinterpretation of the essential plot? Could it be that our authors and illustrators are trying to feed us something they think we want? Have our tastes changed so much?

At times it appears that one way of achieving this "goodness" is to deny the goodness of the *actually* good. Another method is to deny the difference between the goodness and cases that fall short of such goodness. Loeb and Morris summarize this point nicely: "The heroes who live and work around us every day include firemen, police officers, doctors, nurses, and teachers ... But we don't often think of these people as heroes ... We like to think about such people and their jobs that, 'They do it because they like to do it.' And we comfort ourselves that, because of this, 'They're really no better than the rest of us'" (Morris and Morris 13).

Acknowledging that some possibility exists for humans to be better than we currently are entails a responsibility to try to meet that standard. When one is too lazy or afraid to rise to a challenge, like an ostrich he sticks his head in the sand and wonders, "Challenge? What challenge? I already *am* all that anyone should have to be!" Anything that opposes the ostrich's cranial nesting, perhaps a tap on the shoulder from above, shall be buried under the sand with his head before he would ever deign to lift it high and view the possibilities.

Originally superheroes provided us ideals to live up to. Now we resent such greatness. Loeb and Morris hypothesize "ordinary people first welcome superheroes as needed saviors, then come to take them for granted, and finally begin to resent them for their heroically never-ending efforts to do what the rest of the population ought to be doing too" (Morris and Morris 13–14). If Friedrich Nietzsche were alive today, he'd surely say "I told you so." But what would make this uninteresting to him is that ordinary people always behave this way. It is the fact that most people behave this way today that creates the problem. For Nietzsche, the term 'ordinary' did not have to refer to all people. Had enough noblemen lived up to the standards of their role models, the timid and subservient "supers" of *The Incredibles* would never have been written into the film as they are. The supers of *The Incredibles* are a new step in the ongoing revision process. They are the most recent draft. And they do not exemplify obviously better human beings that serve as role models for aspiring fans. Instead, they are people who are secretly better and considerably conscientious of how their superiority could intimidate others.

While the supers in *The Incredibles* denote a draft in superhero revision that virtually depreciates them of all superiority, these supers have roots in earlier superhero depictions. Aeon Skoble notes that two graphic novels published in 1986 predicted the resentment that is in full effect in *The Incredibles*: *The Dark Knight Returns* and *Watchmen* (Morris and Morris 29–41). Skoble points out that, in general, "Superheroes function as a sort of unauthorized police auxiliary unit" (Morris and Morris 30). If Loeb and Morris are accurate in their depiction of police officers as heroes nobody resents because it is easy to downplay their greatness by considering it "something they like to do" or "just their job," then a blatantly altruistic policeman who saves the world (and, as Skoble duly notes, "people from themselves") simply because he's better could become irritating to the common man who resents having to live up to any standard. Living up to standards is not a new issue in superhero revision. Though it may be at its peak, it began its ascent in the '80s.

In *The Dark Knight Returns* superheroes are outlawed and forced to retire. Batman ignores this instruction and continues to be what he is— super. He is contrasted though with Superman, who manages to finagle a job with the government where he actually becomes a condoned law-enforcer who is required to operate in secret. But with such a position, one must submit to the law and its processes as the government sees them. At one point in the graphic novel, Batman chastises Superman for giving in to the ridiculous demands of society that they not be all that they can be as independent superior people: "You sold us out, Clark. You gave them—the *power*—that should have been *ours*.... My parents taught me a *different* lesson ... they showed me that the world only makes sense when you *force* it to" (Miller 38–40). Batman recognizes that the superior humans have a right to assume power. Much like what Nietzsche suggested, Batman believed all value comes from man. Superman, on the other hand, views this fact in a different light. When discussing the common resentful men, Superman comments, "We must not remind them that giants walk the Earth" (Miller 26). He makes it clear that he fears the power of their endless envy. Naturally, this repulses Batman, who cannot comprehend how one who is strong could fear the "power" of the weak.

Superman's character in *The Dark Knight Returns* is the missing link between the noble superhero and those heroes who are continuously surprised to find their efforts unappreciated. Superman was aware of the reasons why common men resented him. The supers in *The Incredibles* appear to have lost sight of this devious motivation altogether. Unlike Superman, they do not recognize the resentment. In fact, in addition to the commoners resenting the supers, the supers begin to admire the commoners, simply because they have the gift of being "normal." These supers are still superior enough to be clearly abnormal—but not so much that they can't hide it.

HUMANITY IN *THE INCREDIBLES*

While the heroes in Brad Bird's Pixar film resemble many of the traditional attributes of superheroes in film, their nature makes them particularly salient to the human situation. These superheroes are actual people who just happen to be endowed with extraordinary abilities. This can be contrasted with some traditional superheroes that are not human. For example, Superman, though from a foreign planet, seemed human at times. He had feelings; he experienced stress and difficulty. Superman, however, was more like the legendary Achilles since he had presumably only one weakness.[11] The heroes in the Pixar film, however, are more like other heroes that can be found in comic books and movies. Like Spiderman, Pixar's heroes are entirely mortal. They simply have some kind of freak genetic code that gives them strange "gifts" that they somehow channel to do good and care for the commoners while living their superior lives.[12]

On the other hand, like the X-Men's "mutants," these supers are born the way that they are. Their talents are natural. This is different from superheroes like Batman who are not only regular human beings, but also choose to meet the challenge of being super. They are super, whether they like it or not. Still, they are not invincible. Unlike Superman, these characters are, for the most part, vulnerable to all the same ills that normal humans are, save for their particular gifts.[13] They too are mortal. There is more than one way to bring about their demise (as opposed to Superman who will live so long as he does not come into contact with Kryptonite). So what is it about them that makes them super?

The superhero in *The Incredibles* is very similar to Frederick Nietzsche's idea of the nobleman, or master. A master is one who is just born in such a way that distinguishes him from the majority. He is stronger and more skilled in various areas of life. The Master is born to rule, and is influential. However, the Master is not of another type of species as the rest of the common people, whom Nietzsche refers to as slaves. While this paper argues that the supers in *The Incredibles* resemble Nietzsche's noblemen, at the same time one must acknowledge that there does seem to be a significant difference between how the supers interact with others in the movie and how Nietzsche insists the nobles ought to act. Namely, the nobles ought to use the slaves to maximize their greatness, whereas the supers use their greatness to maximize the quality of life of the slaves. This is one move that Nietzsche might have known would only lead to trouble.

MOB MENTALITY: THE SLAVE REVOLT AT THE "MACRO" LEVEL

The more the supers in *The Incredibles* care for and help others, the more they are relied upon and, ultimately, taken for granted. Finally, the commoners revolt by blaming the supers for unfortunate consequences that resulted from their attempts to prevent greater ones. For example, at one point in the movie, a man attempts to commit suicide by jumping off a skyscraper. The man's attempt was thwarted by Mr. Incredible; upon seeing the man jump from within a nearby building, Mr. Incredible took one running leap through the window of his building and soared across the divide between the two buildings, thereby catching the would-be pavement artist and safely transporting him through the window of the second building. This man, Oliver Sansweet, later sued Mr. Incredible for interrupting his plan. His lawyer explained to the press, "Mr. Sansweet didn't asked to be saved. Mr. Sansweet didn't want to be saved." Mr. Incredible interjects that he saved Mr. Sansweet's life. To this, Sansweet replies, "You didn't save my life. You ruined my death; that's what you did!" He had not wanted to live and felt it was a crime that anyone rescue him without his asking for help. In addition, he suffered some injuries during the rescue process, for which he blames Mr. Incredible.

After this precedent was set, many others began taking superheroes to court because of rescue-related damages. Citizens can be seen on the news exclaiming complaints like, "It is time for their secret identities to become their only identities," and it is "time for them to join us, or go away!" Protestors display signs with slogans like "Go Save Yourself!" Newspaper headlines such as "Not So Super Anymore" challenge the previous view that the supers are great. In little time, the government answers the pleas of these commoners and bans superhero activity. They develop the Superhero Relocation Program, a top-secret program for helping superheroes integrate into society under the guise of "normal" citizen characters. A later news broadcast addresses the question of what has happened to the super. The broadcast provides the following answer: "They are living among us. Average citizens, average heroes, quietly and anonymously, continuing to make the world a better place." As if refraining from super-hero activity betters anything! As if there were anything "average" about being a hero! There you have it. And mediocrity wins its battle over tal-ent.

This particular example of a slave revolt in the Pixar film seems to be slightly different from that explained by Nietzsche and the rise of religion. The first reason is that the superheroes, while powerful and influential, were not in control of the society. This is why it was possible for the com-moners to do away with them so quickly. Also, this called for little to no redefinition of values. The values were already in place for mediocrity. The society in question resembles current American society, where we are all free to do what we wish and have the right to sue anyone who threat-ens that. This would include the right to do stupid, weak, lazy things. The supers were in a society that was bound to resent them. It was only a mat-ter of time.

IF YOU CAN'T JOIN 'EM, BEAT 'EM:
THE SIDEKICK AND REVOLT AT THE "MICRO" LEVEL

While it is clear that this is one example of a battle successfully won by mediocrity, it was not the most complete and greatest Nietzschean slave revolt in the movie. That came from the greatest hero-worshipper of them all. Buddy's transformation into Incrediboy, and later, Syndrome, marks a complete typical Nietzschean slave revolt where the slave struggles with his own nature, redefines values and compensates for a lack of abilities, and finally looks to a higher power to ensure the permanency of his rise.

The converse of the adage, "if you can't beat 'em, join 'em" is espoused by the character of Incrediboy in the feature film *The Incredibles*. Incredi-boy, allegedly born "Buddy," first appears on the scene in the movie as a young, jovial kid who idolizes the film's main character, Mr. Incredible. Buddy's purpose in life is to be like Mr. Incredible. There is just one slight problem: by nature, Buddy simply is not like Mr. Incredible.

Buddy, or the aspiring Incrediboy, was for the most part like all the other commoners. He was not born with superpowers. He was not related to any supers. However, he had one aspect that stood out from the other commoners. Buddy *wanted* to be super. No other normal humans wanted to be super. Buddy wanted this so much, in fact, that he insisted that he could compensate for the super powers that he lacked. Buddy is an exam-ple of Nietzsche's mysteriously ambitious slave. He complains to Mr. Incred-ible, "You always say 'be true to yourself' but you never say which part of yourself to be true to! Well I've finally figured out who I am. I am your ward, Incrediboy!" Buddy seems to have two parts of himself, each of which he struggled to accommodate. Part of him is ordinary. Another part of him desires to have what Mr. Incredible has. But Mr. Incredible is not ordinary. Buddy continues to try to impress Mr. Incredible with his compensatory inventions. These scientific advances are impressive. They do demonstrate some form of talent. However, as mentioned earlier, it isn't merely talent that makes someone super. One's motive for developing one's talents says a lot about the kind of person he or she is. After many attempts to convince Mr. Incredible that he is a worthy sidekick, Buddy gets put in his place one particular time that would change the course of his life and reveal his true nature. When Mr. Incredible told Buddy, "You're not affiliated with me!" Buddy developed the mentality that, if he couldn't join Mr. Incredible, he would some day beat him.

Let us now see how Incrediboy parallels the Nietzschean slave. First, it is apparent that his character is one of redefinition. We discover that his birth name is Buddy only when Mr. Incredible exclaims it in contempt during an argument. Buddy immediately corrects him, informing him that his name is "Incrediboy." At the outset of the movie, the redefinition and platform for revolt was already set. The name Buddy, as it is commonly understood, has a connotation of inferiority. A Buddy is a friend who helps out. He is not one who is looked up to, or who is in charge. "Buddy" is not a particularly intelligent or sophisticated name. It is common and unexciting. "Buddy" is not a name of someone special. In fact, it is even used as a general condescending name when fighting with a man who has seemed to have overstepped his place (for example, when two drivers are arguing over who cut off whom, the dispute might begin with, "Hey Buddy, what do you think you're doing?!")

Buddy's first attempt to redefine himself is done in Mr. Incredible's image. Still true to his original slavish nature, he wants not to be Mr. Incredible, but to be his sidekick. He wants to help him be and do the best that he can. Buddy has not yet made the complete transformation to deceptive revolt. He does not want to be Mr. Incredible exactly, but he does want to be special, like him. He wants to be special in that he has privileges over other commoners. He wants to stand out. The only example he has of how one does this is Mr. Incredible. Unlike a nobleman, he simply copies Mr. Incredible. Even in redefining himself, in his creation of a more-noble commoner, he cannot resist putting part of Mr. Incredible's name in his own new name, Incrediboy.

Recall how, as Incrediboy, Buddy is rejected by Mr. Incredible. While Buddy assumes that Mr. Incredible's reason for refusing his company is that he doesn't have super powers, he resents this reasoning and does not accept it. He is insulted by Mr. Incredible's refusal to include him. Mr. Incredible views this discrepancy as obvious and natural. Buddy, on the other hand, views Mr. Incredible's rejection as personal, unfair, and prejudiced. In attempts to show Mr. Incredible that he is worthy of the task, Buddy begins to find ways to compensate for the skills that he lacks by nature. He uses his intellectual talents to create artificial means of performing super acts. For example, he designs and builds rocket boots that allow him to "fly." This is the first of many steps towards the use of artificial simulation of superiority that Buddy will make throughout the movie. Alas, as the ability is contingent upon something artificial, and Mr. Incredible is still aware of Buddy's natural differences, he still refuses him as a potential apprentice.

It would appear that this was Buddy's final attempt to join Mr. Incredible. But rather than accepting his natural inferiority and place in life, Buddy does not give up. If he cannot join Mr. Incredible, he will find the means to beat him. At this juncture in the movie, Buddy grows up, renames himself a second time, and begins to plot against the supers. Buddy, now Syndrome, works on his inventions on a private island so that people can buy his gadgets and then everyone will be super, "Because when everyone is super, no one is!" While this was Buddy's original goal, his bitterness develops into something further. It is not enough for him to simply elevate the weaker people. In addition, Buddy wishes to bring down the supers and create the illusion that he is the last super, so that he may enjoy the admiration of all of the commoners he helps. While on the island, he invents an indestructible learning combat machine called Kronos. Like Nietzsche's speculation of the origin of the monotheistic god, Kronos is an invented being intended to rule the supers.[14] Syndrome then lures the supers one by one to his island to see if they can overcome the machine.

The most important significance of Kronos in this movie is towards the end when Syndrome attempts his master plan. Syndrome unleashes the machine on the public, and stages a fight with it where he is supposed to be the victor, thus proving his status among supers to onlookers. The artificial attack routine is not new. In *Watchmen*, Ozymandias stages a similar attack on the planet, but for entirely different reasons. He predicts that the Earth is on the verge of nuclear holocaust, and if humanity is left to its own devices, it will surely destroy itself and the entire planet with it. Ozymandias stages an alien invasion (killing millions) so that the nations of the world will forget their disputes and cooperate. The nations defeat the "aliens" and Ozymandias's plan works. While, like Syndrome, he deceived the public and endangered their lives, he argues that he did it for their own good. Syndrome, on the other hand, stages this attack for two purposes: (1) so that the public will see the supers as inferior and inadequate, and (2) so that he can pretend to save the day and be viewed as the next savior. If he is sincere in his earlier description of his intentions, he will then convince the public to use his technology to elevate the populace. However, the fact that he could have done this without destroying the supers gives cause for suspicion. It is more likely that he will continue selling weapons to sparring armies and benefit from their constant destruction of one another. Regardless of Syndrome's true motives, he certainly does not stage the attack to save the world from nuclear holocaust; in fact, his actions could have led to it.

Unlike Ozymandias's invasion, Syndrome's does not go according to plan. The machine learns in battle that it is essentially Syndrome's slave. When Syndrome injures the machine, it immediately retaliates by striking him in the same way he hit it—indicating that the machine has learned "an eye for an eye." Syndrome was unable to control his own creation. This "God" was going to be no man's slave, despite the fact that it was a machine. In the end, the supers manage to defeat the machine by tricking it into harming itself. Mr. Incredible recognizes that the only thing strong enough to penetrate the machine is itself, perhaps alluding to the idea that the inherent contradictions of certain religions are sufficient in themselves for recognizing their fantastical roots in history. Kronos is dead. Every man is again free to become his own god—to become super ... but will he?

MEDIOCRITY: IS IT A GLASS CEILING?

This part of the movie would seem to indicate that the naturally superior humans both won the war and saved the day. However, the movie does not end here. After much consideration within the Incredibles family, Mr. and Mrs. Incredible decide to allow their son, Dash, to compete in sports. Previously, he was not allowed because his extreme talent and competitive nature were sure to blow the family's cover as "normal" people. While attending one of Dash's track meets, the Incredible family cheers him on, only to instruct him to slow down whenever he pulls too far ahead of the other competitors. Dash is allowed to participate, but he is still expected to hold back and hide his greatness. In addition, the supers are permitted to resume superhero work, but under the guise of "normal" citizens. The fact that the supers are "allowed" to be themselves so long as they do not negatively effect the self-esteem of "normal" people would seem to suggest that mediocrity still rules society. In addition, the supers' compliance with these rules only perpetuates the matter. Why on earth do the supers continue to appease the mob?

Alan Moore's graphic novel *Watchmen* can be viewed as an answer to the question: what would it be like if ordinary people decided to become superheroes? *Watchmen* comes to a similar conclusion as *The Incredibles* in that the remaining superheroes come to a consensus to hide the truth about superhero activity from humans "for their own good." Shortly after Ozymandias's plan to save humanity is executed and successful, the superheroes consider whether what was done was wrong and how to proceed from there. Rorschach disapproves of Ozymandias's deeds and protests letting him get away with it. Dr. Manhattan ends up killing Rorschach because he will not comply with the others. The superheroes in *The Watchmen* are very aware of how humans are likely to react if they learn that some of them are more powerful than the rest and can manipulate their lives and actions to such a degree. So Moore's answer to this question isn't much different from that provided by *The Incredibles*. Laypeople would initially accept the assistance, but quickly resent the help. They would become suspicious of these superior people, and find a way to redefine the value of their acts and outlaw their doings.[15] Then the superheroes continue to protect the interests of the greater good, without its consent. They serve a public that does not want them. They protect people who resent them.

While Moore's answer to this question is similar to the conclusion of *The Incredibles*, one dramatically different element persists: Moore's "watchmen" seem to consider the secrecy solution necessary to micromanaging the public in a rather patronizing way, whereas the supers in *The Incredibles* seem to sympathize more with the insecurities of the average person. The watchmen choose not to let the public know the truth, but they still retain power over them. The supers seem to have a less-dignified place towards the end of their movie. They are perhaps overly sensitive to the fact that Dash's classmates' feelings might be hurt if they really knew how much better Dash is. In addition to risking blowing the family's cover, protecting the feelings of normal kids also appeared to be an incentive for holding Dash back. Earlier in the film, Dash had pleaded with his mother to allow him to play sports. He bargained, "I promise I'll slow up. I'll only be the best by a *tiny* bit." When his mother expressed her doubt that Dash could handle such temptation, he complained, "You always say 'Do your best' but you don't really mean it. Why can't I do the best that I can do?" Helen's response was, "Right now, honey, the world just wants us to fit in. And to fit in we just gotta be like everybody else." Sensitive to the differences of opinion between his mother and father, Dash retorts, "But Dad always said our powers are nothing to be ashamed of. Our powers make us special." Helen replies, "Everyone's special, Dash," to which Dash returns, "Which is another way of saying no one is."

At times, the supers in *The Incredibles* appear to have forgotten entirely that they are better *because* they are super. They hide the truth from the public because they are, in a way, hiding the truth from themselves. While they let Dash compete, they don't allow him to push himself to become better; after all, he isn't likely to improve pretending to race slower runners. While both superhero stories result in sheltering the public from the acts and powers of superheroes, only the supers in *The Incredibles* seem content to be sort-of above average.

Some might say that this assessment is radically pessimistic and unforgiving. Brad Bird's film is a phenomenal one in many ways, and it received reviews that reflect its merits. However, while it is a terrific example of the dangers of mediocrity, it still teaches very little about how to avoid them. Many perceptive critics noticed the allusions to conformity and mediocrity. Roger Ebert called the movie "a critique of modern American uniformity" that "observes its gifted characters trying to dumb down and join the crowd" (Ebert). Indeed, the mention of mediocrity and the pressure to fit in is hard to miss. Nonetheless, reviewers were not interested in commenting on this unsettling aspect of the ending. Some seemed to overlook it altogether. Scott Tobias wrote, "Fortunately, *The Incredibles* and Pixar continue to prevail triumphantly over mediocrity" (Tobias). Peter Travers concludes his review proclaiming, "There's no better expression of family values and fears onscreen right now," and "Bird has crafted a film—one of the year's best—that doesn't ring cartoonish, it rings true" (Travers). Perhaps Travers is correct; the message in *The Incredibles* does ring true. Perhaps Brad Bird subconsciously felt pressure to provide a "normal" ending where all of our children can maintain the illusion that they are as fast as Dash. But all this really does is deny competition to such a degree that none of them ever will be.

Does it have to be this way? Wouldn't Brad Bird's film have received such rave reviews even if he had allowed Dash to race his best and the Incredibles to reveal their identities? Maybe we don't have to succumb to mediocrity just yet. If we recall Nietzsche's description of the ancient nobleman and the man of resentment, one solution surfaces. It may be the case that being super so that one can protect society is a hopeless task. Men of resentment will always resent what they get when they get what they want. Perhaps one cannot be great for the benefit of the weak. The weak will not allow it. They undermine their own benefit so that they do not have to face their own weaknesses.

Instead of being super for others, we could try to be super as the nobles were super—simply because we can. This is not to say that people ought to be super and neglect others. Instead, they should first be super. If that results in an ability to resolve problems when the occasion arises, so be it. But it is the mark of the man of resentment to wait for an occasion against which to react. During his retirement, Mr. Incredible becomes considerably out of shape and depressed. He laments the loss of "the good old days." But did he need them to be super? He should not have. And neither should we.

It is possible that the sands of mediocrity are quick; once one has set foot in them, there is no escaping them. Even the slightly gloomy, slightly disgruntled philosopher Friedrich Nietzsche had hope that this was not the case. Perhaps Nietzsche's optimism for the rebirth of greatness is unrealistic. Is it the case that, after the birth of mediocrity, no return to greatness is possible? If this is true, then there is surely one thing Nietzsche was mistaken about; if mediocrity can permanently depose greatness, then it is not the case that whatever doesn't kill us makes us stronger. If he was right, then it is merely our own resentment that holds us back. We have two choices. We may either return to admiring the great among us and try to be more like them, or we may continue this trend of writing our superheroes as though they are more like us. In Nietzsche's terms, either our resentment or our will to power will win this fight. And there is only one way to find out....

NOTES

1. I mention this because it is an unfortunate reality that Adolf Hitler adopted Friedrich Nietzsche as the national philosopher of the third Reich. It is believed that many of Nietzsche's writings were edited and manipulated so that they supported the agendas of the Holocaust. There are numerous reasons why one might claim that Hitler abused and misinterpreted Nietzsche's philosophy. If the nobleman benefits from the oak tree, there would be no reason to cut it down. Only a man of resentment feels compelled to decimate a race of people. A nobleman is too good and too busy to be preoccupied with such insecurities.

2. While Nietzsche's concern is the rise of mediocrity, it is evident that a completely equal society may not be possible. Even the most egalitarian mediocrities include such discrepancies. Perhaps Nietzsche's concern then was not simply the possibility of mediocrity, but a diverse society where the noble gifts are bestowed upon the wrong people.

3. Incidentally, John Locke, a philosopher most libertarians consider a founding father of the movement, held the position that all men have a natural right to own whatever property they can manage on their own, and that naturally (in the state of nature) no man is entitled to more raw materials than he can possibly mix with his own labor.

4. While I chose Bill Gates as an example here, I would like to add that he is a particularly interesting one in that he elects to donate an incredibly large amount of money to charities all over the world. Incidentally, he has people working beneath him whose sole occupation is managing the charity funds.

5. Nietzsche does not postulate how a slave, one who is naturally inferior, is able to even conceive of the idea of the discrepancy, least of all how to reverse it. He does speculate that the leaders of the revolt were the priests. We are not sure whether the priests were nobleman gone wrong or highly intuitive slaves. My students and I have discussed the implications, which, it would appear, Nietzsche ignored, of such an argument. If the slaves are naturally inferior, how could they ever successfully revolt? If they are smart enough to trick the masters, isn't that a superlative quality that they have over the masters? Does that not make them less slavish and of a more superior nature than originally thought?

6. See also section 3 of the Introduction to *Genealogy of Morals* for further discussion of "ressentiment."

7. While this line is often treated as a cliché, it actually does come directly from a quote in the *Twilight of the Idols*, published, 1889. The German reads: W*as mich nicht umbringt, macht mich starker.* This is most often translated as 'Whatever does not destroy me makes me stronger.'

8. This concept is also discussed in *Beyond Good and Evil*, section 195, note 11.

9. Jeph Loeb is an extremely accomplished American comic book writer and screen and television writer. He has written many works concerning the X-Men, Superman, Batman, and Spider-Man. With Jim Lee he is co-creator of *Batman: Hush*. Loeb is also a writer and producer of *Smallville* and *Lost*. Most recently, he is a writer and co-producer for the series *Heroes*.

10. Tom Morris is a former professor of philosophy at the University of Notre Dame. Morris is the author of several philosophy books and business-success books, including *True Success: a New Philosophy of Excellence, Making Sense of it All, If Aristotle Ran General Motors, Philosophy for Dummies, The Art of Achievement*, and *The Stoic Art of Living*. He is also the chairman of the Morris Institute for Human Values in Wilmington, North Carolina.

11. It is arguable whether Superman had one weakness. At times, he is characterized as being susceptible to magic. On one occasion, a stronger enemy wins a fight with him. Nonetheless, his weaknesses are more limited than those of a human being. I am indebted to a fellow colleague and friend, Emmanuel Andre, for this observation.

12. For example, the strengths the heroes have are used for good to save lives, or to enhance their own everyday lives, like in the scene where Mr. Incredible, while reading, picks up the sofa with one hand to assist Mrs. Incredible (aka Elastigirl) in cleaning.

13. For example, Elastigirl might not be as susceptible to bullets since they could potentially bounce off of her, by virtue of the nature of her special attribute. However, Mr. Incredible, not having that particular feature, would not. In the same light, Elastigirl might not be able to withstand a building falling on top of her, while her husband, Mr. Incredible, has the ability to push it back up, or perhaps even toss it aside.

14. This we also infer by its name. Cronos was the father of all the Greek gods in mythology. Zeus, Cronos' only surviving son, punishes Cronos for eating Zeus' brothers and sisters in an attempt to remain in control of the gods.

15. In this novel, the Keene Act outlawed superhero activity shortly after the general suspicions of the McCarthy era began to pick up speed.

WORKS CITED

Ebert, Roger. "*The Incredibles.*" *Chicago Sun Times.* 5 November 2004. 10 January 2006 http://rogerebert.suntimes.com/apps/pbcs.dll/article?AID=/20041104/REVIEWS/41006004/1023.

The Incredibles. Dir. Brad Bird. Walt Disney Pictures, 2004.

Miller, Frank. *The Dark Knight Returns.* New York: DC Comics, 1986.

Moore, Alan. *Watchmen.* New York: DC Comics, 1987.

Morris, Tom, and Matt Morris. *Superheroes and Philosophy: Truth, Justice, and the Socratic Way.* Peru, Ill.: Open Court, 2005.

Nietzsche, Friedrich. *Beyond Good and Evil.* Trans. R.J. Hollingdale. New York: Penguin, 1972.

_____. *On the Genealogy of Morals.* Trans. Douglas Smith. Oxford: Oxford University Press, 1998.

Roberts, Adam. "Is Superman a Superman?" *The Man From Krypton.* Ed., Glenn Yeffeth. Dallas: Benbella Books, 2005. 115–125.

Tobias, Scott. "*Incredibles.*" *The Onion.* 2 November 2004. 5 January 2006. http://www.theonion.com/content/node/18156.

Travers, Peter. "*Incredibles.*" *Rolling Stone.* 3 November 2004. 5 January 2006. http://www.rollingstone.com/reviews/movie/6131777/the_incredibles.

Afterword: Conclusion to the Never-Ending Story(s)

TERRENCE R. WANDTKE

Setting aside the coy title of this closing section, what you are about to read is merely an afterword and not a conclusion. As stated in the introduction, the goal of this collection is to open debate and therefore, a conclusion that ties together the essays in this volume with a comprehensive idea would be counterproductive. Nevertheless, the afterword needs to be written in order to acknowledge the nature of this collection and to identify the work that has yet to be done.

My intention remains to identify the superhero as a significant innovation of 20th century culture produced by the media that the superhero inhabits (among other cultural forces). With this claim in mind, the fairly conservative design of this collection should be apparent. While completely justified by a relative lack of academic engagement with the medium (which only in recent years is being rectified), the larger part of this collection is devoted to the medium with which superheroes are mostly readily identified: comic books. The rest of this collection is devoted to the two mediums that it could be easily argued rank as the others most readily associated with superheroes: film and television. However, in recent years, the comic book no longer captures popular interest in the same way that it once did (sales have declined and its youth market is disappearing).

That is not to say that the medium is less significant, but it is changing in terms of its general significance, perhaps maturing as it now lives more often than not with a gentrified (and more appropriate) label: graphic novel. And that is to say that other mediums such as video games now control the youth market that once belonged to comic books; superheroes now live in those other mediums in permutations that may someday eclipse those existing in the medium in which they were created. (For some time, both DC and Marvel have made more money licensing their characters than selling their comic books and graphic novels.) Consequently, while the source medium of superheroes should not be forgotten, greater attention must be paid to revisions to the superhero within other media, particularly as media changes due to technological innovation.

231

For instance, as comic books of the past are now being packaged in deluxe bound editions and identified as graphic novels, the experience of those comic books is radically altered. Instead of being monthly pamphlets filled with advertisements, printed on low-quality paper, and generally considered to be disposable, they are comprehensive overviews of complete eras in a superhero's history, featuring introductions by prominent authors, and worthy of display on very discerning coffee tables. The timelessness of the endlessly repeated superhero narrative identified by Umberto Eco may have only existed on an unconscious level for casual readers of comic books in the 1950s—but as issues are set side-by-side and volumes are read entirely in one setting, the "oneiric climate" is obvious to even the casual readers in recent years. As print processes have been refined with 21st century technology, the art (particularly the color and line resolution) in the collected comic books has been radically improved and this quality places superheroes in a different position as something for serious consideration.

Ironically, the nearest approximation of the original reading experience of superhero comic books can be found in Marvel's "40 Years of...." collections[1] which place entire runs of superhero series, scanned as originally printed (complete with advertisements), onto computer DVDs. While the advertisements help to contextualize the comic books and recreate the original reading experience, the very fact that these comic books only exist in virtual space on a computer screen changes the reader's interface with the story. (This is not mention that the DVD allows for a high resolution zoom, enabling fanboys and academics alike to scrutinize these comic books in a way not previously possible.) Even as the history of superheroes in comic books is being preserved, the superhero is being revised.

Although films may have been a subject with which essays in this collection dealt in part, new distribution technologies for film also need to be taken into account, as they are changing the nature of the superhero experience captured on film. For instance, the theatrical release of Mark Steven Johnson's *Daredevil* film was originally cut drastically, eliminating a significant subplot, in order to decrease the time Daredevil spent separated from his love interest. The result was a slightly incoherent work which was only modestly successful at the box office. In a trend not uncommon and used to boost DVD sales, the theatrical version of *Daredevil* was released on DVD and followed about a year later with the "director's cut." While the theatrical version of the DVD has virtually disappeared, the director's cut has not only become the perennially stocked favorite at Blockbuster Video but also it has become the version regularly aired on cable television.

Though the film's theatrical release didn't make enough money to merit the studio machine's immediate move toward developing a sequel, many of those involved in the film hint that a sequel may some day be seen. If so, the obvious question to be addressed would be whether the sequel would be based on the theatrical version (previously understood as the Urtext) or on the more popular director's cut. The revisionism technologically encouraged in an age of downloadable films with alternate endings can be seen in the way that Brian Singer has revised Superman in films. In addition to ignoring the third and fourth Christopher Reeve *Superman* sequels, the DVD release of Singer's *Superman Returns* was synchronized with the release of Richard Donner's director's cut of *Superman II*. Due to creative differences with the producers, Donner was released from the film and Richard Lester came aboard as the film's new director (he would use some of Donner's footage, reshoot some scenes, restructure the plot, and receive sole directing credit). Similar to the *Daredevil* situation, this marketing ploy causes the viewer of Superman films to question which might be the authoritative version of *Superman II* that is supposed to directly precede *Superman Returns*.[2] Again, technology provides a means by which the supposedly static past of superheroes remains in flux and subject to revision.

While the world of video games may be taking what was once the target audience for superhero comic books, video games producers are offering adolescent boys content that is strikingly reminiscent of comic books (although often more graphic). In fact, video games not only craft narratives based in large part on the tropes of superhero narratives (such as the power fantasy) but also regularly implement classic superheroes as part of the worlds created for gamers. The superhero industry has long been engineering multi-media blitzes to accompany the most recent development in a superhero's life. Most recently, this has been seen to accompany the release of major motion pictures featuring superheroes such as the X-Men. One of the video games designed to piggyback on the popularity of Brian Singer's film featured the voices of some actors who played superheroic characters in the film, reinforcing the versions of the superheroes seen in the films. However, the narrative frame in the video game extended beyond that of the film and incorporated some ideas privy only to readers of the X-Men comic books. Consequently, the film version of the X-Men was not authoritatively replacing the comic book version as the video game expanded and revised the film's world by creating a bridge that allows two-way traffic between the film and the comic books.

The simple fact that most video games have narrative frameworks means that another medium now crafts versions of superhero stories that reach the audience most often regarded by the public at large as the appropriate audience for superheroes. Of course, emphasizing the narrative may be ignoring the most important possibility inherent within the directions recently being taken with video games. Many video games are now known for their open-ended structure which lacks a story-driven imperative and which allows gamers to choose their own path, at least to some extent. Such a design can be seen a limited way in the *Superman Returns* video game which allows the game player to simply fly around Metropolis and knock down buildings (if the gamer so chooses); it should be noted this game does retain a traditional moral framework for Superman, as the gamer loses "points" as Superman destroys Metropolis. However, that future may see gamers in which the morality is much more relative and allows the gamer to explore the "what if" questions that have fascinated the writers of Superman's "imaginary" stories.

Finally, one of the things that must be admitted by academics devoted to the study of superheroes is that the line between fan and critic is becoming less distinct. The power of the reader to influence superhero stories was certainly seen in the heyday of comic book letters pages, and while the discussions on letters pages may not be as prevalent or as heated as they once were, they have been forcefully replaced by the discussions in internet chatrooms. In addition, blogs may garner enough attention to receive sponsorship and then become full-fledged websites (which then become trusted on-line journals about comic books, films, and video games). Anyone who argues that such conversations are inconsequential to the new directions of superheroes doesn't understand the power of the consumer in a capitalist economy and also doesn't know of the way superhero creators shamelessly have pillaged popular fanfiction for new ideas. And as digital technology is cheaper than ever before, superhero fanfiction is now taking new forms, manifested as fanfilms.

One of the most popular fanfilms featured at the well known website "Comics2Film" is not really a film per se and thus not only revises superheroes but also revises the idea of the superhero film; it's a faux trailer for a film never made called *Grayson* (as in Dick Grayson, better known as to Batman fans as Robin). Although the trailer doesn't strive for complete narrative coherency (sacrificed at the end of the trailer especially in order to throw in other superheroes such as the Green Lantern), the supposed movie does set forth a story far outside that of the "canonical" Dick Grayson. After Batman is killed, Grayson returns from his costumed retirement to once again look after an out-of-control Gotham City as Robin. In addition to featuring the (re)appearance of essential Batman villains such as the Catwoman and the Joker, the trailer also reveals that Grayson is married to another retired crimefighter (Barbara Gordon, aka Batgirl) who leaves him once he again becomes Robin (an apparent nod to the self-destructiveness regularly associated with Batman's crusade). In addition, a reporter in the crowd is revealed to be none other than Clark Kent, later asked as Superman by the powers-that-be to rein in Robin (a device drawn directly from *The Dark Knight Returns* but substituting Robin for Batman). With the extreme popularity of this darkened version of a traditionally light part of the Batman narrative, one could justifiably expect to see such a "damaged goods" portrayal of Robin in the near future. Moreover, one could justifiably make the case that someone other than the copyright owners of the character named Robin (and those who pay for the right to tell his story) has control over the direction Robin will take.

Undoubtedly, there is work to be done and these examples merely form a meager indication of that work, as superheroes are endlessly revised within the mediums that they inhabit. Thus, in closing, I feel it's important to note that the enlightened academic devoted to the study of superheroes should not focus on the way the educated critic's supposed authority is being usurped by the above mentioned fan. Instead, as the shift occurs that blurs the line between the arbiters of high culture and the advocates of popular culture, the academic should return to aspects of the superhero that made that academic into a superhero fan long before that superhero fan earned a higher degree. And then, without sacrificing any theoretical acumen, that academic can begin to work as part of an enormous community that speaks playfully and seriously about superheroes in the same breath, that writes about superheroes with a fanatic passion that feeds higher thought.

NOTES

1. These collections include: *40 Years of the Amazing Spiderman, 44 Years of the Fantastic Four, 40 Years of the X-Men, 40 Years of the Avengers, 43 Years of Incredible Hulk,* and *41 Years of Captain America* among others.

2. The box set (*The Superman Ultimate Collector's Edition*) gives no clue, as both versions are included. It's not unusual for creative teams to change and choose different directions for characters in film. However, DVD box sets often set extremely disparate visions of superheroes side by side. Consider also the box set of Batman films (*The Batman Anthology*), which places the radically different Tim Burton and Joel Schumacher films alongside one another.

About the Contributors

Audrey Anton has a B.A. in philosophy from Assumption College, an M.A. in philosophy from the State University of New York at Buffalo, and is working towards a Ph.D. in philosophy at Ohio State University. She works primarily in areas of ethics, including normative ethics and metaethics, and free will. Audrey started reading up on superheroes only in 2004 when she came to the disappointing realization that she wasn't one. Her therapist attributes her delusions of grandeur to Audrey's younger days when she and her brother dressed up as Wonder Woman and Superman. Apparently Andrew never let on that it was just a game.

Gerard F. Beritela is a man of many identities, only a few of which are secret. As a long-standing Ph.D. candidate at Syracuse University, a mild mannered adjunct instructor for a great metropolitan college (Le Moyne College) and an only slightly strange minister from an Episcopalian planet, he fights for truth and justice in a decidedly 21st century American way.

Marc Edward DiPaolo, assistant professor of communications and English at Alvernia College, is a narratologist who has written about film, literature, and adaptation theory. A former journalist, DiPaolo earned his doctorate in 18th and 19th century British and American Romanticism from Drew University. He believes that his early exposure to gothic fiction and the television exploits of Batman, Wonder Woman, and Spider-Man helped fuel his imagination and inspire him to a lifelong interest in ethics.

Jason Dittmer is a native of Jacksonville, Florida, and is currently an assistant professor of geography at Georgia Southern University. He collected comic books in junior high school and was remembering them fondly one day when he made the connection between Captain America and his other studies in the field of critical geopolitics. Who knew all that allowance money spent on comics was an investment in an academic career?

Jeff McClelland received his master of arts degree in English from Youngstown State University, where he currently teaches freshman composition. He fell in love with comics (with a particular affinity for the ever-lovin' blue-eyed Thing) after reading his father's copy of *Fantastic Four* #183. And so he says: thanks, Dad.

Robert M. McManus is the McCoy Assistant Professor of Communication and Media Studies at Marietta College, Marietta, Ohio. His interest in superheroes began as a child. He identified with the secret lives of characters such as Clark Kent, a.k.a. Superman, Peter Parker, a.k.a. Spider-Man, and—much to his father's chagrin—Diana Prince, a.k.a. Wonder Woman, much more than the superheroes themselves. The reason why remains a mystery to some.

Dan O'Rourke is an associate professor of communication at Ashland University in Ohio. He put away comics in his youth as a sign of his maturity. Years later, Frank Miller's *Dark Knight* reawakened his interest in the art form. Now he shares his books with his children, Morgan and Devin. He believes superheroes succeed where politicians and social leaders fail; the world will always need tales of mythic heroes.

Lorrie Palmer has a B.A. and an M.A. in film studies (University of Missouri, University of Miami) and is starting her work on a Ph.D. After an earlier incarnation as a musician and singer-songwriter, she is aiming for a university teaching position. Her interests include orphaned genre films (especially the hybrids), the Trek-verse, revisionist superheroes, and action-adventure movies. Her 15 seconds of fame occurred when she was an extra in James Cameron's *Titanic*.

Brendan Riley is an English professor at Columbia College–Chicago and a member of the editorial board of the *Journal of Popular Culture*. His writing has appeared in *Kairos* and *Reconstruction*, as well as the *American Icons* series. Brendan began reading comics the month Brian Michael Bendis began publishing *Powers*—and thus feels like a normal guy in a world full of superheroes.

Pravin A. Rodrigues grew up in Bombay (now Mumbai), India, immersed in British and American comics. Comic books constructed the fantastic worlds he resided in during his childhood and nourished the idealism of his youth. He stills finds comic books engaging and hard to resist. He is an associate professor in the Communication Arts Department at Ashland University, Ohio. His research interests include intercultural communication, rhetoric, and the Asian Indian identity.

Grace R. Waitman is a doctoral student in British and American Literature at Washington University in Saint Louis. She received her master of arts degree in English literature from Indiana University–Bloomington, as well as her bachelor's degree in English and history. The Superman mythos has interested her since the age of eight (or possibly before), and she thinks it rather unfortunate that Indiana doesn't currently offer a degree in flying or a major in invisibility.

Terrence R. Wandtke is an associate professor of literature and media at Judson University, where he teaches a course on comic books and graphic novels (and includes them in as many other courses as he can). He founded and currently directs the Imago Film Festival. Terrence writes extensively on heroic models reinterpreted in contemporary literature, film, and comic books. He is a chair for the Midwest Popular Culture Association in the area of "heroes in contemporary culture." And while being a lifelong reader of superhero comics, he has never had sand kicked in his face by the local bully.

Index

*Numbers in **bold italics** indicate pages with photographs.*